ENVIRONMENTAL PROTECTION LAWS

ENVIRONMENTAL PROTECTION LAWS

S.K. Murthy

ANMOL PUBLICATIONS PVT. LTD.
NEW DELHI-110 002 (INDIA)

ANMOL PUBLICATIONS PVT. LTD.
Regd. Office: 4360/4, Ansari Road, Daryaganj,
New Delhi-110002 (India)
Tel.: 23278000, 23261597, 23286875, 23255577
Fax: 91-11-23280289
Email: anmolpub@gmail.com
Visit us at: www.anmolpublications.com

Branch Office: No. 1015, Ist Main Road, BSK IIIrd Stage
IIIrd Phase, IIIrd Block, Bangalore-560 085 (India)
Tel.: 080-41723429 • Fax: 080-26723604
Email: anmolpublicationsbangalore@gmail.com

Environmental Protection Laws

First Edition, 2010

ISBN 978-81-261-4602-4

PRINTED IN INDIA

Printed at Mehra Offset Press, Delhi.

Contents

Preface

In the present century environmental degradation has emerged as a major global concern for human survival. For this reason environmental issues are intensely debated increasingly often. The law relating to the environment is rapidly growing as a complex regulatory mechanism which increasingly reflects public concern over vital issues such as clean water and air, conservation of forests and wildlife, increasing noise and depletion of other natural resources.

Recent spate of legislations and policy formulations on environmental issues in India reveal sincere efforts of the Government to combat this stupendous problem. The environmental situation after coming into effect of the law and policy is not satisfactorily improving. It is against this background, this book sets-out to provide a broad examination of environmental law and policy in India.

The book which is first of its kind highlights the sources and effects of environmental pollution as well as the legal mechanism for its control. The judicial approach to the environmental law and emergence of public interest litigation finds an elaborated treatment in the study.

Author

Chapter 1

Environment Protection Act

PROTECTION ACT 1986

The main objective of this Act is to provide the protection and improvement of environment (which includes water, air, land, human being, other living creatures, plants, microorganism and properties) and for matters connected therewith. There is a constitutional provision also for the environment protection.

Article 48A, specify that the State shall endeavour to protect and improve the environment and to safeguard the forests and wildlife of the country and every citizen shall protect the environment (51 A).

The Environment (Protection) Act is applicable to whole of India including Jammu & Kashmir. *Environment*: It includes water, air, and land and the inter-relationship which exists among and between water, air and land and human beings, other living creatures, plants, microorganism and property.

ENVIRONMENTAL POLLUTION

It means any solid, liquid or gaseous substances present in such concentration as may be or tend to be injurious to environment and human being are known as pollutant and presence of any pollutant in the environment in such proportion and concentration that has bearing on health and environment is termed as "Environmental Pollution". Handling: In relation to any substance, it means the manufacturing, processing, treatment, packaging, storage, transportation, use, collection, destruction, conversion, offering for sale, etc.

OCCUPIER

It means a person who has control over the affairs of the factory or the premises, and includes, in relation to any substance, the person in possession of the substance. The Act provide power to make rules to regulate environmental pollution, to notify standards and maximum limits of pollutants of air, water, and soil for various areas and purposes,; prohibition and restriction on the handling of hazardous substances and location of industries.

The Central Government is empowered to constitute authority or authorities for the purpose of exercising of performing such of the powers and functions, appoint a person for inspection, for analysis or samples and for selection or notification of environmental laboratories. Such person or agency has power to inspect or can enter in the premises or can take samples for analysis. According to the section, the Central Government may issue directions in writing to any person or officers or any authority to comply. There could be closure, prohibition of the supply of electricity or operation or process; or stoppage or regulation of the supply of electricity or water or any other service. Section empower the government to make rules to achieve the object of the Act.

Persons carrying on industry, operation etc. not to allow emission or discharge of environmental pollutants in excess of the standards. Persons handling hazardous substances must comply with procedural safeguards and occupiers must furnish the information to authority.

PENALTY

Whoever Person or Owner/Occupier of companies, factories or whichever source found to be the cause of pollution may be liable for punishment for a term which may extend to five years or with fine which may extend to one lakh rupees or both. Ir not comply fine of Rs. 5000 per day extra and if not comply for more than one year then imprisonment may extend up to 7 years. Section specify that Head of the department/ in-charge of small unit may be liable for punishment if the owner /occupier produce enough evidence of innocence. The CPCB or state boards have power to close or cancel or deny the authorization to run the factory/institution/hospital whichever is causing pollution. No suit, prosecution or other legal procceings shall lie against govt. officer who has exercise power in good faith in pursuance of this Act. An Act to provide for the protection and improvement of environment and for matters connected there with:

Whereas the decisions were taken at the United NationsConference on the Human Environment held at Stockholm in June, 1972, in which India participated, to take appropriate steps for the protection and improvement of human environment; And whereas it is considered necessary further to implement the decisions aforesaid in so far as they relate to the protection and improvement of environment and the prevention of hazards to human beings, other living creatures, plants and property.

PRELIMINARY

SHORT TITLE

- This Act may be called the Environment (Protection) Act, 1986.
- It extends to the whole of India.
- It shall come into force on such date as the Central Government may, by notification in the Official Gazette, appoint and different dates may be appointed for different provisions of this Act and for different areas.

DEFINITIONS

In this Act, unless the context otherwise requires:

- "Environment" includes water, air and land and the inter- relationship which exists among and between water, air and land, and human beings, other living creatures, plants, micro-organism and property;
- "Environmental pollutant" means any solid, liquid or gaseous substance present in such concentration as may be, or tend to be, injurious to environment;

- "Environmental pollution" means the presence in the environment of any environmental pollutant;
- "Handling", in relation to any substance, means the manufacture, processing, treatment, package, storage, transportation, use, collection, destruction, conversion, offering for sale, transfer or the like of such substance;
- "Hazardous substance" means any substance or preparation which, by reason of its chemical or physico-chemical properties or handling, is liable to cause harm to human beings, other living creatures, plant, micro-organism, property or the environment;
- "Occupier", in relation to any factory or premises, means a person who has, control over the affairs of the factory or the premises and includes in relation to any substance, the person in possession of the substance;
- "Prescribed" means prescribed by rules made under this Act.

POWERS OF GOVERNMENT

Subject to the provisions of this Act, the Central Government, shall have the power to take all such measures as it deems necessary or expedient for the purpose of protecting and improving the quality of the environment and preventing controlling and abating environmental pollution.

In particular, and without prejudice to the generality of the provisions of sub-section, such measures may include measures with respect to all or any of the following matters, namely:

- Co-ordination of actions by the State Governments, officers and other authorities
  - Under this Act, or the rules made thereunder, or
  - Under any other law for the time being in force which is relatable to the objects of this Act;
- Planning and execution of a nation-wide programme for the prevention, control and abatement of environmental pollution;

- Laying down standards for the quality of environment in its various aspects;
- Laying down standards for emission or discharge of environmental pollutants from various sources whatsoever:
  Provided that different standards for emission or discharge may be laid down under this clause from different sources having regard to the quality or composition of the emission or discharge of environmental pollutants from such sources;
- Restriction of areas in which any industries, operations or processes or class of industries, operations or processes shall not be carried out or shall be carried out subject to certain safeguards;
- Laying down procedures and safeguards for the prevention of accidents which may cause environmental pollution and remedial measures for such accidents;
- Laying down procedures and safeguards for the handling of hazardous substances;
- Examination of such manufacturing processes, materials and substances as are likely to cause environmental pollution;
- Carrying out and sponsoring investigations and research relating to problems of environmental pollution;
- Inspection of any premises, plant, equipment, machinery, manufacturing or other processes, materials or substances and giving, by order, of such directions to such authorities, officers or persons as it may consider necessary to take steps for the prevention, control and abatement of environmental pollution;
- Establishment or recognition of environmental laboratories and institutes to carry out the functions entrusted to such environmental laboratories and institutes under this Act;
- Collection and dissemination of information in respect of matters relating to environmental pollution;

- preparation of manuals, codes or guides relating to the prevention, control and abatement of environmental pollution;
- Such other matters as the Central Government deems necessary or expedient for the purpose of securing the effective implementation of the provisions of this Act.

The Central Government may, if it considers it necessary or expedient so to do for the purposes of this Act, by order, published in the Official Gazette, constitute an authority or authorities by such name or names as may be specified in the order for the purpose of exercising and performing such of the powers and functions (including the power to issue directions under section 5) of the Central Government under this Act and for taking measures with respect to such of the matters referred to in sub-section as may be mentioned in the order and subject to the supervision and control of the Central Government and the provisions of such order, such authority or authorities may exercise the powers or perform the functions or take the measures so mentioned in the order as if such authority or authorities had been empowered by this Act to exercise those powers or perform those functions or take such measures.

APPOINTMENT OF OFFICERS AND POWERS

- The Central Government may, by notification in the Official Gazette, make rules in respect of all or any of the matters referred to in section 3.
- In particular, and without prejudice to the generality of the foregoing power, such rules may provide for all or any of the following matters, namely:—
  - The standards of quality of air, water or soil for various areas and purposes;
  - The maximum allowable limits of concentration of various environmental pollutants (including noise) for different areas;
  - The procedures and safeguards for the handling of hazardous substances;

- The prohibition and restrictions on the handling of hazardous substances in different areas;
- The prohibition and restriction on the location of industries and the carrying on process and operations in different areas;
- The procedures and safeguards for the prevention of accidents which may cause environmental pollution and for providing for remedial measures for such accidents.

PREVENTION AND CONTROL

Persons carrying on industry operation, etc.,Not to allow emission or discharge of environmental pollutants in excess of the standards. No person carrying on any industry, operation or process shall discharge or emit or permit to be discharged or emitted any environmental pollutants in excess of such standards as may be prescribed.

Persons handling hazardous substances to comply with procedural safeguards No person shall handle or cause to be handled any hazardous substance except in accordance with such procedure and after complying with such safeguards as may be prescribed.

FURNISHING OF INFORMATION

Where the discharge of any environmental pollutant in excess of the prescribed standards occurs or is apprehended to occur due to any accident or other unforeseen act or event, the person responsible for such discharge and the person in charge of the place at which such discharge occurs or is apprehended to occur shall be bound to prevent or mitigate the environmental pollution caused as a result of such discharge and shall also forthwith.

- Intimate the fact of such occurrence or apprehension of such occurrence; and
- Be bound, if called upon, to render all assistance, to such authorities or agencies as may be prescribed.

On receipt of information with respect to the fact or apprehension on any occurrence of the nature referred to in sub-section, whether through intimation under that sub-section or otherwise, the authorities or agencies referred to in sub-section shall, as early as practicable, cause such remedial measures to be taken as necessary to prevent or mitigate the environmental pollution.

The expenses, if any, incurred by any authority or agency with respect to the remedial measures referred to in sub-section, together with interest (at such reasonable rate as the Government may, by order, fix) from the date when a demand for the expenses is made until it is paid, may be recovered by such authority or agency from the person concerned as arrears of land revenue or of public demand.

POWERS OF ENTRY AND INSPECTION

Subject to the provisions of this section, any person empowered by the Central Government in this behalf shall have a right to enter, at all reasonable times with such assistance as he considers necessary, any place.

- For the purpose of performing any of the functions of the Central Government entrusted to him;
- For the purpose of determining whether and if so in what manner, any such functions are to be performed or whether any provisions of this Act or the rules made there under notice, order, direction or authorization served, made, given or granted under this Act is being or has been complied with;
- For the purpose of examining and testing any equipment, industrial plant, record, register, document or any other material object or for conducting a search of any building in which he has reason to believe that an offence under this Act or the rules made thereunder has been or is being or is about to be committed and for seizing any such equipment, industrial plant, record, register, document or other material object if he has reason to believe that it may furnish evidence of the commission of an offence punishable under this Act or the rules made thereunder or that such seizure is

necessary to prevent or mitigate environmental pollution.

Every person carrying on any industry, operation or process of handling any hazardous substance shall be bound to render all assistance to the person empowered by the Central Government under sub-section (1) for carrying out the functions under that sub-section and if he fails to do so without any reasonable cause or excuse, he shall be guilty of an offence under this Act.

If any person willfully delays or obstructs any persons empowered by the Central Government under sub-section in the performance of his functions, he shall be guilty of an offence under this Act. The provisions of the Code of Criminal Procedure, 1973, or, in relation to the State of Jammu and Kashmir, or an area in which that Code is not in force, the provisions of any corresponding law in force in that State or area shall, so far as may be, apply to any search or seizures under this section as they apply to any search or seizure made under the authority of a warrant issued under section 94 of the said Code or as the case may be, under the corresponding provision of the said law.

Power to Take Sample and Procedure

The Central Government or any officer empowered by it in this behalf, shall have power to take, for the purpose of analysis, samples of air, water, soil or other substance from any factory, premises or other place in such manner as may be prescribed.

The result of any analysis of a sample taken under sub-section shall not be admissible in evidence in any legal proceeding unless the provisions of sub-sections (3) and (4) are complied with.

Subject to the provisions of sub-section (4), the person taking the sample under sub-section (1) shall

- Serve on the occupier or his agent or person in charge of the place, a notice, then and there, in such form as may be prescribed, of his intention to have it so analyzed;

- In the presence of the occupier of his agent or person, collect a sample for analysis;
- Cause the sample to be placed in a container or containers which shall be marked and sealed and shall also be signed both by the person taking the sample and the occupier or his agent or person;
- Send without delay, the container or the containers to the laboratory established or recognized by the Central Government under section 12.

When a sample is taken for analysis under sub-section and the person taking the sample serves on the occupier or his agent or person, a notice under clause (a) of sub-section, then,

- In a case where the occupier, his agent or person wilfully absents himself, the person taking the sample shall collect the sample for analysis to be placed in a container or containers which shall be marked and sealed and shall also be signed by the person taking the sample, and
- In a case where the occupier or his agent or person present at the time of taking the sample refuses to sign the marked and sealed container or containers of the sample as required under clause
- Of sub-section (3), the marked and sealed container or containers shall be signed by the person taking the samples, and the container or containers shall be sent without delay by the person taking the sample for analysis to the laboratory established or recognized under section 12 and such person shall inform the Government Analyst appointed or recognized under section 12 in writing, about the willful absence of the occupier or his agent or person, or, as the case may be, his refusal to sign the container or containers.

ENVIRONMENTAL LABORATORIES

- The Central Government may, by notification in the Official Gazette,
  - Establish one or more environmental laboratories;

- Recognize one or more laboratories or institutes as environmental laboratories to carry out the functions entrusted to an environmental laboratory under this Act.

- The Central Government may, by notification in the Official Gazette, make rules specifying
  - The functions of the environmental laboratory;
  - The procedure for the submission to the said laboratory of samples of air, water, soil or other substance for analysis or tests, the form of the laboratory report thereon and the fees payable for such report;
  - Such other matters as may be necessary or expedient to enable that laboratory to carry out its functions.

GOVERNMENT ANALYSTS

The Central Government may by notification in the Official Gazette, appoint or recognise such persons as it thinks fit and having the prescribed qualifications to be Government Analysts for the purpose of analysis of samples of air, water, soil or other substance sent for analysis to any environmental laboratory established or recognised under sub-section (1) of section 12.

REPORTS OF GOVERNMENT ANALYSTS

Any document purporting to be a report signed by a Government analyst may be used as evidence of the facts stated therein in any proceeding under this Act.

Penalty for contravention of the provisions of the act and the rules, orders and directions: Whoever fails to comply with or contravenes any of the provisions of this Act, or the rules made or orders or directions issued thereunder, shall, in respect of each such failure or contravention, be punishable with imprisonment for a term which may extend to five years with fine which may extend to one lakh rupees, or with both, and in case the failure or contravention continues, with additional fine which may extend to five thousand rupees for every day during which such failure or contravention continues after the conviction for the first such failure or contravention. If the failure or contravention referred to in sub-section continues beyond a period of one year after the date of conviction, the offender shall be punishable with imprisonment for a term which may extend to seven years.

OFFENCES BY COMPANIES

Where any offence under this Act has been committed by a company, every person who, at the time the offence was committed, was directly in charge of, and was responsible to, the company for the conduct of the business of the company, as well as the company, shall be deemed to be guilty of the offence and shall be liable to be proceeded against and punished accordingly:

Provided that nothing contained in this sub-section shall render any such person liable to any punishment provided in this Act, if he proves that the offence was committed without his knowledge or that he exercised all due diligence to prevent the commission of such offence. (2) Notwithstanding anything contained in sub-section (1), where an offence under this Act has been committed by a company and it is proved that the offence has been committed with the consent or connivance of, or is attributable to any neglect on the part of, any director, manager, secretary or other officer of the company, such director, manager, secretary or other officer shall also deemed to be guilty of that offence and shall be liable to be proceeded against and punished accordingly.

Explanation:For the purpose of this section,—

- "Company" means any body corporate and includes a firm or other association of individuals;
- "Director", in relation to a firm, means a partner in the firm.

OFFENCES BY GOVERNMENT DEPARTMENTS

Where an offence under this Act has been committed by any Department of Government, the Head of the Department shall be deemed to be guilty of the offence and shall be liable to be proceeded against and punished accordingly. Provided that nothing contained in this section shall render such Head of the Department liable to any punishment if he proves that the offence was committed without his knowledge or that he exercise all due diligence to prevent the commission of such offence. Notwithstanding anything contained in sub-section (1), where an offence under this Act has been committed by a Department of Government and it is proved that the offence has been committed with the consent or connivance of, or is attributable to any neglect on the part of, any officer, other than the Head of the Department, such officer shall also be deemed to be guilty of that offence and shall be liable to be proceeded against and punished accordingly.

MISCELLANEOUS

PROTECTION OF ACTION

No suit, prosecution or other legal proceeding shall lie against the Government or any officer or other employee of the Government or any authority constituted under this Act or any member, officer or other employee of such authority in respect of anything which is done or intended to be done in good faith in pursuance of this Act or the rules made or orders or directions issued thereunder.

COGNIZANCE OF OFFENCES

No court shall take cognizance of any offence under this Act except on a complaint made by:

- The Central Government or any authority or officer authorised in this behalf by that Government, or
- Any person who has given notice of not less than sixty days, in the manner prescribed, of the alleged offence and of his intention to make a complaint, to the Central Government or the authority or officer authorised as aforesaid.

INFORMATION, REPORTS OR RETURNS

The Central Government may, in relation to its function

under this Act, from time to time, require any person, officer, State Government or other authority to furnish to it or any prescribed authority or officer any reports, returns, statistics, accounts and other information and such person, officer, State Government or other authority shall be bound to do so.

MEMBERS, OFFICERS AND EMPLOYEES

All the members of the authority, constituted, if any, under section 3 and all officers and other employees of such authority when acting or purporting to act in pursuance of any provisions of this Act or the rules made or orders or directions issued thereunder shall be deemed to be public servants within the meaning of section 21 of the Indian Penal Code (45 of 1860).

Bar of Jurisdication

No civil court shall have jurisdiction to entertain any suit or proceeding in respect of anything done, action taken or order or direction issued by the Central Government or any other authority or officer in pursuance of any power conferred by or in relation to its or his functions under this Act.

POWERS TO DELEGATE

Without prejudice to the provisions of sub-section (3) of section, the Central Government may, by notification in the Official Gazette, delegate, subject to such conditions and limitations as may be specified in the notifications, such of its powers and functions under this Act [except the powers to constitute an authority under sub-section of section 3 and to make rules under section 25] as it may deem necessary or expedient, to any officer, State Government or other authority.

EFFECT OF OTHER LAWS

Subject to the provisions of sub-section (2), the provisions of this Act and the rules or orders made therein shall have effect notwithstanding anything inconsistent therewith contained in any enactment other than this Act. Where any act or omission constitutes an offence punishable under this

Act and also under any other Act then the offender found guilty of such offence shall be liable to be punished under the other Act and not under this Act.

POWER TO MAKE RULES

The Central Government may, by notification in the Official Gazette, make rules for carrying out the purposes of this Act. In particular, and without prejudice to the generality of the foregoing power, such rules may provide for all or any of the following matters, namely

- The standards in excess of which environmental pollutants shall not be discharged or emitted under section 7;
- The procedure in accordance with and the safeguards in compliance with which hazardous substances shall be handled or caused to be handled under section 8;
- The authorities or agencies to which intimation of the fact of occurrence or apprehension of occurrence of the discharge of any environmental pollutant in excess of the prescribed standards shall be given and to whom all assistance shall be bound to be rendered under sub-section (1) of section 9;
- The manner in which samples of air, water, soil or other substance for the purpose of analysis shall be taken under sub-section (1) of section 11;
- The form in which notice of intention to have a sample analysed shall be served under clause (a) of sub section (3) of section 11;
- The functions of the environmental laboratories, the procedure for the submission to such laboratories of samples of air, water, soil and other substances for analysis or test; the form of laboratory report; the fees payable for such report and other matters to enable such laboratories to carry out their functions under sub-section (2) of section 12;
- The qualifications of Government Analyst appointed or recognised for the purpose of analysis of samples of air, water, soil or other substances under section 13;

- The manner in which notice of the offence and of the intention to make a complaint to the Central Government shall be given under clause (b) of section 1
- The authority of officer to whom any reports, returns, statistics, accounts and other information shall be furnished under section 20;
- Any other matter which is required to be, or may be, prescribed.

RULES MADE UNDER THIS ACT

Every rule made under this Act shall be laid, as soon as may be after it is made, before each Hose of Parliament, while it is in session, for a total period of thirty days which may be comprised in one session or in two or more successive sessions, and if, before the expiry of the session immediately following the session or the successive sessions aforesaid, both Houses agree in making any modification in the rule or both Houses agree that the rule should not be made, the rule shall thereafter have effect only in such modified form or be of no effect, as the case may be; so, however, that any such modification or annulment shall be without prejudice to the validity of anything previously done under that rule.

- It came into force in the whole of India on 19th November, 1986 vide Notification No. G.S.R. 1198(E) dated 12-11-86 published in the Gazette of India No. 525 dated 12-11-86.
- The Central Government has delegated the powers vested m it under section 5 of the -Act to the State Governments of Andhra Pradesh, Assam, Bihar, Gujarat, Haryana, Himachal Pradesh, Karnatalca, Kerala, Madhya Predesh, Mizoram, Orissa, Rajasthan, Sikkim and Tamil Nadu subject to the condition that the Central Government may revoke such delegation of Powers in respect of all or any one or more of the State Governments or may itself invoke the provisions of section 5 of the Act, if in the opinion of the Central Government such a course of action is necessary in public interest, (Notification

No, S.O. 152 (E) dated 10-2-88 published in Gazette No. 54 of the same date).

These Powers have been delegated to the following State Governments also on the same terms:

- Meghalaya, Punjab and Uttar Pradesh vide Notification No. S.0.389 (E) dated 14-4-88 published in the Gazette No. 205 dated 144-88;
- Maharashtra vide Notification No. S.O. 488(E) dated 17-5-88 published in the Gazette No. 255 dated 17-5-88;
- Goa and Jammu & Kashmir vide Notification No. S.O. 881 (E~ dated 22-9-88; published in the Gazette No. 749 dated 22.9.88.
- West Bengal Manipur vide Notificadon N. S.O. 408 (E) dated 6-6-89; published in the Gazette No. 319 dated 6-6-89;
- Tripura vide Notification No. S.O. 479 (E) dated 25-7-91 published in thc Gazene No. 414 dated 25-7-91.
- For issuing directions see r.4 of Itnviromnent (Protection) Rules, 1986.
- Schedule I lists the standards for emission or discharge of environmental pollutants from the industries, processes or operations and their maximum allowable limits of concentration;
  - Schedule II lists general standards for discharge of effluents and their maximum limits of concentration allowable;
  - Schedule III lists ambient air quality standards in respect of noise and its maximum allowable limits; and
  - Schedule IV lists standards for emission of smoke, vapour etc. from motor vehicles and maximum allowable limits of their emission.
- Environment (Protection) Rules, 1986
  - Hazardous Wastes (Management and Handling) Rules, 1989;
  - Manufacture, Storage and Import of Hazardous Chemicals Rules, 1989; and

Rules for the Manufacture, Use, Import, Export and Storage of Hazardous Micro organisms, Genetically-engineered organisms or Cells.

Rules and Schedule 11, and relevant provisions of Hazardous Wastes (Management and Handling) Rules, Manufacture, Storage and Import of Hazardous Chemicals Rules and Rules for the Manufacture, Use, Import Export and Storage of hazardous Micro-organisms, Genetically Engineered Organisms or Cells.

- For authorities or agencies see r. 12 of Environment (Protection) Rules, 1986 and Schedule
- The Central Govt. has empowered 60 persons listed in the Table vide S.O. 83 (E) published in the Gazette of India No. 66 dated 16-2-87 and S.O. 63 (E) published in the Gazette of India No. 42 dated 18-1-88.
- In excercise of powers conferred under sub-section (i) of section 11 the Central Government has empowered 60 officers listed in the Table vide S.O. 84. (E) published in the Gazette No. 66 dated 16-2-87 and S.O. 62(E) published in the Gazette No. 42 dated 18-l-88.
- For procedure for taking samples.
- The Central Government has delegated its powers under clause (b) of sub-section (i) of section 12 and section 13 of the Act to the Central Pollution Control Board vide Notification No. S.O. 145 (E) dated 21-2-91 published in the Gazette No. 128 dated 27-2-91.
- The list of laboratories/institutes recognised as environmental laboratories: and the persons recognised as Govt. Analysts is given in the table.
- For qualifications of Govt. Analyst.
- In exercise of powers conferred under clause (a) of section l9, the Central-Government has authorised the officers and authorities listed in the Table (p. 238) vide S.O. 394 (E) published in the Gazette No. 185 dated 164-87, S.O. 237(E) published in the Gazette No. 171 dated 29-3-89 and S.O. 656(E) dated 21-8-89 published in the Gazette No. 519 dated 21-8-89.

- For the procedure for submission of samples to laboratories and the form of laboratory report.

S.O.145(E)

In exercise of the powers conferred under Section 23 of the Environment (Protection) Act, 1986, the Central Government hereby issue the following orders namely:-

- The Central Government hereby delegates the powers with respect to grant of recognition to laboratories or institutes as environmental laboratories and to appoint or recognize Analysts as Government Analysts, as conferred by clause (b) of Sub-section (i) of Section 12 and section 13 respectively of the Environment (Protection) Act, 1986 to the Central Pollution Control Board.
- Recognition of private laboratories under clause (b) of sub-section (i) of section 12 of the Environment (Protection)Act, 1986 as well as recognition of their Analysts as Government Analysts under Section 13 of the Environment (Protection) Act, 1986, will continue to be done by the Central Government.
- The laboratories recognized under clause (b) of sub-section (i) of section 12 of the Environment (Protection) Act, 1986 shall be specified as Government/ Autonomous/ Public Sector Undertaking/ Educational Institution/State or Central Pollution Control Board Laboratories.
- The work done by each Laboratories recognized under the Environment (Protection) Act, 1986 shall be included in the Annual Report of the Central Pollution Control Board.
- This notification shall come into force on the date of its publication in the Official Gazette.

PREAMBLE

An Act to provide for the protection and improvement of environment and for matters connected therewith. Whereas decisions were taken at the United Nations Conference on the

Human Environment held at Stockholm in June, 1972, in which India participated, to take appropriate steps for the protection and improvement of human environment; And whereas it is considered necessary further to implement the decisions aforesaid in so far as they relate to the protection and improvement of environment and the prevention of hazards to human being, other living creatures, plants and property; Be it enacted by Parliament in the Thirty-seventh Year of the Republic of India as follows.

SHORT TITLE, EXTENT AND COMMENCEMENT

- This Act may be called the Environment (Protection) Act, 1986.
- It extends to the whole of India.
- It shall come into force on such date 1 as the Central Government may, by notification in the Official Gazette, appoint and different dates may be appointed for different provisions of this Act and for different areas.

DEFINITIONS

In this Act, unless the context otherwise requires:

- "Environment" includes water, air and land and the inter-relationship which exists among and between water, air and land, and human beings, other living creatures, plants, micro-organism and property;
- "Environmental pollutant" means any solid, liquid or gaseous substance present in such concentration as may be, or tend to be, injurious to environment;
- "Environmental pollution" means the presence in the environment of any environmental pollutant;
- "Handling", in relation to any substance, means the manufacture, processing, treatment, package, storage, transportation, use, collection, destruction, conversion, offering for sale, transfer or the like of such substance;
- "Hazardous substance" means any substance or

preparation which, by reason of its chemical or physico-chemical properties or handling, is liable to cause harm to human beings, other living creatures, plants, micro-organism, property or the environment;

- "Occupier", in relation to any factory or premises, means a person who has control over the affairs of the factory or the premises and includes in relation to any substance, the person in possession of the substance;
- "Prescribed" means prescribed by rules made under this Act.

MEASURES TO PROTECT AND IMPROVE ENVIRONMENT

Subject to the provisions of this Act, the Central Government shall have the power to take all such measures as it deems necessary or expedient for the purpose of protecting and improving the quality of the environment and preventing, controlling and abating environmental pollution.

In particular, and without prejudice to the generality of the provisions of sub-section (1), such measures may include measures with respect to all or any of the following matters, namely :

- Co-ordination of actions by the State Governments, officers and other authorities
  - Under this Act, or the rules made there under;
  - Under any other law for the time being in force which is relatable to the objects of this Act;
- Planning and execution of a nation-wide programme for the prevention, control and abatement of environmental pollution;
- Laying down standards for the quality of environment in its various aspects;
- Laying down standards for emission or discharge of environmental pollutants from various sources whatsoever : Provided that different standards for emission or discharge may be laid down under this clause from different sources having regard to the

quality or composition of the emission or discharge of environmental pollutants from such sources;

- Restriction of areas in which any industries, operations or processes, or class of industries, operations or processes shall not be carried out or shall be carried out subject to certain safeguards;
- Laying down procedures and safeguards for the prevention of accidents which may cause environmental pollution and remedial measures for such accidents;
- Laying down procedures and safeguards for the handling of hazardous substances;
- Examination of such manufacturing processes, materials and substances as are likely to cause environmental pollution;
- Carrying out and sponsoring investigations and research relating to problems of environmental pollution;
- Inspection of any premises, plant, equipment, machinery, manufacturing or other processes, materials or substances and giving, by order, of such directions to such authorities, officers or persons as it may consider necessary to take steps for the prevention, control and abatement of environmental pollution;
- Establishment or recognition of environmental laboratories and institutes to carry out the functions entrusted to such environmental laboratories and institutes under this Act;
- Collection and dissemination of information in respect of matters relating to environmental pollution;
- Preparation of manuals, codes or guides relating to the prevention, control and abatement of environmental pollution;
- Such other matters as the Central Government deems necessary or expedient for the purpose of securing the effective implementation of the provisions of this Act.

The Central Government may, if it considers it necessary or expedient so to do for the purposes of this Act, by order, published in the Official Gazette, constitute an authority or authorities by such name or names as may be specified in the order for the purpose of exercising and performing such of the powers and functions (including the power to issue directions under section 5) of the Central Government under this Act and for taking measures with respect to such of the matters referred to in sub-section (2) as may be mentioned in the order and subject to the supervision and control of the Central Government and the provisions of such order, such authority or authorities may exercise the powers or perform the functions or take the measures so mentioned in the order as if such authority or authorities had been empowered by this Act to exercise those powers or perform those functions or take such measures.

APPOINTMENT OF OFFICERS

(1) Without prejudice to the provisions of sub-section (3) of section 3, the Central Government may appoint officers with such designations as it thinks fit for the purposes of this Act and may entrust to them such of the powers and functions under this Act as it may deem fit. (2) The officers appointed under sub-section (1) shall be subject to the general control and direction of the Central Government or, if so directed by that Government, also of the authority or authorities, if any, constituted under sub-section (3) of section 3 or of any other authority or officer.

POWER TO GIVE DIRECTIONS

Notwithstanding anything contained in any other law but subject to the provisions of this Act, the Central Government may, in the exercise of its powers and performance of its functions under this Act, issue directions in writing to any person, officer or any authority and such person, officer or authority shall be bound to comply with such directions.

Explanatione : For the avoidance of doubts, it is hereby declared that the power to issue directions under this section includes the power to direct

- The closure, prohibition or regulation of any industry, operation or process; or

- Stoppage or regulation of the supply of electricity or water or any other service.

REGULATE ENVIRONMENTAL POLLUTION

- The Central Government may, by notification in the Official Gazette, make rules in respect of all or any of the matters referred to in section 3.
- In particular, and without prejudice to the generality of the foregoing power, such rules may provide for all or any of the following matters, namely:
  - The standards of quality of air, water or soil for various areas and purposes;
  - The maximum allowable limits of concentration of various environmental pollutants (including noise) for different areas;
  - The procedures and safeguards for the handling of hazardous substances;
  - The prohibition and restrictions on the handling of hazardous substances in different areas;
  - The prohibition and restrictions on the location of industries and the carrying on of processes and operations in different areas;
  - The procedures and safeguards for the prevention of accidents which may cause environmental pollution and for providing for remedial measures for such accidents.

Persons carrying on industry, operation, etc. Not to allow emission or discharge of environmental pollutants in excess of the standards.

No person carrying on any industry, operation or process shall discharge or emit or permit to be discharged or emitted any environmental pollutant in excess of such standards as may be prescribed.

Persons handling hazardous substances to comply with procedural safeguards. No person shall handle or cause to be handled any hazardous substance except in accordance with such procedure and after complying with such safeguards as may be prescribed.

Fernishing of Infomation to Authorities

Where the discharge of any environmental pollutant in excess of the prescribed standards occurs or is apprehended to occur due to any accident or other unforeseen act or event, the person responsible for such discharge and the person in charge of the place at which such discharge occurs, or is apprehended to occur shall be bound to prevent or mitigate the environmental pollution caused as a result of such discharge and shall also forthwith.

- Intimate the fact of such occurrence or apprehension of such occurrence; and
- Be bound, if called upon, to render all assistance, to such authorities or agencies as may be prescribed.

On receipt of information with respect to the fact or apprehension of any occurrence of the nature referred to in sub-section (1), whether through intimation under that sub-section or otherwise, the authorities or agencies referred to in sub-section (1) shall, as early as practicable, cause such remedial measures to be taken as are necessary to prevent or mitigate the environmental pollution.

The expenses, if any, incurred by any authority or agency with respect to the remedial measures referred to in sub-section (2), together with interest (at such reasonable rate as the Government may, by order, fix) from the date when a demand for the expenses is made until it is paid may be recovered by such authority or agency from the person concerned as arrears of land revenue or of public demand.

POWER OF ENTRY AND INSPECTION

Subject to the provisions of this section, any person empowered by the Central Government in this behalf shall have a right to enter, at all reasonable times with such assistance as he considers necessary, any place.

- For the purpose of performing any of the functions of the Central Government entrusted to him;
- For the purpose of determining whether and if so in what manner any such functions are to be performed or whether any provisions of this Act or the rules

made there under or any notice, order, direction or authorisation served, made, given or granted under this Act is being or has been complied with;

- For the purpose of examining and testing any equipment, industrial plant, record, register, document or any other material object or for conducting a search of any building in which he has reason to believe that an offence under this Act or the rules made there under has been or is being or is about to be committed and for seizing any such equipment, industrial plant, record, register, document or other material object if he has reasons to believe that it may furnish evidence of the commission of an offence punishable under this Act or the rules made there under or that such seizure is necessary to prevent or mitigate environmental pollution.

Every person carrying on any industry, operation or process or handling any hazardous substance shall be bound to render all assistance to the person empowered by the Central Government under sub-section (1) for carrying out the functions under that sub-section and if he fails to do so without any reasonable cause or excuse, he shall be guilty of an offence under this Act. If any person willfully delays or obstructs any person empowered by the Central Government under sub-section (1) in the performance of his functions, he shall be guilty of an offence under this Act.

The provisions of the Code of Criminal Procedure, 1973 in relation to the State of Jammu and Kashmir, or any area in which that Code is not in force, the provisions of any corresponding law in force in that State or area shall, so far as may be, apply to any search or seizure under this section as they apply to any search or seizure made under the authority of a warrant issued under section 94 of the said Code or, as the case may be, under the corresponding provisions of the said law.

SAMPLE AND PROCEDURE

The Central Government or any officer empowered by it in this behalf, shall have power to take, for the purpose of analysis, samples of air, water, soil or othe. rance from any factory, premises or other place in such r as may be prescribed.

The result of any analysis of a sample taken u r sub-section (1) shall not be admissible in evidence in a egal proceeding unless the provisions of sub-sections (3) an (4) are complied with.

Subject to the provisions of sub-section (4), the person taking the sample under sub-section (1) shall

- Serve on the occupier or his agent or person in charge of the place, a notice, then and there, in such form as may be prescribed, of his intention to have it so analysed;
- In the presence of the occupier or his agent or person, collect a sample for analysis;
- Cause the sample to be placed in a container or containers which shall be marked and sealed and shall also be signed both by the person taking the sample and the occupier or his agent or person;
- Send without delay, the container or the containers to the laboratory established or recognised by the Central Government under section 12.

When a sample is taken for analysis under sub-section (1) and the person taking the sample serves on the occupier or his agent or person, a notice under clause (a) of sub-section

Then,

- In a case where the occupier, his agent or person willfully absents himself, the person taking the sample shall collect the sample for analysis to be placed in a container or containers which shall be marked and sealed and shall also be signed by the person taking the sample, and
- In a case where the occupier or his agent or person present at the time of taking the sample refuses to sign the marked and sealed container or containers of the sample as required under clause
- Of sub-section (3), the marked and sealed container or containers shall be signed by the person taking

.nples, and the container or containers shall be ·without delay by the person taking the sample · analysis to the laboratory established or .ecognised under section 12 and such person shall inform the Government Analyst appointed or recognised under section 13 in writing, about the willful absence of the occupier or his agent or person, or, as the case may be, his refusal to sign the container or containers.

ENVIRONMENTAL LABORATORIES

- The Central Government may, by notification in the Official Gazette,
  - Establish one or more environmental laboratories;
  - Recognise one or more laboratories or institutes as environmental laboratories to carry out the functions entrusted to an environmental laboratory under this Act.
- The Central Government may, by notification in the Official Gazette, make rules specifying
  - The functions of the environmental laboratory;
  - The procedure for the submission to the said laboratory of samples of air, water, soil or other substance for analysis or tests, the form of the laboratory report thereon the fees payable for such report;
  - Such other matters as may be necessary or expedient to enable that laboratory to carry out its functions.

GOVERNMENT ANALYSTS

The Central Government may, by notification in the Official Gazette, appoint or recognise such persons as it thinks fit and having the prescribed qualifications to be Government Analysts for the purpose of analysis of sample of air, water, soil or other substance sent for analysis to any environmental laboratory established or recognised under sub-section (1) of section 12.

REPORTS OF GOVERNMENT ANALYSTS

Any document purporting to be a report signed by a Government analyst may be used as evidence of the facts stated therein in any proceeding under this Act.

Penalty for contravention of the provisions of the act and the rules, orders and direction: Whoever fails to comply with or contravenes any of the provisions of this Act, or the rules made or orders or directions issued there under, shall, in respect of each such failure or contravention, be punishable with imprisonment for a term which may extend to five years or with fine which may extend to one lakh rupees, or with both, and in case the failure or contravention continues, with additional fine which may extend to five thousand rupees for every day during which such failure or contravention continues after the conviction for the first such failure or contravention.

If the failure or contravention referred to in sub-section (1) continues beyond a period of one year after the date of conviction, the offender shall be punishable with imprisonment for a term which may extend to seven years.

Offences by Companies

Where any offence under this Act has been committed by a company, every person who, at the time the offence was committed, was directly in charge of, and was responsible to, the company for the conduct of the business of the company, as well as the company, shall be deemed to be guilty of the offence and shall be liable to be proceeded against and punished accordingly :

Provided that nothing contained in this sub-section shall render any such person liable to any punishment provide in this Act, if he proves that the offence was committed without his knowledge or that he exercised all due diligence to prevent the commission of such offence.

Notwithstanding anything contained in sub-section (1), where an offence under this Act has been committed by a company and it is proved that the offence has been committed with the consent or connivance of, or is attributable to any neglect on the part of, any director, manager, secretary or other officer of the company, such director, manager, secretary or other officer shall also deemed to be guilty of that offence and shall be liable to be proceeded against and punished accordingly.

Explanation: For the purposes of this section

- "Company" means any body corporate and includes a firm or other association of individuals;
- "Director", in relation to a firm, means a partner in the firm.

Offences by Government departments

Where an offence under this Act has been committed by the Department of Government, the Head of the Department shall be deemed to be guilty of the offence and shall be liable to be proceeded against and punished accordingly: Provided that nothing contained in this section shall render such Head of the Department liable to any punishment if he proves that the offence was committed without his knowledge or that he exercised all due diligence to prevent the commission of such offence.

Notwithstanding anything contained in sub-section (1), where an offence under this Act has been committed by a Department of Government and it is proved that the offence has been committed with the consent or connivance of, or is attributable to any neglect on the part of, any officer, other than the Head of the Department, such officer shall also be deemed to be guilty of that offence and shall be liable to be proceeded against and punished accordingly.

Protection of Action Taken in Good Faith

No suit, prosecution or other legal proceeding shall lie against the Government or any officer or other employee of the Government or any authority constituted under this Act or any member, officer or other employee of such authority in respect of anything which is done or intended to be done in good faith in pursuance of this Act or the rules made or orders or directions issued there under.

COGNIZANCE OF OFFENCES

No Court shall take cognizance of any offence under this Act except on a complaint made by:

- The Central Government or any authority or officer authorised in this behalf by that Government; or
- Any person who has given notice of not less than sixty days, in the manner prescribed, of the alleged offence and of his intention to make a complaint, to the Central Government or the authority or officer authorised as aforesaid.

Information, Reports or Returns

The Central Government may, in relation to its functions under this Act, from time to time, require any person, officer, State Government or other authority to furnish to it or any prescribed authority or officer any reports, returns, statistics, accounts and other information and such person, officer, State Government or other authority shall be bound to do so.

Members, Officers and Employees of the Authority

All the members of the authority, constituted, if any, under section 3 and all officers and other employees of such authority when acting or purporting to act in pursuance of any provisions of this Act, or the rules made, or orders or directions issued there under, shall be deemed to be public servants within the meaning of section 21 of the Indian Penal Code.

Bar of Jurisdiction

No Civil Court shall have jurisdiction to entertain any suit or proceeding in respect of anything done, action taken or order or direction issued by the Central Government or any authority or officer in pursuance of any power conferred by or in relation to its or his functions under this Act.

POWER TO DELEGATE

Without prejudice to the provisions of sub-section (3) of section 3, the Central Government may, by notification in the

Official Gazette, delegate, subject to such conditions and limitations as may be specified in the notification, such of its powers and functions under this Act, [except the power to constitute an authority under sub-section (3) of section 3 and to make rules under section 25] as it may deem necessary or expedient, to any officer, State Government or other authority.

Effect of Other Laws

Subject to the provisions of sub-section (2), the provisions of this Act and the rules or orders made therein shall have effect notwithstanding anything inconsistent therewith contained in any enactment other than this Act.

Where any act or omission constitutes an offence punishable under this Act and also under any other Act then the offender found guilty of such offence shall be liable to be punished under the other Act and not under this Act.

Power to Make Rules

The Central Government may, by notification in the Official Gazette, make rules for carrying out the purposes of this Act. In particular, and without prejudice to the generality of the foregoing power, such rules may provide for all or any of the following matters, namely :

- The standards in excess of which environmental pollutants shall not be discharged or emitted under section 7;
- The procedure in accordance with and the safeguards in compliance with which hazardous substances shall be handled or caused to be handled under section 8;
- The authorities or agencies to which intimation of the fact of occurrence or apprehension of occurrence of the discharge of any environmental pollutant in excess of the prescribed standards shall be given and to whom all assistance shall be bound to be rendered under sub-section (1) of section 9;
- The manner in which samples of air, water, soil or other substance for the purpose of analysis shall be taken under sub-section (1) of section 11;

- The form in which notice of intention to have a sample analysed shall be served under clause (a) of sub-section (3) of section 11;
- The functions of the environmental laboratories, the procedure for the submission to such laboratories of samples of air, water, soil and other substances for analysis or test; the form of laboratory report; the fees payable for such report and other matters to enable such laboratories to carry out their functions under sub-section (2) of section 12;
- The qualifications of Government Analyst, appointed or recognised for the purpose of analysis of samples of air, water, soil or other substances under section 13;
- The manner in which notice of the offence and of the intention to make a complaint to the Central Government shall be given under clause (b) of section 19;
  - The authority or officer to whom any reports, returns, statistics, accounts and other information shall be furnished under section 20;
- Any other matter which is required to be, or may be, prescribed.

Act to be Laid Before Parliament

Every rule made under this Act shall be laid, as soon as may be after it is made, before each House of Parliament, while it is in session, for a total period of thirty days which may be comprised in one session or in two or more successive sessions, and if, before the expiry of the session immediately following the session or the successive sessions aforesaid, both Houses agree in making any modification in the rule or both House agree that the rule should not be made, the rule shall thereafter have effect only in such modified form or be of no effect, as the case may be; so, however, that any such modification or annulment shall be without prejudice to the validity of anything previously done under that rule.

Chapter 2

Protection Rules 1986

INTRODUCTION

In exercise of the powers conferred by sections 6 and 25 of the Environment (Protection) Act, 1906, the Central Government hereby makes the following rules, namely:

SHORT TITLE AND COMMENCEMENT

- These rules may be called the Environment (Protection) Rules, 1986.
- They shall come into force on the date of their publication in the Official Gazette.

DEFINITIONS

In these rules, unless the context otherwise requires:

- "Act" means the Environment (Protection) Act, 1986 (29 of 1986);
- "Central Board" means the Central Pollution Control Board constituted under section 3 of the Water (Prevention and Control of Pollution) Act, 1974 (6 of 1974);
- "Form" means a form set forth in Appendix A to these rules;
- "Government Analyst" means a person appointed or recognized as such under section 13;
- "Person" in relation to any factory or premises means a person or occupier or his agent who has control over the affairs of the factory or premises and

includes in relation to any substance, the person in possession of the substance.

- "Recipient system" means the part of the environment such as soil, water, air or other which receives the pollutants;
- "State Board" means a State Pollution Control Board constituted under section 4 of the Water (Prevention and Control of Pollution) Act, 1974 or a State Pollution Control Board constituted under section 5 of the Air (Prevention and Control of Pollution) Act, 1981;

DISCHARGE OF ENVIRONMENTAL POLLUTANTS

Standards fr emission or Discharge of Environmental Pollutants:

(1) For the purposes of protecting and improving the quality of the environment and preventing and abating environmental pollution, the standards for emission or discharge of environmental pollutants from the industries, operations or processes shall be as specified in (5)[Schedules I to IV]

(2) Notwithstanding anything contained in sub-rule (1), the Central Board or a State Board may specify more stringent standards from those provided in (7)[Schedules I to IV] in respect of any specific industry, operation or process depending upon the quality of the recipient system and after recording reasons, therefor, in writing.

(3) The standards for emission or discharge of environmental pollutants specified under sub-rule (1) or sub-rule (2) shall be complied with by an industry, operation or process within a period of one year of being so specified.

[(3A) (i) Notwithstanding anything contained in sub-rules (1) and (2), on and from the 1st day of January, 1994, emission or discharge of environmental pollutants from the (10)[industries, operations or processes other than those industries, operations or processes for which standards have been specified in Schedule I shall] not exceed the relevant parameters and standards specified in Schedule VI:

Provided that the State Boards may specify more stringent standards for the relevant parameters with respect to specific industry or locations after recording reasons therefor in writing; (ii) The State Board shall while enforcing the standards specified in Schedule VI follow the guidelines specified in Annexures I and II in that Schedule.]

[(3B) Any emission or discharge of environmental pollutants from the industries, operations or possesses shall not exceed the relevant concentration in ambient air as indicated and set out against each pollutants in (3) to (5) of the Schedule VII.], (4) Notwithstanding anything contained in sub-rule (3), (a) the Central Board or a State Board, depending on the local conditions or nature of discharge of environment pollutants, may, by order, specify a lesser period than a period specified under sub-rule (3) within which the compliance of standards shall be made by an industry, operation or process; (b) the Central Government in respect of any specified industry, operation or process, by order, may specify any period other than a period specified under sub-rule (3)within which the compliance ofstandards shall be made by such industry, operation or process.

(5) Notwithstanding anything contained in sub-rule (3), the standards for emission or discharge of environmental pollutants specified under sub-rule (1) or sub-rule (2) in respect of an industry, operation or process before the commencement of the Environment (Protection) Amendment Rules, 1991, shall be complied with by such industry, operation or process by the 31st day of December, 1991.] (6) Notwithstanding anything contained in sub-rule (3), an industry, operation or process which has commenced production on or before 16th May, 1981 and has shown adequate proof of at least commencement of physical work for establishment of facilities to meet the specified standards within a time-bound programme, to the satisfaction of the concerned, State Pollution Control Board, shall comply with such standards latest by the 31st day of December, 1993. (7) Notwithstanding anything contained in sub-rule (3) or sub-rule (6) an industry, operation or process which has commenced production after the 16th day of May,

1981 but before the 31st day of December, 1991 and has shown adequate proof of at least commencement of physical work for establishment of facilities to meet the specified standards within a time-bound programme, to the satisfaction of the concerned State Pollution Control Board, shall comply with such standards latest by the 31st day of December, 1992.]

PROTECTION RULES, 1986 – DIRECTIONS

Directions

(1) Any direction issued under section 5 shall be in writing. (2) The direction shall specify the nature of action to be taken and the time within which it shall be complied with by the person, officer or the authority to whom such direction is given. [(3-a)] The person, officer or authority to whom any direction is sought to be issued shall be served with a copy of the proposed direction and shall be given an opportunity of not less than fifteen days from the date of service of a notice to file with an officer designated in this behalf the objections, if any, to the issue of the proposed direction.

[(3-b) Where the proposed direction is for the stoppage or regulation of electricity or water or any other service affecting the carrying on any industry, operation or process and is sought to be issued to an officer or an authority, a copy of the proposed direction shall also be endorsed to the occupier of the industry, operation or process, as the case may be, and objections, if any, filed by the occupier with an officer designated in this behalf shall be dealt with in accordance with the procedures under sub-rules (3-a) and (4) of this rule:

Provided that no opportunity of being heard shall be given to the occupier if he had already been beard earlier and the proposed direction referred to in sub-rule (3-b) above for the stoppage or regulation of electricity or water or any other service was the resultant decision of the Central Government after such earlier hearing.]

(4) The Central Government shall within a period of 45 days from the date of receipt of the objections, if any, or from the date up to which an opportunity is given to the person,

officer or authority to file objections whichever is earlier, after considering the objections, if any, received from the person, officer or authority sought to be directed and for reasons to be recorded in writing, confirm, modify or decide not to issue the proposed direction. (5) In a case where the Central Government is of the opinion that in view of the likelihood of a grave injury to the enviromnent it is not expedient to provide an opportunity to file objections against the proposed direction, it may, for reasons to be recorded in writing, issue directions without providing such an opportunity. (6) Every notice or direction required to be issued under this rule shall be deemed to be duly served-

- Where the person to be served is a company, if the document is addressed in the name of the company at its registered office or at its principal office or place of businessand is either,-
  - Sent by registered post; or
  - Delivered at its registered office or at the principal office or place of business;
- Where the person to be served is an officer serving Government, if the document is addressed to the person and a copy thereof is endorsed to the Head of the Department and also to the Secretary to the Government, as the case may be, incharge of the Department in which for the time being the business relating to the Department in which the officer is employed is transacted and is either,-
  - Sent by registered post; or
  - Is given or tendered to him;
- In any other case, if the document is addressed to the person to be served
  - Is given or tendered to him; or
  - If such person cannot be found, is affixed on some conspicuous part of his last known place of residence or business or is given or tendered to some adult member of his family or is affixed on some conspicuous part of the land or building, if any, to which it relates; or

– Is sent by registered post to that person.

Explanation:For the purposes of this sub-rule,

- "Company"means any body corporate and includes a firm or other association of individuals;
- "A servant" is not a member of the family.

PROCEDURE FOR TAKING SAMPLES

Procedure for Taking Samples

The Central Government or the officer empowered to take samples under section 11 shall collect the sample in sufficient quantity to be divided into two uniform parts and effectively seal and suitably mark the same and permit the person from whom the sample is taken to add his own seal or mark to all or any of the portions so sealed and marked. In case where the sample is made up in containers or small volumes and is likely to deteriorate or be otherwise damaged if exposed, the Central Government or the officer empowered shall take two of the said samples without opening the containers and suitably seal and mark the same.

The Central Government or the officer empowered shall dispose of the samples so collected as follows:

- One portion shall be handed over to the person from whom the sample is taken under acknowledgement;
- The other portion shall be sent forth with to the environmental laboratory for analysis.]

Service of Notice

The Central Government or the officer empowered shall serve on the occupier or his agent or person in charge of the place a notice then and there in Form I of his intention to have the sample analysed.

Procedure for submission of samples for analysis, and the form of laboratory report thereon:

- Sample taken for analysis shall be sent by the Central Government or the officer empowered to the environmental laboratory by registered post or through special messenger along with Form II.

- Another copy of Form II together with specimen impression of seals of the officer empowered to take samples along with the seals/marks, if any, of the person from whom the sample is taken shall be sent separately in a sealed cover by registered post or through a special messenger to the environmental laboratory.
- The findings shall be recorded in Form III in triplicate and signed by the Government Analyst and sent to the officer from whom the sample is received for analysis.
- On receipt of the report of the findings of the Government Analyst, the officer shall send one copy of the report to the person from whom the sample was taken for analysis, the second copy shall be retained by him for his records and the third copy shall be kept by him to be produced in the Court before which proceedings, if any are, instituted.

FUNCTIONS OF ENVIRONMENTAL LABORATORIES

The following shall be the functions of environmental laboratories:

- To evolve standardised methods for sampling and analysis of various types of environmental pollutants;
- To analyse samples sent by the Central Government or the officers empowered under sub-section (1) of section 11;
- To carry out such investigations as may be directed by the Central Government to lay down standards for the quality of environment and discharge of environmental pollutants, to monitor and to enforce the standards laid down;
- To send periodical reports regarding its activities to the Central Government;
- To carry out such other functions as may be entrusted to it by the Central Government from time to time.

Qualifications of Government Analyst

A person shall not be qualified for appointment or recognised as a Government Analyst unless he is a-

- Graduate in science from a recognised university with five years'experience in a laboratory engaged in environmental investigations, testing or analysis;
- Post-graduate in science or a graduate in engineering or a graduate in medicine or equivalent with two years'experience in a laboratory engaged in environmental investigations, testing or analysis; or
- Post-graduate in environmental science from a recognized university with two years' experience in a laboratory engaged in environmental investigations, testing or analysis.

FURNISHING OF INFORMATION TO AUTHORITIES

Manner of Giving Notice

The manner of giving notice under clause (b) of section 19 shall be as follows, namely:

- The notice shall be, in writing in Form IV.
- The person giving notice may send notice to,

(a) if the alleged offence has taken place in a Union territory: (A) the Central Board; and (B) the Ministry of Environment and Forests (represented by the Secretary of the Government of India); (b) if the alleged offence has taken place in a State: (A) the State Board; and (B) the Government of the State (represented by the Secretary to the State Government incharge of environment); and (C) the Ministry of Environment and Forests (represented by the Secretary to the Government of India).

- The notice shall be sent by registered post-acknowledgement due.
- The period of sixty days mentioned in clause (b) of section 19 of the Environment (Protection) Act, 1986 shall be reckoned from the date it is first received by one of the authorities mentioned above.

Furnishing of Information to Agencies in Certain Cases

Where the discharge of environmental pollutant in excess of the prescribed standard occurs or is apprehended to occur due to any accident or other unforeseen act or event, the person in charge of the place at which such discharge occurs or is apprehended to occur shall forthwith intimate the fact of such occurrence or apprehension of such occurrence to all the following authorities or agencies, namely:-

- The officer-in-charge of emergency or disaster relief operations in a district or other region of a State or Union territory specified by whatever designation, by the Government of the said State or Union territory, and in whose jurisdiction the industry, process or operation is located;
- The Central Board or a State Board, as the case may be, and its regional officer having local jurisdiction who have been delegated powers under sections 20, 21, 23 of the Water (Prevention and Control of Pollution) Act, 1974 and section 24 of the Air (Prevention and Control of Pollution) Act, 1981 (14 of 1981);
- The Statutory authorities or agencies specified in column 3 in relation to places mentioned in column 2 against thereof of.]

HANDLING OF HAZARDOUS SUBSTANCES

- The Central Government may take into consideration the following factors while prohibiting or restricting the handling of hazardous substances in different areas:
  - The hazardous nature of the substance (either in qualitative or quantitative terms) as far as may be in terms of its damage causing potential to the environment, human beings, other living creatures, plants and property;
  - The substances that may be or likely to be or readily available as substitutes for the substances proposed to be prohibited or restricted;

- The indigenous availability of the substitute, or the state o f technology available in the country for developing a safe substitute;
- The gestation period that may be necessary for gradual introduction of a new substitute with a view to bringing about a total prohibition of the hazardous substance in question; and
- Any other factor as may be considered by the Central Government to be relevant to the protection of environment.

- While prohibiting or restricting the handling of hazardous substances in an area including their imports and exports the Central Government shall follow the procedure hereinafter laid down:-
  - Whenever it appears to the Central Government that it is expedient to impose prohibition or restriction on the handling of hazardous substances in an area, it may, by notification in the Official Gazette and in such other manner as the Central Government may deem necessary from time to time, give notice of its intention to do so.
  - Every notification under clause (i) shall give a brief description of the hazardous substances and the geographical region or the area to which such notification pertains and also specify the reasons for the imposition of prohibition or restriction on the handling of such hazardous substances in that region or area.
  - Any person interested in filing an objection against the imposition of prohibition or restrictions on the handling of hazardous substances as notified under clause (i) may do so in writing to the Central Government within thirty days from the date of publication of the notification in the Official Gazette.
  - The Central Government shall within a period of sixty days from the date of publication of the

notification in the Official Gazette consider all the objections received against such notification and may impose prohibition or restrictions on the handling of hazardous substances in a region or an area.]

SUBMISSION OF ENVIRONMENT

Every person carrying on an industry, operation or process requiring consent under section 25 of the Water (Prevention and Control of Pollution) Act, 1974 (6 of 1974) or under section 21 of the Air (Prevention and Control of Pollution) Act, 1981 (14 of 1981) or both or authorisation under the Hazardous Waters (Management and Handling) Rules, 1989 issued under the Environment (Protection) Act, 1986 (29 of 1986) shall submit an environmental

NOTIFICATION

S.O. 844(E)

In exercise of the powers conferred by sections 6 and 25 of the Environment (Protection) Act, 1906 (29 of 1986), the Central Government hereby makes the following rules, namely:-

Short Title and Commencement

- These rules may be called the Environment (Protection) Rules, 1986.
- They shall come into force on the date of their publication in the Official Gazette.

Definitions

In these rules, unless the context otherwise requires:

- "Act" means the Environment (Protection) Act, 1986 (29 of 1986);
- "Central Board" means the Central Pollution Control Board constituted under section 3 of the Water (Prevention and Control of Pollution) Act, 1974 (6 of 1974);

- "Form" means a form set forth in Appendix A to these rules;
- "Government Analyst" means a person appointed or recognized as such under section 13;
- "person" in relation to any factory or premises means a person or occupier or his agent who has control over the affairs of the factory or premises and includes in relation to any substance, the person in possession of the substance.
- "recipient system" means the part of the environment such as soil, water, air or other which receives the pollutants;
- "section" means a section of the Act;
- "Schedule" means a Schedule appended to these rules;
- "Standards' means standards prescribed under these rules;
- "State Board" means a State Pollution Control Board constituted under section 4 of the Water (Prevention and Control of Pollution) Act, 1974 (6 of 1974) or a State Pollution Control Board constituted under section 5 of the Air (Prevention and Control of Pollution) Act, 1981;

Standards for Emissions or Discharge

(1) For the purpose of protecting and improving the quality of the environment and preventing and abating environmental pollution, the standards for emission or discharge of environmental pollutants from the industries, operations or processes shall be as specified in [Schedule I to IV]. (2) Notwithstanding anything contained in sub-rule (1),the Central Board or a State Board may specify more stringent standards from those provided in [Schedule I to IV] in respect of any specific industry, operation or process depending upon the quality of the recipient system and after recording reasons therefore in writing. (3) The standards for emission or discharge of environmental pollutants specified under sub-rule (1) or sub-rule (2) shall be complied with by an industry,

operation or process within a period of one year of being so specified. [(3A) (i) Notwithstanding anything contained in sub-rules (1) and (2), on and from the 1st day of January, 1994, emission or discharge of environmental pollutants from the [industries, operations or processes other than those industries, operations or processes for which standards have been specified in Schedule-I] shall not exceed the relevant parameters and standards specified in schedule VI.

Provided that the State Boards may specify more stringent standards for the relevant parameters with respect to specific industry or locations after recording reasons therefore in writing; (ii) The State Board shall while enforcing the standards specified in Schedule VI follow the guidelines specified in Annexure I and II in that Schedule]. [(3B)] The combined effect of emission or discharge of environmental pollutants in an area, from industries, operations, process, automobiles and domestic sources, shall not be permitted to exceed the relevant concentration in ambient air as specified against each pollutant in columns (3) to (5) of Schedule VII.] (4) Notwithstanding anything contained in sub-rule (3)- (a) the Central Board or a State Board, depending on the local conditions or nature of discharge of environmental pollutants, may, by order, specify a lesser period than a period specified under sub-rule (3) within which the compliance of standards shall be made by an industry, operation or process (b) the Central Government in respect of any specific industry, operation or process, by order, may specify any period other than a period specified under sub-rule (3) within which the compliance of standards shall be made by such industry, operation or process. (5) Notwithstanding anything contained in sub-rule (3) the standards for emission or discharge of environmental pollutants specified under sub-rule (I) or sub-rule (2) in respect of an industry, operation or process before the commencement of the Environment (Protection) Amendment Rules, 1991, shall be complied by such industry, operation or process by the 31st day of December 1991. [(6) Notwithstanding anything contained in sub-rule (3), an industry, operation or process which has commenced production on or before 16th May, 1981 and has shown adequate proof of at least commencement of physical work for establishment of facilities to meet the specified standards within a time-bound programme, to the satisfaction of the concerned State Pollution Control Board, shall comply with such standards latest by the 31 st day of December, 1993. (7) Notwithstanding anything contained in sub-rule (3) or sub-rule (6) an industry, operation or process which has commenced production after the 16th day of May, 1981 but before the 31st day of December 1991 and has shown adequate proof of at least commencement of physical work for establishment of facilities to meet the specified standards within a time-bound programme, to the satisfaction of the concerned State Pollution Control Board, shall comply with such standards latest by the 31st day of December, 1992.]

Directions

(1) Any direction issued under section 5 shall be in writing. (2) The direction shall specify the nature of action to be taken and the time within which it shall be complied with by the person, officer or the authority to whom such direction is given. (3) (a) The person, officer or authority to whom any direction is sought to be issued shall be served with a copy of the proposed direction and shall be given an opportunity of not less than fifteen days from the date of service of a notice to file with an officer designated in this behalf the objections, if any, to the issue of the proposed direction. (b) Where the proposed direction is for the stoppage or regulation of electricity or water or any other service affecting the carrying on any industry, operation or process and is sought to be issued to an officer or an authority, a copy of the proposed direction shall also be endorsed to the occupier of the industry, operation or process, as the case may be and objections, if any, filed by the occupier with an officer designated in this behalf shall be dealt with in accordance with the procedures under sub-rules (3a) and (4) of this rule: Provided that no opportunity of being heard shall be given to the occupier if he had already been heard earlier and the proposed direction referred to in sub-rule (3b) above for the stoppage or regulation of electricity

or water or any other service was the resultant decision of the Central Government after such earlier hearing. (4) The Central Government shall within a period of 45 days from the date of receipt of the objections, if any or from the date up to which an opportunity is given to the person, officer or authority to file objections whichever is earlier, after considering the objections, if any, received from the person, officer or authority sought to be directed and for reasons to be recorded in writing, confirm, modify or decide not to issue the proposed direction. (5) In case where the Central Government is of the opinion that in view of the likelihood of a grave injury to the environment it is not expedient to provide an opportunity to file objections against the proposed direction, it may, for reasons to be recorded in writing, issue directions without providing such an opportunity. (6) Every notice or direction required to be issued under this rule shall be deemed to be duly served (a) where the person to be served is a company, if the document is addressed in the name of the company at its registered office or at its principal office or place of business and is either.

- Sent by registered post,
- Delivered at its registered office or at the principal office or place of business; (b) where the person to be served is an officer serving Government, if the document is addressed to the person and a copy thereof is endorsed to this Head of the Department and also to the Secretary to the Government, as the case may be, in-charge of the Department in which for the time being the business relating to the Department in which the officer is employed is transacted and is either-
- Sent by registered post, or
- Given or tendered to him; (c) in any other case, if the document is addressed to the person to be served
- Is given or tendered to him, or
- If such person cannot be found, is affixed on some conspicuous part of his last known place of residence or business or is given or tendered to some adult

member of his family or is affixed on some conspicuous part of the land or building, if any, to which it relates, or

- Is sent by registered post to that person;

*Explanation:*For the purpose of this sub-rule,-

- "Company" means any body corporate and includes a firm or other association of individuals;
- "A servant" is not a member of the family.

Prohibitions and Restrictions

(1) The Central government may take into consideration the following factors while prohibiting or restricting the location of industries and carrying on of processes and operations in different areas,

- Standards for quality of environment in its various aspects laid down for an area.
- The maximum allowable limits of concentration of various environmental pollutants (including noise) [or an area.
- The likely emission or discharge of environmental pollutants from an industry, process or operation proposed to be prohibited or restricted.
- The topographic and climatic features of an area.
- The biological diversity of the area which, in the opinion of the Central Government needs to be preserved.
- Environmentally compatible land use.
- Net adverse environmental impact likely to be caused by an industry, process or operation proposed to be prohibited or restricted.
- Proximity to a protected area under the Ancient Monuments and Archaeological Sites and Remains Act, 1958 or a sanctuary, National Park, game reserve or closed area notified as such under the Wild Life (Protection) Act, 1972 or places protected under any treaty, agreement or convention with any other country or countries or in pursuance of any decision made in any international confcrcnce1 association or other body.

- Proximity to human settlements.
- Any other factor as may be considered by the Central Government to De relevant to the protection of the environment in an area.

(2) While prohibiting or restricting the location of industries and carrying on of processes and operations in an area, the Central Government shall follow the procedure hereinafter laid down. (3) (a) Whenever it appears to the Central Government that it is expedient to impose prohibition or restrictions on the locations Of an industry or the carrying on of processes and operations in an area, it may by notification in the Official Gazette and in such other manner as the Central government may deem necessary from time to time, give notice of its intention to do so. (b) Every notification under clause (a) shall give a brief description of the area, the industries, operations, processes in that area about which such notification pertains and also specify the reasons for the imposition of prohibition or restrictions on the locations of the industries and carrying on of process or operations in that area. (c) Any person interested in filing an objection against the imposition of prohibition or restrictions on carrying on of processes or operations as notified under clause (a) may do so in writing to the Central Government within sixty days from the date of publication of the notification in the Official Gazette. (d) The Central Government shall within a period of one hundred and twenty days from the date of publication of the notification in the Official Gazette consider all the objections received against such notification and may [within one hundred and eighty days from such day of publication] impose prohibition or restrictions on location of such industries and the carrying on of any process or operation in an area.

PROCEDURE OF TAKING SAMPLES

The Central Government or the officer empowered to take samples under section 11 shall collect the sample in sufficient quantity to be divided into two uniform parts and effectively seal and suitably mark the same and permit the person from whom the sample is taken to add his own seal or mark to all or any of the portions so sealed and marked. In case where the sample is made up in containers or small volumes and is likely to deteriorate or be otherwise damaged if exposed, the Central Government or the officer empowered shall take two of the said samples without opening the containers and suitably seal and mark the same.

The Central Government or the officer empowered shall dispose of the samples so collected as follows:

- One portion shall be handed over to the person from whom the sample is taken under acknowledgement;
- The other portion shall be sent forthwith to the environmental laboratory or analysis.

Service of Notice

The Central Government or the officer empowered shall serve on the occupier or his agent or person in charge of the place a notice then and there in Form I of his intention to have the sample analyzed.

Procedure for Submission of Samples for Analysis, and the Form of Laboratory Report Thereon

- Sample taken for analysis shall be sent by the Central Government or the officer empowered to the environmental laboratory by registered post or through special messenger along with Form II.
- Another copy of Form II together with specimen impression of seals of the officer empowered to take samples along with the seals/marks, if any, of the person from whom the sample is taken shall be sent separately in a sealed cover by registered post or through a special messenger to the environmental laboratory.
- The findings shall be recorded in Form III in triplicate and signed by the Government Analyst and sent to the officer from whom the sample is received for analysis.
- On receipt of the report of the findings of the Government Analyst, the officer shall send one copy

of the report to the person from whom the sample was taken for analysis, the second copy shall be retained by him for his record and the third copy shall be kept by him to be produced in the Court before which proceedings, if any, are instituted.

Functions of Environmental LaboraTories

The following shall be the functions of environmental laboratories:

- To evolve standardized methods for sampling and analysis of various types of environmental pollutants;
- To analyse samples sent by the Central Government or the officers empowered under sub-section (1) of section 11.
- To carry out such investigations as may be directed by the Central Government to lay down standards for the quality of environment and discharge of environmental pollutants, to monitor and to enforce the standards laid down;
- To send periodical reports regarding its activities to the Central Government;
- To carry out such other functions as may be entrusted to it by the Central Government from time to time.

Qualification of Government Analyst

A person shall not be qualified for appointment or recognized as a Government Analyst unless he is a:

- Graduate in science from a recognized university with five years experience in laboratory engaged in environmental investigation, testing or analysis; or
- Post-graduate in science or a graduate in engineering or a graduate in medicine or equivalent with two years experience in a laboratory engaged in environmental investigations testing or analysis; or
- Post-graduate in environmental science from a recognized university with two years experience in a laboratory engaged in environmental investigations, testing or analysis.

Manner of Giving Notice

The manner of giving notice under clause (b) of section 19 shall be as follows, namely:

- The notice shall be in writing in Form IV.
- The person giving notice may send notice to-

(a) if the alleged offence has taken place in a Union territory (A) the Central Board and (B) Ministry of Environment and Forests (represented by the Secretary to Government of India); (b) if the alleged offence has taken place in a State: (A) the State Board; and (B) the Government of the State (represented by the Secretary to the State Government in-charge of environment); and (C) the Ministry of Environment and Forests (represented by the Secretary to the Government of India);

- The notice shall be sent by registered post acknowledgement due; and
- The period Of sixty days mentioned in clause (b) of section 19 of the Environment (Protection) Act, 1986 shall be reckoned from the date it is first received by one of the authorities mentioned above.

Furnishing of Information to Authorities

Where the discharge of environmental pollutant in excess of the prescribed standards occurs or is apprehended to occur due to any accident or other unforeseen act or event, the person in charge of the place at which such discharge occurs or is apprehended to occur shall forth with intimate the fact of such occurrence or apprehension of such occurrence to all the following authorities or agencies, namely:-

- The officer-in-charge of emergency or disaster relief operation in a district or other region of a state or Union territory specified by whatever designation by the Government of the said State or Union territory, and in whose jurisdiction the industry, process or operation is located.
- Central Board or a State Board as the case may be and its regional officer having local jurisdiction who have been delegated powers under section 20, 21, 23

of the Water (Prevention and Control of Pollution) Act 1974 (6 of 1974)- and section 24 of the Air (Prevention and Control of Pollution) Act, 1981 (14 of 1981).

- The statutory authorities or agencies specified in column 3 in relation to places mentioned in column 2 against thereof of the Schedule II.]

Handling of Hazardous Substances

- The Central Government may take into consideration the following factors while prohibiting or restricting the handling of hazardous substances in different area is-
  - The hazardous nature of the substance (either in qualitative or quantitative terms as far as may be) in terms of its damage causing potential to the environment, human beings, other living creatures, plants and property;
  - The substances that may be or likely to be readily available as substitutes for the substances proposed to be prohibited or restricted;
  - The indigenous availability of the substitute, or the state of technology available in the country for developing a safe substitute;
  - The gestation period that may be necessary for gradual introduction of a new substitute with a view to bringing about a total prohibition of the hazardous substance in question; and
  - Any other factor as may be considered by the Central Government to be relevant to the protection of environment.
- While prohibiting or restricting the handling of hazardous substances in an area including their imports and exports the Central Government shall follow the procedure hereinafter laid down-
  - Whenever it appears to the Central Government that it is expedient to impose prohibition or restriction on the handling of hazardous

substances in an area, it may, by notification in the Official Gazette and in such other manner as the Central Government may deem necessary from time to time, give notice of its intention to do so.

- Every notification under clause (i) shall give a brief description of the hazardous substances and the geographical region or the area to which such notification pertains, and also specify the reasons for the imposition of prohibition or restriction on the handling of such hazardous substances in that region or area.
- Any person interested in filing an objection against the imposition of prohibition or restrictions on the handling of hazardous substances as notified under clause (i) may do so in writing to the Central Government within sixty days from the dale of publication of the notification in the Official Gazette.
- The Central Government shall within a period of ninety days from the date of publication of the notification in the Official Gazette consider all the objections received against such notification and may impose prohibition or restrictions on the handling of hazardous substances in a region or an area.]

Submission of Environmental 16[Statement]

Every person carrying on an industry, operation or process requiring consent under Section 25 of the Water (Prevention and Control of Pollution) Act, 1974 (6 of 1974) or under section 21 of the Air (Prevention and Control of Pollution) Act, 1981 (14 of 1981) or both or authorization under the Hazardous Wastes (Management and Handling) Rules, 1989 issued under the Environment (Protection) Act, *Notes*:

- Clauses (aa), (ee) and (ff) inserted by Notification NO. G.S.R. 931(E) dated 27.10.89 published in the Gazette NO. 564 dated 27.10.89. These rules are- referred to as Principal Rules in all Notifications beginning with S.O. 82(E) published in the Gazette No. 66.

- Substituted by notification G.S.R 422(E) dated 19.5.93, published in the Gazette No. 174.
- Substituted ibid.
- The sub-rule (3) of rule 3 inserted vide S.O. 23(E) dated 16.1.91.
- The sub-rule (3A) of rule 3 inserted by rule 2(a)(iii) of the Environment Protection) Second Amendment Rules, 1993 notified vide G.S.R. 422(E) dated19.5.93, published in the Gazette No.174 dated 19.5.93.
- Substituted by rule 2(a) of the Environment (Protection) Third Amendment Rules, 1993 notified vide Notification G.S.R. 801(E), dated 31.12.93, published in Gazette No.463 dated 31.12.93.
- Substituted by Rule2(a) of the Environment (Protection) Second (Amendment) Rules, 1998 notified by notification G.S.R. 7, dated 22.12.98.
- Sub-rule (6) and (7) of rule 3 were added by the Environment (Protection) Amendment Rule, 1992 vide G.S.R. 95(E) dated 12.02.1992.
- Sub-rule (3) of rule 4 of the Principal Rules was re-numbered as sub-rule 3(a) and sub-rule 3(b) inserted vide Notification No. S.O. 64(E) published in the Gazette No. 42 dated 18.1.88.
- Inserted by Rule 2 of the Environment (Protection) (Third Amendment) Rules, 1992 notified vide G.S.R. 562(E), dated 22.5.1992.
- Substituted by Rule 2 of the Environment (Protection) Fourth Amendment) Rule, 1992 notified vide G.S.R. 636(E), dated 25.6.1992.
- For rule 6 of the principal rules this rule was substitute vide S.O. 64(E) published in the Gazette No. 42 dated 18.1.88.
- Rule 12 inserted vide Notification No. S.O. 32(E) dated 16.2.87 published in the Gazette No. 66 dated 16.2.87.

- Rule 13 inserted vide Notification No G.S.R. 931(E) dated 27.10.89 published in the Gazette No. 564 dated 27.10.89.
- Inserted by Rule 2 of the Environment (Protection) Second Amendment & Rules, 1992 vide G.S.R. 329(E), dated 13.03.92.
- Substituted by Rule 2(a)(i) of the Environment (Protection) Amendment Rules, 1993 vide notification G.S.R. 386(E), dated 22.4.93.

Chapter 3

Hazardous Wastes

In exercise of the powers conferred by sections 6, 8 and 25 of the Environment (Protection) Act, 1986, the Central Government hereby makes the following rules, namely :

SHORT TITLE AND COMMENCEMENT

- These rules may be called the Hazardous Wastes (Management and Handling) Rules, 1989.
- They shall come into force on the date of their publication in the official Gazette.

APPLICATION

These rules shall apply to the handling of hazardous wastes as specified in Schedule and shall not apply to:

- Waste water and exhaust gases as covered under the provisions of the Water (Prevention and Control of Pollution) Act, 1974 (6 of 1974) and the Air (Prevention and Control of Pollution) Act, 1981 (14 of 1981) and rules made thereunder;
- Wastes arising out of the operation from ships beyond five kilometres as covered under the provisions of the Merchant Shipping Act,. 1958 (\44 of 1958) and the rules made thereunder,
- R-adio-active wastes as covered under the provisions of the Atomic Energy Act, 1962 (33 of 1962) and rules made thereunder,

DEFINITIONS

In these rules, unless the context otherwise requires:

- "Act" means the Environment (Protection) Act, 1986 (29 of 1986);
- "Applicant" means a person or an organisation that applies, in Form 1, for granting of authorisation to perform specific activities connected with handling of hazardous wastes;
- "Authorisation" means permission for collection, reception, treatment, transport, storage and disposal of hazardous wastes granted by the competent authority in Form 2;
- "Authorised person" means a person or an organisation authorised by the competent authority to collect, treat, transport, store or dispose of hazardous wastes in accordance with the guidelines to be issued by the competent authority from time to time;
- "Export" with its grammatical variation and cognate expression means taking out of India to a place outside India;
- "Exporter' means any person under the jurisdiction of the expor.6ng country who exports hazardous wastes and the exporting country itself, who exports hazardous wastes'
- "Facility" means any location wherein the processes, incidental to the waste generation collection, reception, treatment, storage and disposal are carried out;
- "Form" means Form appended to these rules;
- "Hazardous wastes" means, (a) Waste Substances which are generated in the process indicated in column-2 of Schedule-1 and consists of wholly or partly of the waste substances referred to in column - 3 of the same schedule; (b) Waste substances which consists wholly or partly of substances indicated in Schedule-2, unless the concentration of the substances is less than the limit indicated in the same schedule: and (c) Waste substances indicated in Part-A, List 'A' and 'B' of Schedule -3 applicable only to rule 12, 13 and 14 unless they do not possess any of the

hazardous characteristicsin Part-B of the same schedule.

- "Hazardous wastes site" means a place for collection, reception, treatment, storage and disposal of hazardous wastes which has been duly approved by the competent authority;
- "Import" with its grammatical variations and cognate expressions, means bringing into India from a place outside India;
- "Importer" means an occupier or any person who imports hazardous wastes;
- "Operator of a facility" means a person who owns or operates a facility for collection. reception, treatment, storage and disposal of hazardous wastes;
- "Schedule" means Schedule appended to these rules;
- "State Pollution Control Board" means the Board appointed under sub-section of the section 4 of the Water (Prevention and Control of Pollution) Act 1974 (6 of 1974); and under Section 4 of the Air (Prevention and Control of Pollution3 Act, 1981 (14 of 1981);
- "Transboundary movement" means any movement of hazardous wastes or other wastes from an area under the national jurisdiction of one country to or through an area under the national jurisdiction of another country or to or through an area not under the national jurisdiction of any country, provided at least two countries are involved in the movement;
- "Disposal" means deposit, treatment, storage and recovery of any hazardous wastes;}
- "Manifest" means transporting document originated and signed by the occupier in accordance with rule 7(4) and 7(5);
- "State Government" means State Government and in relation to Union Territory the Administrator thereof appointed under Article 239 of the Constitution;
- "Storage" means keeping hazardous wastes for a temporary period, at the end of which the hazardous waste is treated and disposed off;

- "Transport" means movement of hazardous waste by air, rail, road or water;
- "Transporter" means a person engaged in the off-site transportation of hazardous waste by air, rail, road or water;
- "Treatment" means a method, technique or process, designed to change the physical, chemical or biological characteristics or composition of any hazardous waste so as to render such wastes harmless;
- "Environmentally sound management of hazardous wastes" means taking all steps to ensure that the hazardous wastes are managed in a manner which will protect human health and the environment against the adverse effects which may result from such wastes;
- "Illegal traffic" means any transboundary movement of hazardous wastes as specified in rule 15;
- The words and expressions used in these rules and not defined but defined in the Act, shall have the meanings respectively assigned to them in the Act.

RESPONSIBILITY OF OCCUPIER AND OPERATOR

- The occupier and the operator of a facility shall be responsible for proper collection, reception, treatment, storage and disposal of hazardous wastes listed in Schedule 1,2 and 3.
- The occupier or any other person acting on his behalf who intends to get his hazardous waste treated by the operator of a facility under sub-rule (1), shall give to the operator of a facility, such information as may be specified by the State Pollution Control Board.
- It shall be the responsibility of the occupier and the operator of a facility, to take all steps to ensure that the wastes listed in schedules -1, 2 and 3 are properly handled, and disposed of without any adverse effects to the environment.

Duties

It shall be the duty of the occupier and the operator of a

facility to take adequate steps while handling hazardous waste to Contain contaminants and prevent accidents and limit their consequences on human and the environment; and Provide persons working on the site with information, training and equipment necessary to ensure their safety.

Duties of the Authority

Subject to the provisions of these rules, the authority shall also perform duties as specified in Column 3 of Schedule 4.

AUTHORISATION FOR HANDLING HAZARDOUS WASTES

(1) Hazardous wastes shall be collected, treated, stored and disposed of only in such facilities as may be authorised for this purpose. (2) Every occupier generating hazardous wastes and having a facility for collection, reception, treatment, transport storage and disposal of such wastes shall make an application in Form 1 along with a sum of rupees seven thousand five hundred only for processing application for authorization and analysis fee, if required, as prescribed under the Environment (Protection) Act, 1986 to the State Pollution Control Board for the grant of authorisation for any of the above ctivities: Provided that the occupier not having a facility for the collection, reception, treatment, transport, storage and disposal of hazardous wastes shall make an application to the Member-Secretary, State Pollution Control Board or any officer designated by the Board in Form 1 for the grant of authorisation within a period of six months from the date of commencement of these rules. (3) Any person who intends to be an operator of a facility for the collection, reception, treatment, transport, storage and disposal of hazardous wastes, shall make an application in Form 1 along with a sum of rupees seven thousand five hundred only for processing application for authorization and analysis fee, if required, as prescribed under the Environment (Protection) Act, 1986 to the Member-Secretary, State Pollution Control Board or any officer designated by the Board for the grant of authorisation for any of the above activities: Provided that the operator engaged in

the business of the collection, reception, treatment, transport, storage and disposal of hazardous wastes shall make an application to the Member-Secretary, State Pollution Control Board or any officer designated by the Board in Form 1 for the grant of authorisation within a period of six months from the date of commencement of these rules. (4) The State Pollution Control Board shall not issue an authorisation unless it is satisfied that the operator of a facility or an occupier, as the case may be, possesses appropriate facilities, technical capabilities and equipment to handle hazardous wastes safely. (4A) the authorisation application complete in all respects shall be processed by the State Pollution Control Boards within ninety days of the receipt of such application (5) The authorisation to operate a facility shall be issued in Form 2 and shall be subject to conditions laid down therein. (6) (i) An authorisation granted under this rule shall unless sooner suspended or cancelled, be in force for a period of five years from the date of issue or from the date of renewal. (ii) An application for the renewal of an authorisation shall be made in Form lr before its expiry. (iii) The authorisation shall continue to be in force until it is renewed or revoked. (7) The Member-Secretary, State Pollution Control Board or any officer designated by the Board, may, after giving reasonable opportunity of being heard to the applicant refuse to grant any authorisation. (8) The Member-Secretary, State Pollution Control Board or any officer designated by the Board shall renew the authorisation granted under sub rule (6), after examining each case on merit, subject to the following: (i) on submission of annual returns by the occupier or operator of facility in Form 4; (ii) on steps taken, wherever feasible, for reduction in waste generated or recycled or reused; (iii) on fulfilment of conditions prescribed in the authorisation regarding management in an environmentally sound manner of wastes; and (iv) on remittance of a processing application fee and analysis fee, as the case may be.

POWER TO SUSPEND OR CANCEL

- The State Pollution Control Board or Committee may

cancel an authorisation issued under these rules or suspend it for such period as it thinks fit, if in its opinion, the authorised person has failed to comply with any of the conditions of the authorisation or with any provisions of the Act or these rules, after giving the authorised person an opportunity to show cause and after recording reasons therefor.

- Upon suspension or cancellation of the authorisation and during the pendency of an appeal under rule 12, the State Pollution Control Board or Committee may give directions to the persons whose authorisation has been suspended or cancelled for the safe storage of the hazardous wastes, and such person shall comply with such directions.

PACKAGING, LABELLING AND TRANSPORT

- The occupier or operator of a facility shall ensure that the hazardous wastes are packaged, based on the composition in a manner suitable for handling, storage and transport and the labelling and packaging shall be easily visible and be able to withstand physical conditions and climatic factors.
- Packaging, labelling and transport of hazardous wastes shall be in accordance with the provisions of the rules made by Central Government under the Motor Vehicles Act, 1988 and other guidelines issued from time to time.
- All hazardous waste containers shall be provided with a general label as given in Form 8.
- No transporter shall accept hazardous wastes from an occupier for disposal unless it is accompanied by five copies of the manifest (Form 9) as per the colour codes. The transporter shall give a copy of the manifest signed and dated to the occupier and retain the remaining four copies to be used as prescribed in sub- rule (5).
- Occupier shall provide the transporter with six copies of the manifest as per the colour codes indicated below:

Copy 1(White) forwarded to the Pollution Control Board by the occupier Copy 2(Light Yellow) signed by the transporter and retained by the occupier. Copy 3 (Pink) retained by the operator of a facility. Copy 4(Orange) returned to transporter by the operator of facility after accepting waste. Copy 5 (green) orward to Pollution Control Board by operator of facility after disposal. Copy 6 (Blue) returned to the occupier by the operator of the facility after disposal.

- The occupier shall obtain necessary nc-objection certificate from State Pollution Control Boards in the respective states involved in case of any inter and intra State transport of hazardous wastes;
- The occupier shall provide the transporter with relevant information in Form 10, regarding thehazardous nature of the wastes and measures to be taken in case of an emergency.

DISPOSAL SITES

- The occupier or any operator of a facility shall be responsible for identifying sites for establishing hazardous wastes disposal facility;
- The State Government, operator of a facility or any association of occupiers shall identify sites for common hazardous wastes disposal facility in the state;
- The State Government, occupier or any association shall after preliminary impactassessment studies identify possible sites for disposal facility. They shall then undertake an Environmental Impact Assessment of these sites for selecting an appropriate site for hazardous waste disposal facility;
- The occupier or any association after identification as prescribed in sub-rule (3) shall inform the State Government to take necessary action for notifying of the site;
- The State Government shall after identification or on receipt of information regarding identification by

such occupier or any such association shall cause a public notice inviting objections and suggestions within thirty days;

- The state Government shall on receipt of any objection conduct a public hearing as per the procedure notified for Environmental Impact Assessment;
- The state Government shall then, acquire or inform such occupier or any such association to acquire the site before notifying the same. It shall also undertake to compile and publish periodically an inventory of such disposal sites in the state;

Design and Setting up of Disposal Facility

- The occupier, any association or operator of a facility, as the case may be shall design and set up disposal facility as per the guidelines issued by the Central Government or the State Government as the case may be;
- The occupier, any association or operator, shall before setting up a disposal facility get the design and the layout of the facility approved by the State Pollution Control Board;
- The State Pollution Control Board shall monitor the setting up and operation of a facility regularly.

Operation and Closure of Landfill Site

- The occupier or the operator as the case may be, shall be responsible for safe and environmentally sound operation of the facility as per design approved under Rule 8A by the State Pollution Control Board;
- The occupier or the operator shall ensure that the closure of the landfill is as per the design approved under Rule 8A by the State Pollution Control Board.

Records and Returnes

- The occupier generating hazardous waste and operator of a facility for collection, reception, treatment, transport, storage and disposal of hazardous waste shall maintain records of such operations in Form 3.

- The occupier and operator of a facility shall send annual returns to the State Pollution Control Board or Committee in Form 4.

ACCIDENT REPORTING AND FOLLOW-UP[H]

Where an accident occurs at the facility or on a hazardous waste site or during transportation of hazardous wastes, the occupier or operator of a facility shall report immediately to the State Pollution Control Board or Committee about the accident in Form 5.

IMPORT AND EXPORT OF HAZARDOUS WASTES

- Import of hazardous wastes from any country to India and export of hazardous wastes from India to any country for dumping or disposal shall not be permitted.
- The exporting country or the exporter as the case may be, of hazardous wastes shall communicate in Form 6 to the Central Government (the Ministry of Environment and Forests) of the proposed trans-boundary movement of hazardous wastes.
- The Central Government shall, after examining the communication received under sub-rule(2) and on being satisfied that the import of such hazardous wastes is to be used for processing or reuse as raw material grant permission for the import of such wastes subject to such conditions as the Central Government may specify in this behalf and if, however, the Central Government is not satisfied with the communication received under sub-rule (2), may refuse permission t-o import such hazardous wastes.
- Any importer importing hazardous wastes shall provide necessary information as to the type of hazardous wastes he is to import, in Form 6, to the

concerned State Pollution Control Board/the Central Pollution Control Board in the case of Union Territories.

- The State-Pollution Control Board shall examine the information received under the sub-rule (4) and issue such instructions to the importers as it considers necessary.
- The Central Government or the State Pollution Control Board, as the case may be, shall inform the concerned Port Authority to take appropriate steps regarding the safe handling of the hazardous wastes at the time of off-loading the same.
- Any person importing hazardous wastes shall maintain the records of the hazardous wastes imported as specified in Form 7 and the records so maintained shall be open for inspection by the State Pollution Control Board/the Ministry of Environment and Forests/the Central Pollution Control Board in the case of Union Territories or an officer appointed by them in this behalf.

Import and Export of Hazardous Wastes

- Import and/or export of hazardous wastes rule 3(i)(c) shall only be permitted as raw material for recycling or reuse;
- The Ministry of Environment and Forests shall be the nodal Ministry to deal with transboundary movement of hazardous waste;
- For regulation of export and import the authorities mentioned in Schedule 4 shall be responsible;
- The decision of the Central Government in respect of grant of permission for import or export shall be final;
- Any occupier importing or exporting hazardous waste shall provide detailed information in Form 7A to the Customs authorities.
- Any occupier exporting or importing hazardous waste from or to India shall comply with the articles

of the Basel Convention to which the Central Government is a signatory.

IMPORT OF HAZARDOUS WASTE

- Every occupier importing hazardous waste shall apply to the State Pollution Control Board, one hundred twenty days in advance in Form-6 for permission to import along with a minimum fee of rupees thirty thousand payable to Ministry of Environment and Forests, Govt. of India for imports upto five hundred metric tonnes and for every additional five hundred metric tones or part thereof of waste imported an additional sum of rupees five thousand will be payable;
- The State Pollution Control Board shall examine the application received from the occupier within thirty days and forward the application with recommendation and requisite stipulations for safe transport, storage and processing, to the Ministry of Environment and Forests;
- The Ministry of Environment and Forests, Government of India will examine the application received from the State Pollution Control Board and after satisfying itself will grant permission for imports subject to the following;
  a. Environmentally friendly/ appropriate technology used for re-processing;
  b. The capability of the importer to handle and reprocess hazardous wastes in an environmentally sound manner;
  c. Presence of adequate facility for treatment and disposal of wastes generated; and
  d. Approvals, no objection certificates and authorisations from all concerned authorities; and e. remittance of a processing application fee;
- The Ministry of Environment & Forests, Government of India, shall forward a copy of the permission granted, to the Central Pollution Control Board, the

State Pollution Control Board and the concerned Port and Customs authorities for ensuring compliance of the conditions of imports and to take appropriate steps for safe handling of the waste at the time of off-loading;

- An application for licence to the Directorate General of Foreign Trade for import shall be accompanied with the permission granted by the Ministry of Environment and Forests, Government of India under sub-rule (3) to the importer and an authenticated copy of Form 7 of the Exporter under sub rule (3) of rule 14;
- The Port and Custom authorities shall ensure that the shipping document is accompanied with an authenticated copy of Form 7 and the test report from an accredited laboratory of analysis of the hazardous waste shipped;
- The occupier having valid permission to import shall inform the State and Central Pollution Control Board and the Port authorities of the arrival of the consignment of hazardous wastes ten days in advance;
- The occupier importing hazardous waste shall maintain the records of hazardous waste imports as specified in Form 6A and the record so maintained shall be available for inspection;

EXPORT OF HAZARDOUS WASTE

- The exporting country or the exporter as the case may be, of hazardous waste shall apply ninety days in advance in Form 7 to the Ministry of Environment and Forests, Government of India, seeking permission for the proposed export and transboundary movement;
- The Ministry of Environment and Forests, Government of India, on receipt of such Form 7 from an exporter or an exporting country shall examine the case on merit and grant or refuse permission for export to India;

- The Ministry of Environment and Forests, shall communicate the grant of permission by authentication on Form 7 to the exporter and the exporting country and endorse a copy of the same to the Central Pollution Control Board and the State Pollution Control Board;
- The exporter shall ensure that no consignment is shipped prior to the requisite authentication being received. The exporter shall also ensure that the shipping document is accompanied with Form 7A, an authenticated copy of Form 7 and an authenticated copy of the test report from an accredited laboratory of analysis of the hazardous waste;
- The occupier, exporting hazardous waste to any other country shall seek permission from the competent authority of that country prior to any shipment;
- Every occupier exporting hazardous waste shall inform the Central Government of the permission sought for exporting, permission granted for export and details of the export in Form 7.

ILLEGAL TRAFFIC

- The movement of hazardous wastes from or to the country shall be considered illegal:
  - If it is without prior permission of the Central Government; or
  - If the permission has been obtained through falsification, mis- representation or fraud; or
  - It does not conform to the shipping details provided in the document;
- In case of illegal movement, the hazardous wastes in question;
  - Shall be shipped back within thirty days either to the exporter or to the exporting country;
  - Shall be disposed of within thirty days from the date of off-loading subject to inability to comply with Sub-rule 2(i) above.

- In case of illegal transboundary movement of hazardous wastes, the occupier exporting hazardous waste from the country or the exporter exporting hazardous waste to the country and importer importing hazardous waste into the country shall ensure that the wastes in question is safely stored and shipped or disposed off in an environmentally sound manner within thirty days from the date of off-loading;
- The exporting country shall bear the costs incurred for the disposal of such wastes.

LIABILITY OF OCCUPIER

- The occupier, transporter and operator of a facility shall be liable for damages caused to the environment resulting due to improper handling and disposal of hazardous waste listed in schedule 1, 2 and 3;
- The occupier and operator of a facility shall also be liable to reinstate or restore damaged or destroyed elements of the environment;
- The occupier and operator of a facility shall be liable to pay a fine as levied by the State Pollution Control Board with the approval of the Central Pollution Control Board for any violation of the provisions under these rules.

TRANSITIONAL PROVISIONS

Where:

- On the date of coming into operation of these rules, an occupier handling hazardous wastes who is required to comply with the provisions of these rules, it will be sufficient compliance if the occupier and the authorities do so within three months after the date of coming into force of these rules;
- State Pollution Control Boards and Pollution Control Committees are required to oversee the compliance.

APPEAL

- An appeal shall lie, against any order of grant or

refusal of an authorisation by the Member- Secretary, State Pollution Control Board or any officer designated by the Board to the Secretary, Department of Environment of the State Government by whatever name called.

- Every appeal shall be in writing and shall be accompanied by a copy of the order appealed against and shall be presented within thirty days of the receipt of the order passed.

S.O. 553 (E)

In exercise of the powers conferred clause (d) of sub-section (2) of section 6 and sections 8 and 25 of the Environment (Protection) Act, 1986 (29 of 1986), read with rule 13 of Environment Protection Rules, 1986, the following draft of certain rules further to amend the Hazardous Wastes (Management and Handling) Rules, 1989, is hereby published as draft rules, for information of all persons likely to be affected thereby and notice is hereby given that the said rules will be taken into consideration after the expiry of sixty days from the date on which the Gazette copies containing this notification are made available to the public; Any objections or suggestions which may be received from any person in respect of the said draft rules before expiry of the period specified above, will be taken into consideration by the Central Government.

RULES

(1) These rules may be called the Hazardous Wastes (Management and Handling) Amendment Rules, 2002; (2) They shall come into force on the date of their- publication-in the Official Gazette; 2. In the Hazardous Wastes (Management and Handling) Rules, 1989 (herein after referred to as the said rules), in rule 2, after clause (c), the following clauses shall be inserted namely: "(d) the bio-medical wastes covered under the Bio-medical Wastes (Management and Handling) Rules, 1998 made under the Act; (e) wastes covered under the Municipal Solid Wastes (Management and Handling) Rules,

2000 made under the Act; and (f) the lead acid batteries covered under the Batteries (Management and Handling) Rules, 2001 made under the Act". 3. For rule 3 of the said rules, the following shall be substituted, namely: - (1) "Act" means the Environment (Protection) Act, 1986 (29 of 1986); (2) "applicant" means a person or an organisation that applies, in Form 1, for granting of authorisation to perform specific activities connected with handling of hazardous wastes; (3) "auction" means bulk sale of wastes by invitation of tenders or auction, contract or negotiation by individual(s), companies or government departments. (4) "auctioneer means a person who auctions wastes; (5) "authorisation" means permission for collection, reception, treatment, transport, storage'and disposal of hazardous wastes, granted by the competent authority; (6) "authorised person" means a person or an organisation authorised by the competent authority to collect, treat, transport, store or dispose of hazardous wastes in accordance with the guidelines to be issued by the competent authority from time to time; (7) "Central Pollution Control Board" means the Central Board appointed under subsection (1) of section 3 of the Water (Prevention and Control of Pollution) Act, 1974 (6 of 1974); and under section 3 of the Air (Prevention and Control of Pollution) Act, 1981 (14 of 198 1)" (8) "disposal" means deposit, treatment, storage and recovery of any hazardous wastes; (9) "export" with its grammatical variations and cognate expressions, means taking out of India to a place outside India: (10) "exporter' means any person under the jurisdiction of the exporting country who exports hazardous wastes and the exporting country itself, who exports hazardous wastes; (11) "environmentally sound management of hazardous wastes" means taking all steps to ensure that the hazardous wastes are managed in a manner which will protect human health and the environment against the adverse effects which may result from such wastes; (12) "facility" means any location wherein the processes incidental to the waste generation, collection, reception, treatment, storage and disposal are carried out; (13) "form" means a Form appended to these rules; (14) "hazardous waste" means, any waste which by reason of any of its physical, chemical, reactive, toxic, flammable, explosive or corrosive characteristics causes danger or is likely to cause danger to health or environment, whether alone or when in contact with other wastes or substances, and shall include: (a) wastes listed in column (3) of Schedule-1 generated in the process listed in column (2) of the said Schedule; (b) wastes listed in Schedule (2) unless their concentration is less than the limit indicated therefor in the said Schedule; and (c) Wastes listed in Lists 'A' and 'B' of Part A Schedule-3 applicable only in case(s) of export/import of hazardous wastes in accordance with rules12, 13 and 14 only if they possess any of the hazard characteristics listed in Part-B of the said Schedule". "[Explanation: All wastes mentioned in column 3 of Schedule-1 are hazardous wastes, irrespective of concentration limits/classes given in Schedule - 2.

Schedule - 2 shall be applicable only for wastes not covered in Schedule 1. Schedule-3 is applicable only in cases of export or import.]" (15) "hazardous wastes site" means a place for collection, reception, treatment, storage and disposal of hazardous wastes which has been duly approved by the competent authority; (16) "illegal traffic" means any transboundary movement of hazardous wastes as specified in rule 15; (17) "import" with its grammatical variations and cognate expressions, means bringing into India from a place outside India; (18) "importer" means an occupier or any person who imports hazardous wastes; (19) "manifest" means transporting document originated and signed by the occupier in accordance with rule 7(4) and 7(5); (20) "non-ferrous metal wastes" means wastes listed in Schedule 4 of these rules. (21) "operator of facility" means a person who owns or operates a facility for collection, reception, treatment, storage and disposal of hazardous wastes; (22) "recycler" means an occupier who processes wastes for recovery. (23) "registered recycler" means a recycler registered with the Ministry of Environment and Forests or an agency designated by it for reprocessing wastes, (24) "schedule" means Schedule appended to these rules; (25) "State Government" means State Government and in relation to Union Territory the

Administrator thereof appointed under Article 239 of the Constitution; (26) "State Pollution Control Board/Committee" - means the Board/Committee appointed under sub-section (1) of section 4 of the Water (Prevention and Control of Pollution) Act, 1974 (6 of 1974); and under section 4 of the Air (Prevention and Control of Pollution) Act, 1981 (14 of 1981); (27) "storage" means keeping hazardous wastes for a temporary period, at the end of which the hazardous wastes is treated and disposed off, (28) "transboundary movement" means any movement of hazardous waste or other wastes from an area under the national jurisdiction of one country to or through an area under the national jurisdiction of another country or to or through an area not under the national jurisdiction of any country, provided at least two countries are involved in the movement; (29) "transport' means movement of hazardous waste by air, rail, road or water; (30) "transporter" means a person engaged in the off-site transportation of hazardous waste by air, rail, road or water; (31) "treatment" means a method, technique or process, designed to change the physical, chemical or biological characteristics or composition of any hazardous waste so as to render such wastes harmless; (32) "used oil" - means any used lubricating oil that has been derived from crude oil and mixtures containing synthetic oil and includes used engine oils, gear oils, hydraulic oils, turbine oils, compressor oils, industrial gear oils, heat transfer oils, transformer oils, spent oils, etc.

Used lubricating oils are suitable for re-refining provided the final product meets the specifications laid down in Schedule 5; (33) "waste oil" - means any oil that is contaminated so as to make it unsuitable for recycling. It includes spills of crude oil, tank bottom sludge, emulsions, etc. and can be used as fuel in furnaces and cement kilns. 4. For Rule 5 of the said rules, (a) in sub-rule (2), the following shall be substituted namely:- "(2) Every occupier or a recycler generating or recycling hazardous wastes shall make an application in Form 1 along with an application processing fee, as may be prescribed by the State Pollution Control Board/ Committee to the Member Secretary, State Pollution Control

Board/Committee or any officer designated by the Board/ Committee for the grant of authorization for any of the above activities: Provided that an occupier or a recycler not having a hazardous wastes treatment and disposal facility of his own and is operating in an area under the jurisdiction assigned by the State Pollution Control Board/Committee.

For a Common Treatment, Storage and Disposal Facility (TSDF) shall become a member of this facility, pay charges as may be required and take all other necessary steps to ensure proper treatment and disposal of hazardous wastes generated failing which the authorization granted to the said occupier or recycler in accordance with sub rule (2) above shall be cancelled after giving a reasonable opportunity to be heard or shall not to ' be granted by the State Pollution Control Board/ Committee as the case may be." (b) in sub-rule (3), the following shall be substituted namely:- "(3) Any person who intends to be an operator of a facility for the collection, reception, treatment, transport, storage and disposal of hazardous wastes, shall make an application in Form 1 along with A application processing fee as may be prescribed by the State pollution Control Board/Committee to the Member Secretary, State Pollution Control Board/Committee or any officer designated by the Pollution control Board/Committee for the grant of authorization for any of the above activities". (c) in sub-rule (6), for clause(i), the following clause shall be substituted namely:- "(i) An authorization granted under this rule shall unless sooner suspended or cancelled, be in force during the period of its validity as may be prescribed by the State Pollution Control Board/Committee from the date of issue or from the date of renewal." (d) in sub-rule (8), for clause (ii), the following clause shall be substituted, namely:- "On steps taken, wherever feasible, for reduction and prevention in the waste generated or recycled or reused"; (e) after sub-rule (8), the following sub-rule shall be inserted, namely:- "(9) Every State Pollution Control Board/Committee shall maintain a register containing particulars of the conditions Imposed under these rules for any disposal of hazardous wastes, from any land or premises and it shall be open for inspection during office hours by any person interested or affected or a person authorized by him in this behalf. The entries in the register shall be conclusive proof of the grant of authorisation for disposal of hazardous wastes from such land or premises and the conditions subject to which it was granted.

In rule 12 of the said rules, (a) in sub-rule (3), shall be substituted". (b) after sub-rule(6), the following sub-rules shall be inserted, namely:- "(7) The import or export of hazardous wastes or substances containing or contaminated with such hazardous wastes listed in Schedule 6 is prohibited".

In rule 13 of the said rules, (a) for sub-rule (1), the following sub-rule shall be substituted, namely:- "(1) Every occupier seeking to import hazardous wastes shall apply to the State Pollution Control Board/Committee 120 days in advance of the intended date of commencement of the shipment in Form 6 for permission to import hazardous wastes along with an application fee, as may be prescribed by the State pollution Control Board/Committee to the Member-Secretary, State Pollution Control Board/Committee or any officer designated by the Pollution Control Bdard/Committee". (b) in sub-rule (3), clause (e) shall be omitted. (C) after sub-rule (8), the following sub-rule shall be inserted, namely: (9) An occupier importing hazardous wastes listed under Open General Licence of the Directorate General of Foreign Trade is required to be registered with the Ministry of Environment and Forests in accordance with the procedure laid down under rule 19". Sub-rule 2 rule 15, in clause (ii), the following shall be added, namely:- "in accordance with the procedure laid down by the Central Board in consultation with Ministry of Environment & Forests".

In rule 16 of the said rules, after sub-rule (3), the following sub-rule shall be added, namely:- "(4) The occupier and operator of a facility, as the case may be, shall be liable to pay entire cost of remediation/restoration and pay in advance an amount equal to the estimate computed by State Pollution Control Board/Committee. Thereafter, the Board/committee shall plan and cause to be executed the programme for remediation/restoration. The advance paid to State Pollution

Control Board/Pollution Control Committee towards the cost of remediation/restoration shall be adjusted once actual cost of remediation/restoration is finally determined and the remaining if any, shall be recovered from the occupier and/or operator of the facility". In rule 18 of the said rules, after sub-rule (2), the following sub-rule shall be inserted, namely:"(3) every appeal filed under the said rule shall be disposed of within a period of sixty days from the date of such filing".

After rule 18 of the said rules, the following rules shall be added, namely:- "19. Procedure for registration/renewal of registration of recyclers:- (1) Registration procedure shall be applicable to recyclers of non-ferrous metal wastes as given in Schedule 4 and used lubricating oil; (2) Only recyclers registered with the Ministry of Environment & Forests shall be entitled to undertake recycling; (3) Every recycler of wastes shall make an application in Form II along with the following documents to the Joint Secretary, Ministry of Environment and Forests or any officer or other authority designated by the Ministry for the grant of registration or renewal: (a) a copy of the valid consents under the Water (Prevention and Control of Pollution) Act, 1974, and the Air (Prevention and Control of Pollution) Act, 1981, as amended; (b) a copy of the valid authorisation under Hazardous Wastes (Management and Handling) Rules, 1989; (c) a copy of valid certificate of registration with District Industries Centre; (d) a copy of the proof of installed capacity of plant and machinery issued by either State Pollution Control Board or the District Industries Centre; and (e) proof of compliance of effluent/emission standards and disposal of treated wastes as stipulated by SPCB. (4) The Joint Secretary, Ministry of Environment and Forests or any officer or other authority designated by the Ministry shall ensure that the recyclers possess requisite facilities, technical capabilities, and equipment to recycle the wastes and dispose of the hazardous wastes generated; (5) The Joint Secretary, Ministry of-Environment and Forests or any officer or other authority designated by the Ministry shall dispose of the application for registration within 120 days of receipt of application form with complete details; (6) The registration granted under this rule shall be in force for a period of two years from the date of issue or from the date of renewal unless suspended or cancelled earlier; (7) An application for the renewal of registration shall be made in Form II atleast six months before its expiry.

The Joint Secretary, Ministry of Environment and Forests or any officer designated by the Ministry or an agency designated by it shall renew the registration of the recycler granted under sub-rule (v) of this rule, after examining each case on merit; (8) The Joint Secretary, Ministry of Environment and Forests or any officer or other authority designated by the Ministry may, after giving reasonable opportunity to the applicant of being heard, refuse to grant registration; (9) The Joint Secretary, Ministry of Environment and Forests or any officer or other authority designated by the Ministry may cancel or suspend a registration issued under these rules, if in his/her opinion the registered recycler has failed to comply with any of the conditions of registration, or with any provisions of the Act or rules made thereunder after giving him an opportunity to explain and after recording the reasons therefor; (10) An appeal shall lie against any order of suspension or cancellation or refusal of registration passed by the Joint Secretary to the Ministry of Environment and Forests or other authority designated by the Ministry.

The appeal shall be in writing and shall be accompanied with a copy of-the order appealed against and shall be presented within 30 days of passing of the order. (11) In pursuance of these rules, recyclers already registered with the Ministry of Environment & Forests -need not apply again. (12) In case of-units registered with the Ministry of Environment & Forests for items placed under "free category" in Notification nos. 22(RE-99) 1997-2002 dated 3& July, 1999; 26((RE-99) 1997-2002 dated 10'h September, 1999; 38 (RE2000) 1997-2002 dated 10th October, 2000 and 6(RE 200 1) dated 31st March, 2001 issued by the Directorate General of Foreign Trade and other similar notifications issued in future based on the Ministry of Environment & Forests' advice, prior import permission from the Ministry will not be required. (13) Recyclers registered with

MoEF shall maintain a record of wastes purchased, CL processed and sold and shall file six monthly returns in Form-12 to the respective State Pollution Control Board/Pollution Control Committee latest by 30th June and 31st December of every year.

Responsibilities of waste generator/auctioneer (i) Waste generators of non-ferrous metal wastes shall ensure that such non-ferrous metal wastes, as given in Schedule 6 auctioned sold to the registered - recyclers only; (ii) Major used, oil generators namely State Road Transport, Corporations, Railways, fence Establishments, Shipping Companies, Ports, Power Plants, Fertilizer Industry Electricity Boards, etc. shall auction/sell used oil only to registered recyclers.

All other generators of used oil generating used oil in quantities equal to or more than tons per annum. shall also auction/sell used lubricating oil only to registered recyclers; (iii) The waste generators/auctioneers shall ensure that at the time of auction or sale, balance validity period of registration of waste purchasers unit should be sufficient to reprocess the quantity of wastes being sold/auctioned. (iv) The waste generators/auctioneers shall maintain a record of such auctions/sale and make these records available to the State Pollution Control Board or committee for inspections. (v) The waste generators/auctioneers shall file a half-yearly return of auction/sale in form latest by 30th June and 31st December of every year to the respective State Pollution Control Board/ Pollution Control, Committee.

Techology and standards for recycling - (i) Recyclers shall use only environmentally sound technologies while recycling/ reprocessing non-ferrous metal wastes or used lubricating oil. In case of used lubricating oil, reprocessors using acid clay process/modified acid clay process shall switch over within one year from the date of the notification to other environmentally sound technologies as under: (a) Vacuum distillation with clay treatment (b) Vacuum distillation with hydrotreating (c) Thin film evaporation process (d) Any other technology approved by the Ministry of Environment & Forests (ii) The Recyclers registered with the Ministry of

Environment & Forest in accordance with the procedure laid down under rule 19 of these rules, shall file a compliance report of having adopted one of the technologies mentioned in sub-rule (i) of rule 21 above by the due date. Units registered with the Ministry of Environment & Forests who fail to comply with the provisions mentioned in sub rule (i) of rule 21 above shall automatically cease to be registered with effect from the due date. (iii) The SPCB/PCC shall inspect the units with upgraded technology within three months of the expiry of the one year period and submit a compliance report to MoEF. (iv) The Ministry of Environment & Forests shall notify from time to time product specifications and standards to be followed by recyclers and reprocessors. 11. Schedules 1,2,3 and 4 appended to the said rules shall be substituted respectively by Schedules 1,2,3 and 7. 12. For Form 1 appended to the said rules, the revised Form 1 shall be substituted.

HANDLING RULES

SHORT TITLE AND COMMENCEMENT

- These rules may be called the Hazardous Wastes (Management and Handling) Rules, 1989, as amended in January 6, 2000 and May 21, 2003.
- They shall come into force on the date of their publication in the Official Gazette.

APPLICATION

These rules shall apply to the handling of hazardous wastes as specified in Schedules and shall not apply to:

- Waste water and exhaust gases as covered under the provisions of the Water (Prevention and Control of Pollution) Act. 1974 (6 of 1974) and the Air (Prevention and Control of Pollution) Act, 1981 (14 of 1981) and rules made thereunder;
- Wastes arising out of the operation from ships beyond five kilometers as covered under the provisions of the Merchant Shipping Act, 1958 (44 of 1958) and the rules made thereunder.

- Radio-active wastes as covered under the provisions of the Atomic Energy Act, 1962 (33 of 1962) and rules made thereunder.
- Bio-medical wastes covered under the Bio-Medical Wastes (Management and Handling) Rules, 1998 made under the Act;
- Wastes covered under the Municipal Solid Wastes (Management and Handling) Rules, 2000 made under the Act; and
- The lead acid batteries covered under the Batteries (Management and Handling) Rules, 2001, made under the Act.

DEFINITIONS

In these rules, unless the context otherwise requires:

(1) "Act" means the Environment (Protection) Act, 1986 (29 of 1986); (2) "applicant" means a person or an organisation that applies, in Form 1, for granting of authorisation to perform specific activities connected with handling of hazardous wastes; (3) "auction" means bulk sale of wastes by invitation of tenders or auction, contract or negotiation by individual(s), companies or Government departments; (4) "auctioneer" means a person or an organisation that auctions wastes; (5) "authorisation" means permission for colection, transport, treatment, reception, storage and disposal of hazardous wastes, granted by the competent authority in Form-2; (6) "authorised person" means a person or an organisation authorised by the competent authority; (7) "Central Pollution Control Board" means the Central Board constituted under sub-section (1) of section 3 of Water (Prevention and Control of Pollution) Act, 1974 (6 of 1974); (8) "dispoal" means deposit, treatment, recycling and recovery of any hazardous wastes; (9) "export" means with its grammatical variations and cognate expressions, means taking out of India to a place outside India; (10) "exporter" means any person under the jurisdiction of the exporting country who exports hazardous wastes and the exporting country itself, who exports hazardous wastse to India; (11) "environmentally sound management of

hazardous wastes" means taking all steps required to ensure that the hazardous wastes are managed in a manner which will protect health and the environment against the adverse effects which may result from such wastes; (12) "facility" means any location wherein the processes incidental to the waste generation, collection, reception, treatment, storage and disposal are carried out; (13) "form" means a Form appended to these rules; (14) "hazardous waste" means any waste which by reason of any of its physical, chemical, reactive, toxic, flammable, explosive or corrosive characteristics causes danger or is likely to cause danger to health or environment, whether alone or when in contact with other wastes or substances, and shall include- (a) wastes listed in cloumn (3) of Schedule-1; (b) wastes having constituents listed in Schedule-2 of their concentration is equal to or more than the limit indicated in the said Schedule; and (c) wastes listed in Lists 'A' and 'B' of Schedule-3 (Part-A) applicable only in case(s) of import or export of hazardous wastes in accordance with rules 12, 13 and 14 if they possess any of the hazardous characteristics listed in Part-B of Schedule-3.

Explanation:For the purposes of this clause- (i) all wastes mentioned in column (3) of Schedule-1 are hazardous wastes irrespective of concentration limits given in Schedule-2 except as otherwise indicated and Schedule-2 shall be applicable only for wastes or waste constituents not covered under column (3) of Schedule-1 (ii) Schedule-3 shall be applicable only in case(s) of import or export; (15) "hazardous waste site" means a place for collection, reception, treatment, storage and disposal of hazardous wastes which has been duly approved by the competent authority; (16) "illegal traffic" means any transboundary movement of hazardous wastes as specified in rule 15; (17) "import" with its grammatical variations and cognate expressions, means bringing into India from a place outside India; (18) "importer" means an occupier or any person who imports hazardous wastes; (19) "manifest" means transporting document(s) prepared and signed by the occupier in accordance with rule 7; (20) "non-ferrous metal wastes" means wastes listed in Schedule 4; (21) "operator of facility" means a person who owns or operates a facility for collection, reception, treatment, storage or disposal of hazardous wastes; (22) "recycler" means an occupier who procures and processes wastes for recovery; (23) "recycling of waste oil" means reclamation by way of treatment to separate solids and water from waste oils using methods such as heating, filtering, gravity, settling, centrifuging, dehydration, viscosity and specific gravity adjustment; (24) "registered re-refiner or recyler" means a re-refiner or recycler registered for reprocessing wastes with the Minister of Environment and forests or the Central Pollution Control Board as the case may be fore reprocessing wastes; (25) "re-refining of used oil" means applying a process to the material composed of used oil so as to produce high quality base stock for further manufacture of lubricants or for other petroleum products by blending or any other process; (26) "schedule" means a Schedule appended to these rules; (27) "State Government" means a State Government and in relation to a Union territory, the Administrator thereof appoined under article 239 of the Constitution; (28) "State Pollution Control Board or Committee" means the Board or Committee constituted under sub-section (1) of section 4 of the Water (Prevention and Control of Pollution) Act, 1974 (6 of 1974). (29) "storage" means storing hazardous wastes for temporary period, at the end of which the hazardous wastes is treated and disposed off; (30) "transboundary movement" means any movement of hazardous waste or other wastes from an area under the national jurisdiction of one country to or through an area under the national jurisdiction of another country or to or through an area not under the national jurisdiction of any country, provided at least two countries are involved in the movement; (31) "transport" means off-site movement of hazardous waste by air, rail, road or water; (32) "transporter" means a person engaged in the off-site transporation of hazardous waste by air, rail, road or water; (33) "treatment" means a method, technique or process, designed to change the physical, chemical or biological characteristics or composition of any hazardous waste so as to render such wastes harmless; (34)

"used oil" means any oil- (i) derived from crude oil or mixtures containing synthetic oil including used engine oil, gear oil, hydraulic oil, turbine oil, compressor oil, industrial gear oil, heat transfer oil, transformer oil, spent oil and their tank bottom sluidges; and (ii) suitable for re-refining if it meets the specifications laid daown in Schedule 5, but does not include waste oil; (35) "waste oil" means any oil- (i) which includes spills of crude oil, emulsions, tank bottom sludge and slop oil generated from petroleum refineries, installations or ships; and(ii) is unsuitable for re-refining but can be used as fuel in furnaces if it meets the specifications laid down in Schedule 6; (36) words and expressions used in these rules and not defined but defined in the Act shall have the meanings respectively assigned to them in the Act.'

RESPONSIBILITY

- The occupier and the operator of a facility shall be responsible for proper collection, reception, treatment, storage and disposal of hazardous wastes listed in Schedule 1, 2 and 3.
- The occupier or any other person acting on his behalf who intends to get his hazardous waste treated by the operator of a facility under sub-rule(1), shall give, to the operator of a facility, such information as may be specified by the State Pollution Control Board.
- It shall be the responsibility of the occupeir and the operator of a facility, to take all steps to ensure that the wastes listed in schedules-1, 2 and 3 are properly handled, and disposed of without any adverse effects to the environment.

Duties of the Occupier and Operatory

It shall be the duty of the occupier and the operator of a facility to take adequate stpes while handling hazardous waste to-

- Contain contaminants and prevent accidents and limit their consequences on human and the environment; and

- Provide persons working on the site with information, training and equipment necessary to ensure their safety.

GRANT OF AUTHORISATION

- Hazardous wastes shall be collected, treated, stored and disposed of only in such facilites as may be authorised for this purpose
- Every occupeir handling, or a recycler recycling, hazardous wastes shall make an application in Form 1 to the Member Secretary, State Pollution Control Board or Committee, as the case may be or any officer designated by the State Pollution Control Board or Committee for the grant of authorization for any of the said activities: Provided that an occupier or a recycler not having a hazardous wastes treatment and disposal facility of his own and is operating in an area under the jurisdiction assigned by the State Pollution Control Board or Committee, as the case may be, for a Common Treatment, Storage and Disposal Facility (TSDF) shall become a member of this facility and send his waste to this facility to ensure proper treatment and disposal of hazardous wastes generated failing which the authorization granted to the said occupier or recycler in accordance with sub-rule may be cancelled after giving a reasonable opportunity to such occupier or recycler as the case may be, of being heard or shall not to be granted by the State Pollution Control Board or Committee, as the case may be.;
- Any person who intends to be an operator of a facility for the collection, reception, treatment, transport, storage and disposal of hazardous wastes, shall make an application in Form 1 to the Member Secretary, State Pollution Control Board or Committee for the grant of authorization for all or any of the above activities specified in this rule.
- The Member Secretary, State Pollution Control Board

or any officer designated by the Board or Committee shall not issue an authorisation unless he is satisfied that the operator of a facility or an occupier, as the case may be, possesses appropriate facilities, technical capabilities and equipment to handle hazardous wastes safely.

- The authorisation application complete in all respect shall be processed by the State Pollution Control Boards within ninety days of the receipt of such application.

- The authorisation to operate a facility shall be issued in Form 2 and shall be subject to conditions laid down therein.
- An authorisation granted under this rule shall, unless suspended or cancelled, be in force during the period of its validity as specified by the State Pollution Control Board or Committee from the date of issue or from the date of renewal, as the case may be.
  An application for the nrenewal of an authorisation shall be made in Form 1 before its expiry.
  The authoirsation shall continue to be in force until it is renewed or revoked.
- The Member Secretary, State Pollution Control Board or any officer designated by the Board or Committee, may, after giving reasonable opportunity of being heard to the applicant refuse to grant any, authorisation.
- The Member Secretary, State Pollution Control Board or any officer designated by the Board shall renew the authorisation granted under sub-rule (6), after examining each case on merit, subject to the following-
  - On submission of annual returns by the occupier or operator of facility in Form 4;
  - On steps taken, by the applicant whereever feasible, for reduction and prevention in the waste generated or recycling or reuse;
  - On fulfillment of conditions prescribed in the

authorisation regarding management in an environmentally sound manner of wastes.

- Ever State Pollution control Board or Committee shall maintain a register containing particulars of the condiditons imposed under these rules for any disposal of hazardous wastes, on any land or premises and it shall be open for inspection during office hours to any person interested or affected or a person authorized by him in this behalf. The entries in the register shall be conclusive proof of grant of authorisation for management and handling of hazardous wastes on such land or premises and the conditions subject to which it was granted.

POWER TO SUSPEND OR CANCEL

- The State Pollution Control Board or Committee may cancel an authorisation issued under these rules or suspend it for such period as it thinks fit, if in its opinion, the authorised person has failed to comply with any of the conditions of the authorisation or with any provisions of the act or these rules, after giving the authorised person an opportunity to show cause and after recording reasons therefor.
- Upon suspension or/cancellation of the authorisation and during the pendency of an appeal under rule 12, the State Pollution Control Board or Committee may give directions to the persons whose authorisation has been suspended or cancelled for the safe storgae of the hazardous wastes, and such person shall comply with such directions.

PACKAGING, LABELLING AND TRANSPORT OF HAZARDOUS WASTES

(1) The occupier or operator of a facility shall ensure that the hazardous wastes are packages, based on the composition in a manner suitable for handling, storage and transport and the labelling and packaging shall be easily visible and be able to withstand physical conditions and climatic factors. (2)

Packaging, labelling and transport of hazardous wastes shall be in accordance with the provisions of the rules made by the Central Government under the Motor Vehicles Act, 1988 and other guidelines issued from time to time. (3) All hazardous waste containers shall be provided with a general label as given in Form 8. (4) The occupier shall prepare six copies of the manifest in Form 9 comprising of colour code indicated below (all six copies to be signed by the transporter): Copy number with colour code Purpose Copy 1 (White) to be forwarded by the occupier to the State Pollution Control Board or Committee Copy 2 (Yellow) to be retained by the occupier after taking signature on it from the transporter and rest of the four copies to be carried by the transpoter Copy 3 (Pink) to be retained by the operator of the facility after signature Copy 4 (Orange)to be returned to the transporter by the operator of facility after accepting waste Copy 5 (Green) to be returned by the operator of the facility to State Pollution Control Board/Committee after treatment and disposal of wastes.

Copy 6 (Blue)to be returned by the operator of the facility to the occupier after treatment and disposal of wastes (5) The occupier shall forward copy number 1 (white) to the State Pollution Control Board or Committee and in case the hazardous waste is likely to be transported through any transit State, the occupier shall prepare an additional copy each for such State and forward the same to the concerned State Pollution Control Board or Committee before the hands over the hazardous waste to the transporter.

No transporter shall accept hazardous wastes from an occupier for transport unless it is accompanied by copy number 2 to 5 of the manifest. The transporter shall return copy number 2 (yellow) of the manifest signed with date to the occupier as token of receipt of the other four copies of the manifest and retain the remaining four copies to the carried and handed over to respective agencies as specified in sub-rule (4). (6) In case of transport of hazardous wastes to a facility for treatment, storage and disposal existing in a State other than the State where hazardous wastes are generated, the occupier shall obtain 'No Objection Certificate' from the State Pollution Control Board or Committee of the concerned State or Union Territory Administration where the facility is existing. (7) the occupier shall provide the transporter with relevant information in Form 10, regarding the hazardous nature of the wastes and measures to be taken in case of an emergency.

DISPOSAL SITES

(1) The occupier or operator of a facility or any association of occupiers, shall be jointly and severally responsible for identifying sites for establishing the facility for treatment, storage and disposal of hazardous wastes. (2) The State Government, operator of a facility or any association of occupiers shall jointly and severally be responsible for and identify sites for common facility for treatment, storage and disposal of hazardous wastes in the State. (3) The operator of a facility, occupier or any association of occupiers shall undertake an environmental impact assessment (EIA) of the selected site(s) and shall submit the EIA report to the State Pollution Control Board or Committee. (4) The State Pollution Control Board or Committee shall on being satisfied with the EIA report, cause a public notice for conducting a public hearing as per the procedure contained in the Environmental Impact Assessment Notification, 1994 published vide S.O. 60(E) dated 27th January, 1994 as amended from time to time. (5) The State Pollution Control Board or Committee shall forward to the State Government or Union territory Administrator, as the case may be, the project report including EIA report and details of public hearing alonwith its recommendations within a period of 30 days from the last date of public hearing. (6) The State Government shall complete the assessment within a period of thirty days from the date of receipt of the documents mentioned in sub-rule (5) and convey the decision of its approval of site(s) or otherwise within 30 days thereafter to the concerned operator of the facility, occupier or any association of occupiers. (7)After approval of the site or sites, the State Government shall acquire the site or

inform the occupiers to acquire the site(s) for settling up the facility for treatment, storage and disposal of hazardous wastes. The State Government shall simultaneously notify such sites. The State Government shall also compile and publish periodically an inventory of such hazardous wastes disposal sites and facilities; (8) Setting up of an on-site facility for treatment, storage and disposal of hazardous wastes for captive use shall be govenred by the authorisation procedure laid down in rule 5.

Design and Setting up of Disposal Facility

- The occupier any association or operator of a facility, as the case may be shall design and set up disposal facility as per the guidelines issued by the Central Government or the State Government as the case may be.
- The occupier, any association or operator, shall before setting up a disposal facility get the design and the layout of the facility approved by the State Pollution Control Board.
- The State Pollution control Board shall monitor the setting up and operation of a facility regularly.

Operation and Closure of Landfill Site

- The occupier or the operator as the case may be, shall be responsible for safe and environmentally sound operation of the facility as per design approved under Rule 8A by the State Pollution Control Board.
- The occupier or the operator shall ensure that the closure of the landfill is as per the desgn approved under Rule 8A by the State Pollution Control Board.

RECORDS AND RETURNS

(1) The occupier generating hazardous waste and operator of a facility for collection, reception, treatment, transport, storage and disposal of hazardous waste shall maintain records of such operations in Form 3. (2) The occupier and operator of a facility shall send annual returns to the State Pollution

Control Board or Committee in Form 4. (3) The State Pollution Control Board or Committee shall prepare an inventory of hazardous wastes, as early as possible as per Form 4, within its jurisdiction and compile other related information like treatment and disposal of hazardous wastes based on the returns filed by respective occupier and operator of facility as per sub-rule(2).

ACCIDENT REPORTING AND FOLLOW-UP

Where an accident occurs at the facility or on a hazardous waste site or during transporation of hazardous waste, the occupier or operator of a facility shall report immediately to the State Pollution control Board or Committee about the accident in Form 5.

IMPORT AND EXPORT OF HAZARDOUS WASTES FOR DUMPING AND DISPOSAL

(1) Import of hazardous wastes from any country to India and export of hazardous wastes from India to any country for dumping or disposal shall not be permitted. (2) The exporting country or the exporter or the exporter as the case may be of hazardous wastes shall communicate in Form 6 to the Central Government (the Ministry of Environment & Forests) of the proposed trans-boundary movement of hazardous wastes. (3) The Central Government shall, after examining the communication received under sub-rule (2) and on being satisfied that the import of such hazardous wastes is to be used for processing or reuse as raw material grant permission for the import of such wastes subject to such conditions as the Central Government may specify in this behalf and if, however the Central Government is not satisfied with the communication received under sub-rule (2), may refuse permission to import such hazardous wastes. (4) Any importer importing hazardous waste shall provide necessary information as to the type of hazardous wastes he is to import, in Form 6, to the concerned State Pollution Control Board or Committee/the Central Pollution Control Board in the case of Union Territories. (5) The State Pollution Control Board or

Committee shall examine the information received under the sub-rule (4) and issue instruction to the importers as its considers necessary. (6) The Central Government or the State Pollution Control Board or Committee, as the case may be, shall inform the concerned Port Authority to take appropriate steps regarding the safe handling of the hazardous wastes at the time of off-loading the same. (7) Any person importing hazardous wastes shall maintain the records of the hazardous wastes imprted as specified in Form 7 and the records so maintained shall be open for inspection by the State Pollution Control Board or Committee/the Ministry of Environment and Forests/the Central Polltion Control Board in the case of Union Territories or an officer appointed by them in this behalf.

IMPORT AND EXPORT OF HAZARDOUS

(1) No person shall import or export hazardous wastes or substances containing or contaminated with such hazardous wastes as specified in Schedule 8, even for recycling. (2) The Ministry of Environment and forests shall be the Nodal Ministry to deal with the trans-boundary movement of hazardous wastes and to grant permission of transit of hazardous wastes through any part of India. (3) Import and export of hazardous wastes shall be permitted only as raw materials for recycling or reuse. (Schedule 3, 4). (4) The authorities mentioned in column 2 of Schedule 7 shall be responsible for regulation of export and import of hazardous wastes. (5) Any occupier importing or exporting hazardous wastes shall provide detailed information in Form 7A to the Customs authorities. (6) Any occupier importing or exporting hazardous wastes shall comply with the articles of the Basel Convention to which the Central Government is a signatory. (7) In case of any dispute as the grant of permission to import or export of hazardous wastes, the matter shall be referred to the Central Government for a decision..

IMPORT OF HAZARDOUS WASTE

- Every occupier seeking to import hazardous wastes shall apply to the State Pollution Control Board or

Committee at least 120 days in advance of the intended date of commencement of the shipment;

- The State Pollution Control Board shall examine the application received from the occupier within thirty days and forward the application with recommendation and requisite stipulations for safe transport, storage and processing, to the Ministry of Environment and Forests;
- The Ministry of Environment and Forests, Government of India will examine the application received from the State Pollution Control Board and after satisfying itself will grant permission for imports subject to the following:
  - Environmentally friendly/appropriate technology used for re-processing;
  - The capability of the importer to handle and reprocess hazardous wastes in an environmentally sound manner;
  - Presence of adequate facility for treatment and disposal of wastes generated; and
  - Approvals, no objection certificates and authorisation from all concerned authorities.
- The Ministry of Environment & Forests, Government of India, shall forward a copy of the permission granted, to the Central Pollution Control Board, the State Pollution Control Board and the concerned Port and Customs authorities for ensuring compliance of the conditions of imports and to take appropriate steps for safe handling of the waste at the time of off-loading;
- An application for licence to the directorate General of Foreign Trade for import shall be accompanied with the permission granted by the Ministry of Environment & Forests, Government of India under sub-rule (3) to the importer and an authenticated copy of Form 7 of the Exporter under sub-rule (3) of rule 14;
- The Port and Custom authorities shall ensure that

the shipping document is accompanied with an authenticated copy of Form 7 and the test report from an accredited laboratory of analysis of the hazardous waste shipped;

- The occupier having valid permission to import shall inform the State and Central Pollution Control Board and the Port authorities of the arrival of the consignment of hazardous wastes ten days in advance;
- The occupier importing hazardous waste shall maintain the records of hazardas wastes imports as specified in Form 6A and the record so maintained shall be available for inspection;
- An occupier importing hazardous wastes listed under an Open General Licence of the Directoral General of Foreign Trade shall register himself with the Ministry of Environment and Forests or any other authority or agency such as the Central Pollution Control Board designed by it in accordance with the procedure laid down under rule 19.

EXPORT OF HAZARDOUS WASTE

- The exporting country or the exporter as the case may be of hazardous waste shall apply ninety days in advance in Form 7 to the Ministry of Environment and Forests, Government of India, seeking permission for the proposed export and transboundary movement;
- The Ministry of Environment and Forests, Government of India, on receipt of such Form 7 from an exporter or an exporting country shall examine the case on merit and grant or refuse permission for export to India;
- The Ministry of Environment and Forests, shall communicate the grant of permission by authentication on Form 7 to the exporter and the exporting country and endorse a copy of the same to the Central Pollution Control Board and the State

Pollution Control Board.

- The exporter shall ensure that no consignment is shipped prior to the requisite authentication being received. The exporter shall also ensure that the shipping document is accompanied with Form 7A, an authenticated copy of Form 7 and an authenticated copy of the test report from an accredited laboratory of analysis of the hazardous waste.
- The occupier, exporting hazardous waste to any other country shall seek permission from the competent authority of that country prior to any shipment.
- Every occupier exporting hazardous waste shall inform the Central Government of the permission sought for exporting, permission granted for export and details of the export in Form 7.

ILLEGAL TRAFFIC

- The movement of hazardous wastes from or to the country shall be considered illegal:
  - If it is without prior permission of the Central Government; or
  - If the permission has been obtained through falsification, mis-representation or fraud; or
  - It does not conform to the shipping details provided in the document;
- In case of illegal movement, the hazardous wastes in question;
  - Shall be shipped back within thirty days either to the exporter or to the exporting country;
  - Shall be disposed of within thirty days from the date of off-loading subject to inability to comply with sub-rule 2(i) above in accordance with the procedures laid down by the State Pollution Control Board or Committee in constitution with Central Pollution Control Board.
- In case of illegal transboundary movement of hazardous wastes, the occupier exporting hazardous waste from the country or the exporter exporting

hazardous waste to the country and importer importing hazardous waste into the country shall ensure that the waste in question is safely stored and shipped or disposed off in an environmentally sound manner within thirty days from the date of off-loading.

- The exporter shall bear the costs incurred for the disposal of such wastes.

LIABILITY OF THE TRANSPORTER

- The occupier, transporter and operator of a facility shall be liable for damages caused to the environment resulting due to improper handling and disposal of hazardous waste listed in Schedule 1, 2 and 3;
- The occupier and operator of a facility shall also be liable to reinstate or restore damaged or destroyed elements of the environment at his cost, failing which the occupier or the operator of a facility, as the case may be, sahll be liable to pay the entire cost of remediation or restoration and pay in advance an amount equal to the cost estimated by the State Pollution Control Board or Committee. Thereafter the Board or Committee shall plan an cause to be executed the programme for remediation or restoration. The advance paid to State Pollution Control Board or Committee towards the cost of remediation or restoration shall be adjusted once the actual cost of remediation or restoration is finally determined and the remaining amount, if any, shall be recovered from the occupier or the operator of the facility.
- The occupier and operator of a facility shall be liable to pay a fine as levied by the State Pollution Control Board with the approval of the Central Pollution Control Board for any violation of the provisions under these rules.

TRANSITIONAL PROVISIONS

- On the date of coming into operation of these rules,

an occupier handling hazardous wastes who is required to comply with the provisions of these rules, it will be sufficient compliance if the occupier and the authorities do so within three months after the date of coming into force of these rules;

- State Pollution Control Board and Pollution Control Committee are required to oversee the compliance.

APPEAL

- An appeal shall lie, against any order of grant or refusal of an authorisation by the Member Secretary, State Pollution Control Board or any officer designated by the Board or the Secretary, Department of Environment of the State Government by whatever name called.
- Ever appeal shall be in writing and shall be accompanied by a copy of the order appealed against and shall be presented within thirty days of the receipt of the order passed.
- Ever appeal filed under this rule shall be disposed of within a period of sixty days from the date of such filing.

REGISTRATION AND RENEWAL

(1) Every person desirous of recycoling or re-refining non-ferrous metal wastes as specified in Schedule 4 or used oil or waste oil shall register himself with the Central Pollution Control Board Provided that no ownder or occupier of an industrial unit having captive recycling or non-ferrous metals or recycling or waste oil or re-refining oil or used oil facility shall be required to register under these rules. Provided further that no person who has registered with the Ministry of Environment & Forests before the commencement of the Hazardous Wastes (Management and Handling) Amendment rules, 2003, shall, unless such registration is cancelled or ceases to operate under sub- rule (3) of rule 21, be required to register under this sub-rule as given in the certificate of registraion. (2) Every application for registration under this rule shall be

made in Form 11 along with a copy of each of the following doucments to the Central Pollution Control Board for the grant of such registration or renewal: (a) letter of consent granted under the Water (Prevention and Control of Pollution) Act, 1974 and the Air (Prevention and Control of Pollution) Act, 1981; (b) authorisation granted under rule 5 of these rules; (c) certificate of registration with Distrcit Industries Centre; (d) proof of installed capacity of plant and machinery issued by either State Pollution Control Board or Committee or the District Industries Centre; and (e) report from the State Pollution Control Board or Committee regarding proof of compliance of effluent and emission standards and treatment and disposal of hazardous wastes as stipulated by that Board or Commiittee. (3) If the Central Pollution Control Board is satisfied that the recyclers or re-refiners possess requisite facilities, technical capabilities, and equipment to recycle or re-refine the wastes and dispose of the hazardous wastes generated, it shall grant a certificate of registration to such recycler or re-refiner, as the case may be. (4) The Central Pollution Control Board shall dispose of the application for registration within 120 days of receipt of such application with complete details. (5) The certificate of registration granted under sub-rule(3) shall be valid for a period of two years from the date of its issue unless suspended or cancelled earlier. (6) Every application for renewal of registration ofa a certificate of registration granted under sub-rule(3) shall me made in Form 11 along with the documents mentioned in such-rule(2) atleast two monts before the expiry of the period of validity of such certificate.

The Central Pollution Control Board shall renew the registration of the recycler or re-refiner granted under sub-rule(3) after examing each case on merit. (7) The Central Pollution Control Board may, after giving reasonable opportunity to the applicant of being heard, by order, refuse to grant certificate of registration of renewal. (8) The Central Pollution Control Board may cancel or suspend a registration or renewal granted under these rules, if in its opinion the registered recycler has failed to comply with any of the conditions of registration, or with any provisions of the act or rules made thereunder after giving him an opportunity of being heared and after recording the reasons therefor; (9) An appeal against any order of suspension or cancellation or refusal of registration or renewal passed by Central Pollution Control Board shall lie with the Secretary, Ministry of Environment and Forests (hereafter referred to as the appellate authority). (10) The memorandum of appeal under sub-rule (9) shall be in writing and shall be accompanied with a copy of the order appealed against and shall be presented within 30 days of passing of the order; Provided that the appellate authority may allow a memorandum of appeal to be filed after the expiry of the said period of thirty days, but in no case later than 45 days if the appellate authority is satisfied that there exists sufficient cause for not preferring the appeal in time. (11) On receipt of a memorandum of appeal under sub-rule (9) the appellate authority shall within ninty days from the date of receipt of such memorandum of appeal and after giving the appellant an opportunity of being heard pass such order as he may deem fit. (12) In case of units registered with the Ministry of Environment and Forests or the Central Pollution Control Board for items placed under "free category" in Notification nos. 22(RE-99), 1997-2002 dated 30th July, 1999; 26 (RE-99) 1997-2002 dated 10th September, 1999; 38(RE-2000) 1997-2002 dated 16th October, 2000 and 6(RE-2001) dated 31stMarch, 2001 issued by the Directorate General of Foreign Trades and oterh similar notifications issued based on the advice of Ministry of Environment and Forests, prior import permission from that Ministry shall not be required. (13) Recyclers and re-refiners registered with the Government of India in the Ministry of Environment and Forests or the Central Pollution Control Board shall maintain a record of wastes purchased, processed and sold and shall file an annual return in Form 12 to the respective State Pollution Control Board or Committee, as the case may be, latest by 31st January of every year.

RESPONSIBILITY OF WASTE GENERATOR

- No owner or occupier generating non-ferrous metal

waste specified in Schedule 4 or generating used oil or waste oil of ten tons or more per annum shall sell or acution such non-ferrous metal wastes, used oil or waste oil except to registered re-refiner or recycler, as the case may be, who undertakes to re-refine or recycle the waste within the period of validity of his certificate of registration.

- Any waste oil which does not meet the specifications laid down in Schedule 6 shall not be auctioned or sold but shall be disposed of in hazardous wastes incineratory installed with air pollution control devices and meeting emission standards.
- The persons generating wase or auctioneers shall ensure that at the time of auction or sale, he period of validity of the certifciate of registration of the registered re-refiner or recycler is sufficient to reprocess the quantity of wastes being sold or acutioned to him.
- The waste generators and auctioneers shall ensure that the wastes are not allowed to be stored for more than ninety days and shall maintain a record of auctions and sale of such wastes and make there records available to the State Pollution Control Board or Committee for inspections.
- The waste generators and auctioneers shall file annual returns of auctions and sale in Form 13 latest by 31st day of January of every year to the respective State Pollution Control Board or Committee.

TECHNOLOY AND STANDARDS

- Re-refiners and recyclers shall use only environmetally sound technologies while recycling and re-refining non-ferrous metal wastes or used oil or waste oil. In case of used oil, re-refiners using acid clay process or modified acid clay process shall switch over within six months from the date of commencement of the Hazardous Waste (Management and Handling) Amendements Rules,

2003 to other environmentally sound technologies as under:

- Vaccum distillation with clay tretament;
- Vaccum distillation with hydrotreating;
- Thin film evaporation process; or
- Any other technology approved by the Ministry of Environment and Forests.

- The re-refiners and recyclers registered with the Ministry of Environment and Forests or the Central Pollution Control Board in accordance with the procedure laid down in rule 19 shall file a compliance report of having adpoted one of the technologies mentioned in sub-rule (1) within six months from the date of commencement of the Hazardous Wastes (Management and Handling) Amendment Rules, 2003. (3) Notwithstanding anything contained in a certificate of registration granted to a recycler or re-refiner, such registration with the Ministry of Environment and Forests shall cease to be valid if he fails to comply with sub-rule (1).
- The State Pollution Control Board or Committee shall inspect the re-refining and recycling units withing three months of the expiry of the six months period referred to in sub-rule(1) and submit a compliance report to the Central Pollution Control Board which shall compile such information and furnish the same to the Ministry of Environment and Forests on a regular basis.
- The Ministry of Environment and Forests shall notify time-to-time specifications and standards to be followed by recyclers and re-refiners.

Chapter 4

Basel Convention

DEFINITION

The Basel Convention lays down rules to control, at an international level, transboundary movements of wastes hazardous to human health and the environment, and their disposal. In March 1989, 116 states assembled in Basel, Switzerland, to adopt the first global environmental treaty regulating transboundary movements and disposal of hazardous waste, the Basel Convention. Switzerland is proud to welcome the Fifth Conference of the Parties to the Convention again to Basel, to celebrate the achievements of the last decade and to chart the course for future work. The Basel Convention constitutes an important step in dealing with a problem of global dimensions, aiming at protecting human health and the environment against the ill-effects of hazardous wastes. Significant achievements have been made in implementing and developing the Convention during the last decade. However, its objectives have yet to be reached.

We do not know the exact amount of hazardous wastes generated in the world today, but estimates indicate a volume of 300 to 400 million tonnes a year, mostly produced in industrialized countries. Shipments of hazardous wastes from OECD to non-OECD countries have been prohibited under the Convention, thus protecting the latter from unwanted waste imports – but illegal traffic still poses a serious threat to the environment and human health. Enhanced efforts are needed to achieve environmentally sound management of hazardous wastes worldwide. First, we must strengthen our cooperation with developing countries and countries in transition. They require continued assistance from industrialized countries in building up institutional infrastructures and in building or improving installations for the environmentally sound treatment of wastes.

This includes information exchange, pilot projects on state-of-the-art or best available technologies, training and technology transfer. In certain cases – such as the problem of obsolete pesticide stocks – industrialized countries may even have a moral duty to assist developing countries by taking back wastes and disposing of them. Switzerland, as a nation hosting the headquarters of several multinational chemical companies, is working on a number of projects to help solve this problem. Second, we must strengthen our efforts to prevent the generation of hazardous wastes, which mainly stem from industrial production processes and products. This requires strategies for cleaner production processes and more environmentally sound products. Such strategies cannot be developed and implemented successfully without the active participation of industry. Given the high cost of disposing of hazardous wastes, it seems much more economically profitable to invest money in cleaner technologies (which simultaneously save raw materials and energy), than to spend it on the residues of the production process.

Preventing the generation of hazardous wastes concerns countries, but, again, developing countries and countries in transition need special assistance. To this end, Switzerland supports close cooperation between existing national centres for cleaner production and regional and subregional centres for the training and technology transfer established under the Basel Convention.

Finally, given the close linkages between hazardous waste and chemicals management, the international community should develop a global regulation network in these areas, comprising the Basel Convention and the new agreements on chemicals which are currently being negotiated. Switzerland will continue to support the existing competence centre for chemicals and the Secretariat of the Basel Convention in Geneva as the main components of such a network

ACT

Council Decision 93/98/EEC of 1 February 1993 on the conclusion, on behalf of the Community, of the Convention on the control of transboundary movements of hazardous wastes and their disposal (Basel Convention). Council Decision 97/640/EC of 22 September 1997 on the approval, on behalf of the Community, of the amendment to the Convention on the control of transboundary movements of hazardous wastes and their disposal (Basel Convention), as laid down in Decision III/1 of the Conference of the Parties.

SUMMARY

The EEC approves the Convention on the control of transboundary movements of hazardous wastes and their disposal. The Convention came into force for the EEC on 7 February 1994. The Convention (text attached as annex) aims, in introducing a system for controlling the export, import and disposal of hazardous wastes and their disposal, to reduce the volume of such exchanges so as to protect human health and the environment. It defines hazardous wastes. Each party may add to the list other wastes listed as hazardous in its national legislation. A transboundary movement is any movement of hazardous wastes or other wastes from an area under the national jurisdiction of one State to or through an area under the national jurisdiction of another State, or to or through an area not under the national jurisdiction of any State, provided at least two States are involved in the movement.

General obligations:

- It is prohibited to export or import hazardous wastes or other wastes to or from a non-party State;
- No wastes may be exported if the State of import has not given its consent in writing to the specific import;
- Information about proposed transboundary movements must be communicated to the States

concerned, by means of a notification form, so that they may evaluate the effects of the proposed movements on human health and the environment;

- Transboundary movements of wastes must only be authorised where there is no danger attaching to their movement and disposal;
- Wastes which are to be the subject of a transboundary movement must be packaged, labelled and transported in conformity with international rules, and must be accompanied by a movement document from the point at which a movement commences to the point of disposal;
- Any party may impose additional requirements that are consistent with the provisions of the Convention. The Convention establishes notification procedures regarding:
- Transboundary movements between parties;
- Transboundary movements from a party through the territory of States which are not parties.

It sets out those cases where there is a duty to re-import hazardous wastes, especially if they have been the subject of illegal trafficking. Parties to the Convention must cooperate with each other in order to improve and achieve environmentally sound management of hazardous wastes and other wastes. The aim is to implement all practical measures to ensure that wastes covered by the Convention are handled in such a way that protection of human health and the environment from their harmful effects is guaranteed.

Parties may enter into bilateral, multilateral or regional agreements or arrangements regarding transboundary movements of hazardous wastes, with parties or non-parties, provided that these do not derogate from the principles defined by the Convention. A Conference of the Parties is established and is charged with overseeing the effective implementation of the Convention. Provisions on the settlement of disputes between Parties. Under Decision II/1 the Parties provided for an amendment to the Convention to immediately prohibit transboundary movements of hazardous wastes destined for final disposal and prohibit as from 01.01.1998 transboundary movements of hazardous wastes destined for recovery operations from States listed in Annex VII to the Convention, namely, "Members of the European Organisation for Cooperation and Development (OECD), the European Community and Liechtenstein", to States not listed in Annex VII to the Convention. This amendment to the Convention and Annex VII have not yet entered into force for lack of sufficient ratification.

RELATED ACTS

Regulation (EC) No 1013/2006of the European Parliament and of the Council of 14 June 2006 on shipments of waste [Official Journal L 190, 12.7.2006].This Regulation will replace Regulation (EEC) No 259/93 from 12 July 2007. It is designed to strengthen, simplify and spell out the current control procedures for waste shipments, thus reducing the risk of shipments of uncontrolled waste. It also incorporates into Community legislation the amendments to the waste lists annexed to the Basel Convention and the revision adopted by the Organisation for Economic Cooperation and Development (OECD) in 2001.

BASEL CONVENTION ON THE CONTROL

Transboundary Movements of Hazardous Wastes and Their Disposal) is an international treaty to reduce the movements of hazardous waste between nations. It focuses particularly on reducing movement of hazardous waste from developed countries to less developed countries (LCDs) that lack the administrative, monitoring and other capacities to safely manage these wastes.

The treaty does not, however, address radioactive waste. In addition to regulating the transfer of wastes, the Convention is also intended to minimize the amount and toxicity of wastes generated, to ensure wastes are managed as closely as possible to the source of generation, and to assist LDCs (e.g., with technical assistance) in environmentally sound management of the hazardous and other wastes they generate. Better management of wastes can help achieve climate change and energy production objectives. The Convention has been linked to climate change mitigationthrough the recognition that enhancing practices for the environmentally sound management of hazardous and other wastes can help achievement objectives relating to climate change and energy production and use.

In turn, there is the potential for the Clean Development Mechanism established under the Kyoto Protocol to the United Nations Framework Convention on Climate Change (UNFCCC), as well as other mechanisms, to contribute new and additional financial resources to support the environmentally sound management of wastes. The Convention was opened for signature on March 22, 1989, and entered into force on May 5, 1992. A list of parties to the Convention, and their ratification status, can be found on the Basel Secretariat's web page. Of the 170 parties to the Convention, Afghanistan, Haiti, and the United States have signed the Convention but have not yet ratified it.

The Basel Convention on the Control of Transboundary Movements of Hazardous Wastes and their Disposal is the most comprehensive global environmental agreement on hazardous and other wastes. The Convention has 172 Parties and aims to protect human health and the environment against the adverse effects resulting from the generation, management, transboundary movements and disposal of hazardous and other wastes.

The Basel Convention came into force in 1992. This website contains documents and information used by the Parties to the Basel Convention and other stakeholders. A special section for the general public and other newcomers to the issues addressed by the Convention is also available.

TEXT OF THE BASEL CONVENTION

Basel Convention on the Control of Transboundary Movements of Hazardous Wastes and Their Disposal Basel convention on the control of transboundary movements of hazardous wasters and their disposal·

PREAMBLE

The Parties to this Convention

Aware of the risk of damage to human health and the environment caused by hazardous wastes and other wastes and the transboundary movement thereof, Mindful of the growing threat to human health and the environment posed by the increased generation and complexity, and transboundary movement of hazardous wastes and other wastes, Mindful also that the most effective way of protecting human health and the environment from the dangers posed by such wastes is the reduction of their generation to a minimum in terms of quantity and/or hazard potential, Convinced that States should take necessary measures to ensure that the management of hazardous wastes and other wastes including their transboundary movement and disposal is consistent with the protection of human health and the environment whatever the place of disposal, Noting that States should ensure that the generator should carry out duties with regard to the transport and disposal of hazardous wastes and other wastes in a manner that is consistent with the protection of the environment, whatever the place of disposal, Fully recognizing that any State has the sovereign right to ban the entry or disposal of foreign hazardous wastes and other wastes in its territory, Recognizing also the increasing desire for the prohibition of transboundary movements of hazardous wastes and their disposal in other States, especially developing countries, Convinced that hazardous wastes and other wastes should, as far as is compatible with environmentally sound and efficient management, be disposed of in the State where they were generated, Aware also that transboundary movements of such wastes from the State of their generation to any other State should be permitted only when conducted under conditions which do not endanger human health and the environment, and under conditions in conformity with the provisions of this Convention, Considering that enhanced control of transboundary movement of hazardous wastes and other wastes will act as an incentive for their environmentally sound management and for the reduction of the volume of such transboundary movement, Convinced that States should take measures for the proper exchange of information on and control of the transboundary movement of hazardous wastes and other wastes from and to those States, Noting that a number of international and regional agreements have addressed the issue of protection and preservation of the environment with regard to the transit of dangerous goods, Taking into account the Declaration of the United Nations Conference on the Human Environment (Stockholm, 1972), the Cairo Guidelines and Principles for the Environmentally Sound Management of Hazardous Wastes adopted by the Governing Council of the United Nations Environment Programme (UNEP) by decision 14/30 of 17 June 1987, the Recommendations of the United Nations Committee of Experts on the Transport of Dangerous Goods (formulated in 1957 and updated biennially), relevant recommendations, declarations, instruments and regulations adopted within the United Nations system and the work and studies done within other international and regional organizations, Mindful of the spirit, principles, aims and functions of the World Charter for Nature adopted by the General Assembly of the United Nations at its thirty-seventh session (1982) as the rule of ethics in respect of the protection of the human environment and the conservation of natural resources, Affirming that States are responsible for the fulfilment of their international obligations concerning the protection of human health and protection and preservation of the environment, and are liable in accordance with international law, Recognizing that in the case of a material breach of the provisions of this Convention or any protocol thereto the relevant international law of treaties shall apply, Aware of the need to continue the development and implementation of environmentally sound low-waste technologies, recycling options, good house-keeping and management systems with a view to reducing to a minimum the generation of hazardous wastes and other wastes, Aware also of the growing international concern about the need for stringent control of transboundary movement of hazardous wastes and other wastes, and of the need as far as possible to reduce such movement to a minimum, Concerned about the problem of illegal transboundary traffic in hazardous wastes and other wastes, Taking into account also the limited capabilities of the developing countries to manage hazardous wastes and other wastes, Recognizing the need to promote the transfer of technology for the sound management of hazardous wastes and other wastes produced locally, particularly to the developing countries in accordance with the spirit of the Cairo Guidelines and decision 14/16 of the Governing Council of UNEP on Promotion of the transfer of environmental protection technology, Recognizing also that hazardous wastes and other wastes should be transported in accordance with relevant international conventions and recommendations, Convinced also that the transboundary movement of hazardous wastes and other wastes should be permitted only when the transport and the ultimate disposal of such wastes is environmentally sound, and Determined to protect, by strict control, human health and the environment against the adverse effects which may result from the generation and management of hazardous wastes and other wastes. *Have agreed as follows*:

SCOPE OF THE CONVENTION

- The following wastes that are subject to transboundary movement shall be "hazardous wastes" for the purposes of this Convention: (a)Wastes that belong to any category contained in Annex I, unless they do not possess any of the characteristics contained in Annex III; and (b) Wastes that are not covered under paragraph (a) but are defined as, or are considered to be, hazardous wastes by the domestic legislation of the Party of export, import or transit.
- Wastes that belong to any category contained in Annex II that are subject to transboundary movement shall be "other wastes" for the purposes of this Convention.

- Wastes which, as a result of being radioactive, are subject to other international control systems, including international instruments, applying specifically to radioactive materials, are excluded from the scope of this Convention.
- Wastes which derive from the normal operations of a ship, the discharge of which is covered by another international instrument, are excluded from the scope of this Convention.

DEFINITIONS

For the purposes of this Convention:

- "Wastes" are substances or objects which are disposed of or are intended to be disposed of or are required to be disposed of by the provisions of national law;
- "Management" means the collection, transport and disposal of hazardous wastes or other wastes, including after-care of disposal sites;
- "Transboundary movement" means any movement of hazardous wastes or other wastes from an area under the national jurisdiction of one State to or through an area under the national jurisdiction of another State or to or through an area not under the national jurisdiction of any State, provided at least two States are involved in the movement;
- "Disposal" means any operation specified in Annex IV to this Convention;
- "Approved site or facility" means a site or facility for the disposal of hazardous wastes or other wastes which is authorized or permitted to operate for this purpose by a relevant authority of the State where the site or facility is located;
- "Competent authority" means one governmental authority designated by a Party to be responsible, within such geographical areas as the Party may think fit, for receiving the notification of a transboundary movement of hazardous wastes or

other wastes, and any information related to it, and for responding to such a notification, as provided in Article 6;

- "Focal point" means the entity of a Party referred to in Article 5 responsible for receiving and submitting information as provided;
- "Environmentally sound management of hazardous wastes or other wastes" means taking all practicable steps to ensure that hazardous wastes or other wastes are managed in a manner which will protect human health and the environment against the adverse effects which may result from such wastes;
- "Area under the national jurisdiction of a State" means any land, marine area or airspace within which a State exercises administrative and regulatory responsibility in accordance with international law in regard to the protection of human health or the environment;
- "State of export" means a Party from which a transboundary movement of hazardous wastes or other wastes is planned to be initiated or is initiated;
- "State of import" means a Party to which a transboundary movement of hazardous wastes or other wastes is planned or takes place for the purpose of disposal therein or for the purpose of loading prior to disposal in an area not under the national jurisdiction of any State;
- "State of transit" means any State, other than the State of export or import, through which a movement of hazardous wastes or other wastes is planned or takes place;
- "States concerned" means Parties which are States of export or import, or transit States, whether or not Parties;
- "Person" means any natural or legal person;
- "Exporter" means any person under the jurisdiction of the State of export who arranges for hazardous wastes or other wastes to be exported;

- "Importer" means any person under the jurisdiction of the State of import who arranges for hazardous wastes or other wastes to be imported;
- "Carrier" means any person who carries out the transport of hazardous wastes or other wastes;
- "Generator" means any person whose activity produces hazardous wastes or other wastes or, if that person is not known, the person who is in possession and/or control of those wastes;
- "Disposer" means any person to whom hazardous wastes or other wastes are shipped and who carries out the disposal of such wastes;
- "Political and/or economic integration organization" means an organization constituted by sovereign States to which its member States have transferred competence in respect of matters governed by this Convention and which has been duly authorized, in accordance with its internal procedures, to sign, ratify, accept, approve, formally confirm or accede to it;
- "Illegal traffic" means any transboundary movement of hazardous wastes or other wastes as specified in Article 9.

HAZARDOUS WASTES

- Each Party shall, within six months of becoming a Party to this Convention, inform the Secretariat of the Convention of the wastes, other than those listed in Annexes I and II, considered or defined as hazardous under its national legislation and of any requirements concerning transboundary movement procedures applicable to such wastes.
- Each Party shall subsequently inform the Secretariat of any significant changes to the information it has provided pursuant to paragraph 1.
- The Secretariat shall forthwith inform all Parties of the information it has received pursuant to paragraphs 1 and 2.

- Parties shall be responsible for making the information transmitted to them by the Secretariat under paragraph 3 available to their exporters.

GENERAL OBLIGATIONS

1. (a) Parties exercising their right to prohibit the import of hazardous wastes or other wastes for disposal shall inform the other Parties of their decision pursuant to Article 13. (b) Parties shall prohibit or shall not permit the export of hazardous wastes and other wastes to the Parties which have prohibited the import of such wastes, when notified pursuant to subparagraph (a) above. (c) Parties shall prohibit or shall not permit the export of hazardous wastes and other wastes if the State of import does not consent in writing to the specific import, in the case where that State of import has not prohibited the import of such wastes. 2. Each Party shall take the appropriate measures to: (a) Ensure that the generation of hazardous wastes and other wastes within it is reduced to a minimum, taking into account social, technological and economic aspects; (b) Ensure the availability of adequate disposal facilities, for the environmentally sound management of hazardous wastes and other wastes, that shall be located, to the extent possible, within it, whatever the place of their disposal; (c) Ensure that persons involved in the management of hazardous wastes or other wastes within it take such steps as are necessary to prevent pollution due to hazardous wastes and other wastes arising from such management and, if such pollution occurs, to minimize the consequences thereof for human health and the environment; (d) Ensure that the transboundary movement of hazardous wastes and other wastes is reduced to the minimum consistent with the environmentally sound and efficient management of such wastes, and is conducted in a manner which will protect human health and the environment against the adverse effects which may result from such movement; (e) Not allow the export of hazardous wastes or other wastes to a State or group of States belonging to an economic and/or political integration organization that are Parties, particularly developing

countries, which have prohibited by their legislation all imports, or if it has reason to believe that the wastes in question will not be managed in an environmentally sound manner, according to criteria to be decided on by the Parties at their first meeting; (f) Require that information about a proposed transboundary movement of hazardous wastes and other wastes be provided to the States concerned, according to Annex V A, to state clearly the effects of the proposed movement on human health and the environment; (g) Prevent the import of hazardous wastes and other wastes if it has reason to believe that the wastes in question will not be managed in an environmentally sound manner; (h) Co-operate in activities with other Parties and interested organizations, directly and through the Secretariat, including the dissemination of information on the transboundary movement of hazardous wastes and other wastes, in order to improve the environmentally sound management of such wastes and to achieve the prevention of illegal traffic. 3. The Parties consider that illegal traffic in hazardous wastes or other wastes is criminal. 4.Each Party shall take appropriate legal, administrative and other measures to implement and enforce the provisions of this Convention, including measures to prevent and punish conduct in contravention of the Convention. 5. A Party shall not permit hazardous wastes or other wastes to be exported to a non-Party or to be imported from a non-Party. 6. The Parties agree not to allow the export of hazardous wastes or other wastes for disposal within the area south of 60° South latitude, whether or not such wastes are subject to transboundary movement. 7. Furthermore, each Party shall: (a) Prohibit all persons under its national jurisdiction from transporting or disposing of hazardous wastes or other wastes unless such persons are authorized or allowed to perform such types of operations; (b) Require that hazardous wastes and other wastes that are to be the subject of a transboundary movement be packaged, labelled, and transported in conformity with generally accepted and recognized international rules and standards in the field of packaging, labelling, and transport, and that due account is taken of relevant internationally recognized practices; (c) Require that hazardous wastes and other wastes be accompanied by a movement document from the point at which a transboundary movement commences to the point of disposal. 8. Each Party shall require that hazardous wastes or other wastes, to be exported, are managed in an environmentally sound manner in the State of import or elsewhere. Technical guidelines for the environmentally sound management of wastes subject to this Convention shall be decided by the Parties at their first meeting. 9. Parties shall take the appropriate measures to ensure that the transboundary movement of hazardous wastes and other wastes only be allowed if: (a) The State of export does not have the technical capacity and the necessary facilities, capacity or suitable disposal sites in order to dispose of the wastes in question in an environmentally sound and efficient manner; or (b) The wastes in question are required as a raw material for recycling or recovery industries in the State of import; or (c) The transboundary movement in question is in accordance with other criteria to be decided by the Parties, provided those criteria do not differ from the objectives of this Convention. 10. The obligation under this Convention of States in which hazardous wastes and other wastes are generated to require that those wastes are managed in an environmentally sound manner may not under any circumstances be transferred to the States of import or transit. 11. Nothing in this Convention shall prevent a Party from imposing additional requirements that are consistent with the provisions of this Convention, and are in accordance with the rules of international law, in order better to protect human health and the environment. 12. Nothing in this Convention shall affect in any way the sovereignty of States over their territorial sea established in accordance with international law, and the sovereign rights and the jurisdiction which States have in their exclusive economic zones and their continental shelves in accordance with international law, and the exercise by ships and aircraft of all States of navigational rights and freedoms as provided for in international law and as reflected in relevant international instruments. 13. Parties shall undertake to review periodically the possibilities for the reduction of the amount and/or the pollution potential of hazardous wastes and other wastes which are exported to other States, in particular to developing countries.

COMPETENT AUTHORITIES AND FOCAL POINT

To facilitate the implementation of this Convention, the Parties shall:

- Designate or establish one or more competent authorities and one focal point. One competent authority shall be designated to receive the notification in case of a State of transit.
- Inform the Secretariat, within three months of the date of the entry into force of this Convention for them, which agencies they have designated as their focal point and their competent authorities.
- Inform the Secretariat, within one month of the date of decision, of any changes regarding the designation made by them under paragraph 2 above.

TRANSBOUNDARY MOVEMENT BETWEEN PARTIES

- The State of export shall notify, or shall require the generator or exporter to notify, in writing, through the channel of the competent authority of the State of export, the competent authority of the States concerned of any proposed transboundary movement of hazardous wastes or other wastes. Such notification shall contain the declarations and information specified in Annex V A, written in a language acceptable to the State of import. Only one notification needs to be sent to each State concerned.
- The State of import shall respond to the notifier in writing, consenting to the movement with or without conditions, denying permission for the movement, or requesting additional information. A copy of the final response of the State of import shall be sent to the

competent authorities of the States concerned which are Parties.

- The State of export shall not allow the generator or exporter to commence the transboundary movement until it has received written confirmation that:
  - The notifier has received the written consent of the State of import; and
  - The notifier has received from the State of import confirmation of the existence of a contract between the exporter and the disposer specifying environmentally sound management of the wastes in question.
- Each State of transit which is a Party shall promptly acknowledge to the notifier receipt of the notification. It may subsequently respond to the notifier in writing, within 60 days, consenting to the movement with or without conditions, denying permission for the movement, or requesting additional information. The State of export shall not allow the transboundary movement to commence until it has received the written consent of the State of transit. However, if at any time a Party decides not to require prior written consent, either generally or under specific conditions, for transit transboundary movements of hazardous wastes or other wastes, or modifies its requirements in this respect, it shall forthwith inform the other Parties of its decision pursuant to Article 13. In this latter case, if no response is received by the State of export within 60 days of the receipt of a given notification by the State of transit, the State of export may allow the export to proceed through the State of transit.
- In the case of a transboundary movement of wastes where the wastes are legally defined as or considered to be hazardous wastes only:
  - By the State of export, the requirements of paragraph 9 of this Article that apply to the importer or disposer and the State of import shall

apply mutatis mutandis to the exporter and State of export, respectively;
- By the State of import, or by the States of import and transit which are Parties, the requirements of paragraphs 1, 3, 4 and 6 of this Article that apply to the exporter and State of export shall apply mutatis mutandis to the importer or disposer and State of import, respectively; or
- By any State of transit which is a Party, the provisions of paragraph 4 shall apply to such State.

- The State of export may, subject to the written consent of the States concerned, allow the generator or the exporter to use a general notification where hazardous wastes or other wastes having the same physical and chemical characteristics are shipped regularly to the same disposer via the same customs office of exit of the State of export via the same customs office of entry of the State of import, and, in the case of transit, via the same customs office of entry and exit of the State or States of transit.
- The States concerned may make their written consent to the use of the general notification referred to in paragraph 6 subject to the supply of certain information, such as the exact quantities or periodical lists of hazardous wastes or other wastes to be shipped.
- The general notification and written consent referred to in paragraphs 6 and 7 may cover multiple shipments of hazardous wastes or other wastes during a maximum period of 12 months.
- The Parties shall require that each person who takes charge of a transboundary movement of hazardous wastes or other wastes sign the movement document either upon delivery or receipt of the wastes in question. They shall also require that the disposer inform both the exporter and the competent authority of the State of export of receipt by the disposer of

the wastes in question and, in due course, of the completion of disposal as specified in the notification. If no such information is received within the State of export, the competent authority of the State of export or the exporter shall so notify the State of import.

- The notification and response required by this Article shall be transmitted to the competent authority of the Parties concerned or to such governmental authority as may be appropriate in the case of non-Parties.
- Any transboundary movement of hazardous wastes or other wastes shall be covered by insurance, bond or other guarantee as may be required by the State of import or any State of transit which is a Party.

Transboundary Movement

The Convention shall apply mutatis mutandis to transboundary movement of hazardous wastes or other wastes from a Party through a State or States which are not Parties.

DUTY TO RE-IMPORT

When a transboundary movement of hazardous wastes or other wastes to which the consent of the States concerned has been given, subject to the provisions of this Convention, cannot be completed in accordance with the terms of the contract, the State of export shall ensure that the wastes in question are taken back into the State of export, by the exporter, if alternative arrangements cannot be made for their disposal in an environmentally sound manner, within 90 days from the time that the importing State informed the State of export and the Secretariat, or such other period of time as the States concerned agree.

To this end, the State of export and any Party of transit shall not oppose, hinder or prevent the return of those wastes to the State of export.

ILLEGAL TRAFFIC

- For the purpose of this Convention, any

transboundary movement of hazardous wastes or other wastes:

- Without notification pursuant to the provisions of this Convention to all States concerned; or
- Without the consent pursuant to the provisions of this Convention of a State concerned; or
- With consent obtained from States concerned through falsification, misrepresentation or fraud; or
- That does not conform in a material way with the documents; or
- That results in deliberate disposal (e.g. dumping) of hazardous wastes or other wastes in contravention of this Convention and of general principles of international law, shall be deemed to be illegal traffic.

- In case of a transboundary movement of hazardous wastes or other wastes deemed to be illegal traffic as the result of conduct on the part of the exporter or generator, the State of export shall ensure that the wastes in question are:

- Taken back by the exporter or the generator or, if necessary, by itself into the State of export, or, if impracticable,
- Are otherwise disposed of in accordance with the provisions of this Convention, within 30 days from the time the State of export has been informed about the illegal traffic or such other period of time as States concerned may agree. To this end the Parties concerned shall not oppose, hinder or prevent the return of those wastes to the State of export.

- In the case of a transboundary movement of hazardous wastes or other wastes deemed to be illegal traffic as the result of conduct on the part of the importer or disposer, the State of import shall ensure that the wastes in question are disposed of in an environmentally sound manner by the importer or disposer or, if necessary, by itself within 30 days from the time the illegal traffic has come to the attention of the State of import or such other period of time as the States concerned may agree. To this end, the Parties concerned shall co-operate, as necessary, in the disposal of the wastes in an environmentally sound manner.

- In cases where the responsibility for the illegal traffic cannot be assigned either to the exporter or generator or to the importer or disposer, the Parties concerned or other Parties, as appropriate, shall ensure, through co-operation, that the wastes in question are disposed of as soon as possible in an environmentally sound manner either in the State of export or the State of import or elsewhere as appropriate.
- Each Party shall introduce appropriate national/ domestic legislation to prevent and punish illegal traffic. The Parties shall co-operate with a view to achieving the objects of this Article.

INTERNATIONAL CO-OPERATION

- The Parties shall co-operate with each other in order to improve and achieve environmentally sound management of hazardous wastes and other wastes.
- *To this end, the Parties shall*:
  - Upon request, make available information, whether on a bilateral or multilateral basis, with a view to promoting the environmentally sound management of hazardous wastes and other wastes, including harmonization of technical standards and practices for the adequate management of hazardous wastes and other wastes;
  - Co-operate in monitoring the effects of the management of hazardous wastes on human health and the environment;
  - Co-operate, subject to their national laws, regulations and policies, in the development and implementation of new environmentally sound low-waste technologies and the improvement of

existing technologies with a view to eliminating, as far as practicable, the generation of hazardous wastes and other wastes and achieving more effective and efficient methods of ensuring their management in an environmentally sound manner, including the study of the economic, social and environmental effects of the adoption of such new or improved technologies;

- Co-operate actively, subject to their national laws, regulations and policies, in the transfer of technology and management systems related to the environmentally sound management of hazardous wastes and other wastes. They shall also co-operate in developing the technical capacity among Parties, especially those which may need and request technical assistance in this field;
- Co-operate in developing appropriate technical guidelines and/or codes of practice.

- The Parties shall employ appropriate means to co-operate in order to assist developing countries in the implementation of subparagraphs a, b, c and d of paragraph 2 of Article.
- Taking into account the needs of developing countries, co-operation between Parties and the competent international organizations is encouraged to promote, inter alia, public awareness, the development of sound management of hazardous wastes and other wastes and the adoption of new low-waste technologies.

BILATERAL AND MULTILATERAL AGREEMENTS

- Notwithstanding the provisions of Article 4 paragraph 5, Parties may enter into bilateral, multilateral, or regional agreements or arrangements regarding transboundary movement of hazardous wastes or other wastes with Parties or non-Parties provided that such agreements or arrangements do not derogate from the environmentally sound management of hazardous wastes and other wastes as required by this Convention. These agreements or arrangements shall stipulate provisions which are not less environmentally sound than those provided for by this Convention in particular taking into account the interests of developing countries.

- Parties shall notify the Secretariat of any bilateral, multilateral or regional agreements or arrangements referred to in paragraph 1 and those which they have entered into prior to the entry into force of this Convention for them, for the purpose of controlling transboundary movements of hazardous wastes and other wastes which take place entirely among the Parties to such agreements. The provisions of this Convention shall not affect transboundary movements which take place pursuant to such agreements provided that such agreements are compatible with the environmentally sound management of hazardous wastes and other wastes as required by this Convention.

CONSULTATIONS ON LIABILITY

The Parties shall co-operate with a view to adopting, as soon as practicable, a protocol setting out appropriate rules and procedures in the field of liability and compensation for damage resulting from the transboundary movement and disposal of hazardous wastes and other wastes.

TRANSMISSION OF INFORMATION

- The Parties shall, whenever it comes to their knowledge, ensure that, in the case of an accident occurring during the transboundary movement of hazardous wastes or other wastes or their disposal, which are likely to present risks to human health and the environment in other States, those States are immediately informed.
- The Parties shall inform each other, through the Secretariat, of:

- Changes regarding the designation of competent authorities and/or focal points,
- Changes in their national definition of hazardous wastes, pursuant to Article 3;

  and, as soon as possible,
- Decisions made by them not to consent totally or partially to the import of hazardous wastes or other wastes for disposal within the area under their national jurisdiction;
- Decisions taken by them to limit or ban the export of hazardous wastes or other wastes;
- Any other information required pursuant to paragraph 4 of this Article.

• The Parties, consistent with national laws and regulations, shall transmit, through the Secretariat, to the Conference of the Parties established under Article 15, before the end of each calendar year, a report on the previous calendar year, containing the following information:
  - Competent authorities and focal points that have been designated by them pursuant to Article 5;
  - Information regarding transboundary movements of hazardous wastes or other wastes in which they have been involved, including:
  - The amount of hazardous wastes and other wastes exported, their category, characteristics, destination, any transit country and disposal method as stated on the response to notification;
  - The amount of hazardous wastes and other wastes imported, their category, characteristics, origin, and disposal methods;
  - Disposals which did not proceed as intended;
  - Efforts to achieve a reduction of the amount of hazardous wastes or other wastes subject to transboundary movement;
  - Information on the measures adopted by them in implementation of this Convention;
  - Information on available qualified statistics

which have been compiled by them on the effects on human health and the environment of the generation, transportation and disposal of hazardous wastes or other wastes;
- Information concerning bilateral, multilateral and regional agreements and arrangements entered into pursuant to Article 11 of this Convention;
- Information on accidents occurring during the transboundary movement and disposal of hazardous wastes and other wastes and on the measures undertaken to deal with them;
- Information on disposal options operated within the area of their national jurisdiction;
- Information on measures undertaken for development of technologies for the reduction and/or elimination of production of hazardous wastes and other wastes; and
- Such other matters as the Conference of the Parties shall deem relevant.

- The Parties, consistent with national laws and regulations, shall ensure that copies of each notification concerning any given transboundary movement of hazardous wastes or other wastes, and the response to it, are sent to the Secretariat when a Party considers that its environment may be affected by that transboundary movement has requested that this should be done.

FINANCIAL ASPECTS

- The Parties agree that, according to the specific needs of different regions and subregions, regional or sub-regional centres for training and technology transfers regarding the management of hazardous wastes and other wastes and the minimization of their generation should be established. The Parties shall decide on the establishment of appropriate funding mechanisms of a voluntary nature.
- The Parties shall consider the establishment of a

revolving fund to assist on an interim basis in case of emergency situations to minimize damage from accidents arising from transboundary movements of hazardous wastes and other wastes or during the disposal of those wastes.

CONFERENCE OF THE PARTIES

- A Conference of the Parties is hereby established. The first meeting of the Conference of the Parties shall be convened by the Executive Director of UNEP not later than one year after the entry into force of this Convention. Thereafter, ordinary meetings of the Conference of the Parties shall be held at regular intervals to be determined by the Conference at its first meeting.
- Extraordinary meetings of the Conference of the Parties shall be held at such other times as may be deemed necessary by the Conference, or at the written request of any Party, provided that, within six months of the request being communicated to them by the Secretariat, it is supported by at least one third of the Parties.
- The Conference of the Parties shall by consensus agree upon and adopt rules of procedure for itself and for any subsidiary body it may establish, as well as financial rules to determine in particular the financial participation of the Parties under this Convention.
- The Parties at their first meeting shall consider any additional measures needed to assist them in fulfilling their responsibilities with respect to the protection and the preservation of the marine environment in the context of this Convention.
- The Conference of the Parties shall keep under continuous review and evaluation the effective implementation of this Convention, and, in addition, shall:

  Promote the harmonization of appropriate

policies, strategies and measures for minimizing harm to human health and the environment by hazardous wastes and other wastes;

- Consider and adopt, as required, amendments to this Convention and its annexes, taking into consideration, inter alia, available scientific, technical, economic and environmental information;
- Consider and undertake any additional action that may be required for the achievement of the purposes of this Convention in the light of experience gained in its operation and in the operation of the agreements and arrangements.
- Consider and adopt protocols as required; and
- Establish such subsidiary bodies as are deemed necessary for the implementation of this Convention.

- The United Nations, its specialized agencies, as well as any State not Party to this Convention, may be represented as observers at meetings of the Conference of the Parties. Any other body or agency, whether national or international, governmental or non-governmental, qualified in fields relating to hazardous wastes or other wastes which has informed the Secretariat of its wish to be represented as an observer at a meeting of the Conference of the Parties, may be admitted unless at least one third of the Parties present object. The admission and participation of observers shall be subject to the rules of procedure adopted by the Conference of the Parties.
- The Conference of the Parties shall undertake three years after the entry into force of this Convention, and at least every six years thereafter, an evaluation of its effectiveness and, if deemed necessary, to consider the adoption of a complete or partial ban of transboundary movements of hazardous wastes and other wastes in light of the latest scientific, environmental, technical and economic information.

SECRETARIAT

- The functions of the Secretariat shall be:
  - To arrange for and service meetings provided for in Articles 15 and 17;
  - To prepare and transmit reports based upon information received in accordance with Articles 3, 4, 6, 11 and 13 as well as upon information derived from meetings of subsidiary bodies established under Article 15 as well as upon, as appropriate, information provided by relevant intergovernmental and non-governmental entities;
  - To prepare reports on its activities carried out in implementation of its functions under this Convention and present them to the Conference of the Parties;
  - To ensure the necessary coordination with relevant international bodies, and in particular to enter into such administrative and contractual arrangements as may be required for the effective discharge of its function;
  - To communicate with focal points and competent authorities established by the Parties in accordance with Article 5 of this Convention;
  - To compile information concerning authorized national sites and facilities of Parties available for the disposal of their hazardous wastes and other wastes and to circulate this information among Parties;
  - To receive and convey information from and to Parties on:
    a. Sources of technical assistance and training;
    b. Available technical and scientific know-how;
    c. Sources of advice and expertise; and
    d. Availability of resources with a view to assisting them, upon request, in such areas as:
    e. The handling of the notification system of this Convention;

f. The management of hazardous wastes and other wastes;
g. Environmentally sound technologies relating to hazardous wastes and other wastes; such as low- and non-waste technology;
h. The assessment of disposal capabilities and sites;
j. The monitoring of hazardous wastes and other wastes; and
k. Emergency responses;

- To provide Parties, upon request, with information on consultants or consulting firms having the necessary technical competence in the field, which can assist them to examine a notification for a transboundary movement, the concurrence of a shipment of hazardous wastes or other wastes with the relevant notification, and/or the fact that the proposed disposal facilities for hazardous wastes or other wastes are environmentally sound, when they have reason to believe that the wastes in question will not be managed in an environmentally sound manner. Any such examination would not be at the expense of the Secretariat;
- To assist Parties upon request in their identi-fication of cases of illegal traffic and to circulate immediately to the Parties concerned any information it has received regarding illegal traffic;
- To co-operate with Parties and with relevant and competent international organizations and agencies in the provision of experts and equipment for the purpose of rapid assistance to States in the event of an emergency situation; and
- To perform such other functions relevant to the purposes of this Convention as may be determined by the Conference of the Parties.

• The secretariat functions will be carried out on an interim basis by UNEP until the completion of the first meeting of the Conference of the Parties held pursuant .

- At its first meeting, the Conference of the Parties shall designate the Secretariat from among those existing competent intergovernmental organizations which have signified their willingness to carry out the secretariat functions under this Convention. At this meeting, the Conference of the Parties shall also evaluate the implementation by the interim Secretariat of the functions assigned to it, in particular under paragraph 1 above, and decide upon the structures appropriate for those functions.

AMENDMENT OF THE CONVENTION

- Any Party may propose amendments to this Convention and any Party to a protocol may propose amendments to that protocol. Such amendments shall take due account, inter alia, of relevant scientific and technical considerations.
- Amendments to this Convention shall be adopted at a meeting of the Conference of the Parties. Amendments to any protocol shall be adopted at a meeting of the Parties to the protocol in question. The text of any proposed amendment to this Convention or to any protocol, except as may otherwise be provided in such protocol, shall be communicated to the Parties by the Secretariat at least six months before the meeting at which it is proposed for adoption. The Secretariat shall also communicate proposed amendments to the Signatories to this Convention for information.
- The Parties shall make every effort to reach agreement on any proposed amendment to this Convention by consensus. If all efforts at consensus have been exhausted, and no agreement reached, the amendment shall as a last resort be adopted by a three-fourths majority vote of the Parties present and voting at the meeting, and shall be submitted by the

Depositary to all Parties for ratification, approval, formal confirmation or acceptance.

- The procedure mentioned in paragraph 3 above shall apply to amendments to any protocol, except that a two-thirds majority of the Parties to that protocol present and voting at the meeting shall suffice for their adoption.
- Instruments of ratification, approval, formal confirmation or acceptance of amendments shall be deposited with the Depositary. Amendments adopted in accordance with paragraphs 3 or 4 above shall enter into force between Parties having accepted them on the ninetieth day after the receipt by the Depositary of their instrument of ratification, approval, formal confirmation or acceptance by at least three-fourths of the Parties who accepted them or by at least two thirds of the Parties to the protocol concerned who accepted them, except as may otherwise be provided in such protocol. The amendments shall enter into force for any other Party on the ninetieth day after that Party deposits its instrument of ratification, approval, formal confirmation or acceptance of the amendments.
- For the purpose of this Article, "Parties present and voting" means Parties present and casting an affirmative or negative vote.

ADOPTION AND AMENDMENT

- The annexes to this Convention or to any protocol shall form an integral part of this Convention or of such protocol, as the case may be and, unless expressly provided otherwise, a reference to this Convention or its protocols constitutes at the same time a reference to any annexes thereto. Such annexes shall be restricted to scientific, technical and administrative matters.
- Except as may be otherwise provided in any protocol with respect to its annexes, the following procedure

shall apply to the proposal, adoption and entry into force of additional annexes to this Convention or of annexes to a protocol: (a)Annexes to this Convention and its protocols shall be proposed and adopted according to the procedure laid; (b)Any Party that is unable to accept an additional annex to this Convention or an annex to any protocol to which it is party shall so notify the Depositary, in writing, within six months from the date of the communication of the adoption by the Depositary. The Depositary shall without delay notify all Parties of any such notification received. A Party may at any time substitute an acceptance for a previous declaration of objection and the annexes shall thereupon enter into force for that Party; (c) On the expiry of six months from the date of the circulation of the communication by the Depositary, the annex shall become effective for all Parties to this Convention or to any protocol concerned, which have not submitted a notification in accordance with the provision of subparagraph (b) above.

- The proposal, adoption and entry into force of amendments to annexes to this Convention or to any protocol shall be subject to the same procedure as for the proposal, adoption and entry into force of annexes to the Convention or annexes to a protocol. Annexes and amendments thereto shall take due account, inter alia, of relevant scientific and technical considerations.
- If an additional annex or an amendment to an annex involves an amendment to this Convention or to any protocol, the additional annex or amended annex shall not enter into force until such time the amendment to this Convention or to the protocol enters into force.

VERIFICATION

Any Party which has reason to believe that another Party

is acting or has acted in breach of its obligations under this Convention may inform the Secretariat thereof, and in such an event, shall simultaneously and immediately inform, directly or through the Secretariat, the Party against whom the allegations are made. All relevant information should be submitted by the Secretariat to the Parties.

SETTLEMENT OF DISPUTES

- In case of a dispute between Parties as to the interpretation or application of, or compliance with, this Convention or any protocol thereto, they shall seek a settlement of the dispute through negotiation or any other peaceful means of their own choice.
- If the Parties concerned cannot settle their dispute through the means mentioned in the preceding paragraph, the dispute, if the Parties to the dispute agree, shall be submitted to the International Court of Justice or to arbitration under the conditions set out in Annex VI on Arbitration. However, failure to reach common agreement on submission of the dispute to the International Court of Justice or to arbitration shall not absolve the Parties from the responsibility of continuing to seek to resolve it by the means referred to in paragraph 1.
- When ratifying, accepting, approving, formally confirming or acceding to this Convention, or at any time thereafter, a State or political and/or economic integration organization may declare that it recognizes as compulsory ipso facto and without special agreement, in relation to any Party accepting the same obligation:
  - Submission of the dispute to the International Court of Justice; and/or
  - Arbitration in accordance with the procedures set out in Annex VI.

Such declaration shall be notified in writing to the Secretariat which shall communicate it to the Parties.

SIGNATURE

This Convention shall be open for signature by States, by Namibia, represented by the United Nations Council for Namibia, and by political and/or economic integration organizations, in Basel on 22 March 1989, at the Federal Department of Foreign Affairs of Switzerland in Berne from 23 March 1989 to 30 June 1989 and at United Nations Headquarters in New York from 1 July 1989 to 22 March 1990.

RATIFICATION, ACCEPTANCE, FORMAL CONFIRMATION OR APPROVAL

- This Convention shall be subject to ratification, acceptance or approval by States and by Namibia, represented by the United Nations Council for Namibia, and to formal confirmation or approval by political and/or economic integration organizations. Instruments of ratification, acceptance, formal confirmation, or approval shall be deposited with the Depositary.
- Any organization referred to in paragraph 1 above which becomes a Party to this Convention without any of its member States being a Party shall be bound by all the obligations under the Convention. In the case of such organizations, one or more of whose member States is a Party to the Convention, the organization and its member States shall decide on their respective responsibilities for the performance of their obligations under the Convention. In such cases, the organization and the member States shall not be entitled to exercise rights under the Convention concurrently.
- In their instruments of formal confirmation or approval, the organizations referred to in paragraph 1 above shall declare the extent of their competence with respect to the matters governed by the Convention. These organizations shall also inform the Depositary, who will inform the Parties of any

substantial modification in the extent of their competence.

ACCESSION

- This Convention shall be open for accession by States, by Namibia, represented by the United Nations Council for Namibia, and by political and/or economic integration organizations from the day after the date on which the Convention is closed for signature. The instruments of accession shall be deposited with the Depositary.
- In their instruments of accession, the organizations referred to in paragraph 1 above shall declare the extent of their competence with respect to the matters governed by the Convention. These organizations shall also inform the Depositary of any substantial modification in the extent of their competence.
- The provisions of Article 22, paragraph 2, shall apply to political and/or economic integration organizations which accede to this Convention.

RIGHT TO VOTE

- Except as provided for in paragraph 2 below, each Contracting Party to this Convention shall have one vote.
- Political and/or economic integration organizations, in matters within their competence, in accordance with Article 22, paragraph 3, and Article 23, paragraph 2, shall exercise their right to vote with a number of votes equal to the number of their member States which are Parties to the Convention or the relevant protocol. Such organizations shall not exercise their right to vote if their member States exercise theirs, and vice versa.

ENTRY INTO FORCE

- This Convention shall enter into force on the ninetieth day after the date of deposit of the twentieth instrument of ratification, acceptance, formal confirmation, approval or accession.

- For each State or political and/or economic integration organization which ratifies, accepts, approves or formally confirms this Convention or accedes thereto after the date of the deposit of the twentieth instrument of ratification, acceptance, approval, formal confirmation or accession, it shall enter into force on the ninetieth day after the date of deposit by such State or political and/or economic integration organization of its instrument of ratification, acceptance, approval, formal confirmation or accession.
- For the purpose of paragraphs 1 and 2 above, any instrument deposited by a political and/or economic integration organization shall not be counted as additional to those deposited by member States of such organization.

RESERVATIONS AND DECLARATIONS

- No reservation or exception may be made to this Convention.
- State or political and/or economic integration organization, when signing, ratifying, accepting, approving, formally confirming or acceding to this Convention, from making declarations or statements, however phrased or named, with a view, inter alia, to the harmonization of its laws and regulations with the provisions of this Convention, provided that such declarations or statements do not purport to exclude or to modify the legal effects of the provisions of the Convention in their application to that State.

WITHDRAWAL

- At any time after three years from the date on which this Convention has entered into force for a Party, that Party may withdraw from the Convention by giving written notification to the Depositary.

- Withdrawal shall be effective one year from receipt of notification by the Depositary, or on such later date as may be specified in the notification.

DEPOSITORY

The Secretary-General of the United Nations shall be the Depository of this Convention and of any protocol thereto.

AUTHENTIC TEXTS

The original Arabic, Chinese, English, French, Russian and Spanish texts of this Convention are equally authentic. In Witness Where of the undersigned, being duly authorized to that effect, have signed this Convention. Done at Basel on the 22 day of March 1989 Annexes VI .

CATEGORIES OF WASTES TO BE CONTROLLED

Waste Streams:

Y1	Clinical wastes from medical care in hospitals, medical centers and clinics
Y2	Wastes from the production and preparation of pharmaceutical products
Y3	Waste pharmaceuticals, drugs and medicines
Y4	Wastes from the production, formulation and use of biocides and phytopharmaceuticals
Y5	Wastes from the manufacture, formulation and use of wood preserving chemicals
Y6	Wastes from the production, formulation and use of organic solvents
Y7	Wastes from heat treatment and tempering operations containing cyanides
Y8	Waste mineral oils unfit for their originally intended use
Y9	Waste oils/water, hydrocarbons/water mixtures, emulsions
Y10	Waste substances and articles containing or contaminated with polychlorinated biphenyls (PCBs) and/or polychlorinated terphenyls (PCTs)

and/or polybrominated biphenyls (PBBs)

Y11 Waste tarry residues arising from refining, distillation and any pyrolytic treatment

Y12 Wastes from production, formulation and use of inks, dyes, pigments, paints, lacquers, varnish

Y13 Wastes from production, formulation and use of resins, latex, plasticizers, glues/adhesives

Y14 Waste chemical substances arising from research and development or teaching activities which are not identified and/or are new and whose effects on man and/or the environment are not known

Y15 Wastes of an explosive nature not subject to other legislation

Y16 Wastes from production, formulation and use of photographic chemicals and processing materials

Y17 Wastes resulting from surface treatment of metals and plastics

Y18 Residues arising from industrial waste disposal operations

Wastes having as constituents:

Y19 Metal carbonyls

Y20 Beryllium; beryllium compounds

Y21 Hexavalent chromium compounds

Y22 Copper compounds

Y23 Zinc compounds

Y24 Arsenic; arsenic compounds

Y25 Selenium; selenium compounds

Y26 Cadmium; cadmium compounds

Y27 Antimony; antimony compounds

Y28 Tellurium; tellurium compounds

Y29 Mercury; mercury compounds

Y30 Thallium; thallium compounds

Y31 Lead; lead compounds

Y32 Inorganic fluorine compounds excluding calcium fluoride

Y33 Inorganic cyanides

Y34 Acidic solutions or acids in solid form

Y35 Basic solutions or bases in solid form

Y36	Asbestos (dust and fibres)
Y37	Organic phosphorus compounds
Y38	Organic cyanides
Y39	Phenols; phenol compounds including chlorophenols
Y40	Ethers
Y41	Halogenated organic solvents
Y42	Organic solvents excluding halogenated solvents
Y43	Any congenor of polychlorinated dibenzo-furan
Y44	Any congenor of polychlorinated dibenzo-p-dioxin
Y45	Organohalogen compounds other than substances referred to in this Annex (e.g. Y39, Y41, Y42, Y43, Y44)

(a) To facilitate the application of this Convention, and subject to paragraphs (b), (c) and (d), wastes listed in Annex VIII are characterized as hazardous pursuant to Article 1, paragraph 1 (a), of this Convention, and wastes listed in Annex IX are not covered by, paragraph 1 (a), of this Convention. (b) Designation of a waste on Annex VIII does not preclude, in a particular case, the use of Annex III to demonstrate that a waste is not hazardous pursuant to Article 1, paragraph 1 (a), of this Convention. (c) Designation of a waste on Annex IX does not preclude, in a particular case, characterization of such a waste as hazardous pursuant to Article1, paragraph1 (a), of this Convention if it contains Annex I material to an extent causing it to exhibit an Annex III characteristic. (d) Annexes VIII and IX do not affect the application of Article 1, paragraph1 (a), of this Convention for the purpose of characterization of wastes.

ARBITRATION

Unless the agreement referred to in Article 20 of the Convention provides otherwise, the arbitration procedure shall be conducted in accordance with Articles 2 to 10 below. The claimant Party shall notify the Secretariat that the Parties have agreed to submit the dispute to arbitration pursuant to paragraph 2 or paragraph 3 of Article 20 and include, in particular, the Articles of the Convention the interpretation or application of which are at issue. The Secretariat shall forward the information thus received to all Parties to the Convention. The arbitral tribunal shall consist of three members. Each of the Parties to the dispute shall appoint an arbitrator, and the two arbitrators so appointed shall designate by common agreement the third arbitrator, who shall be the chairman of the tribunal.

The latter shall not be a national of one of the Parties to the dispute, nor have his usual place of residence in the territory of one of these Parties, nor be employed by any of them, nor have dealt with the case in any other capacity.

- If the chairman of the arbitral tribunal has not been designated within two months of the appointment of the second arbitrator, the Secretary-General of the United Nations shall, at the request of either Party, designate him within a further two months period.
- If one of the Parties to the dispute does not appoint an arbitrator within two months of the receipt of the request, the other Party may inform the Secretary-General of the United Nations who shall designate the chairman of the arbitral tribunal within a further two months' period. Upon designation, the chairman of the arbitral tribunal shall request the Party which has not appointed an arbitrator to do so within two months. After such period, he shall inform the Secretary-General of the United Nations, who shall make this appointment within a further two months' period.
- The arbitral tribunal shall render its decision in accordance with international law and in accordance with the provisions of this Convention.
- Any arbitral tribunal constituted under the provisions of this Annex shall draw up its own rules of procedure.
- The decisions of the arbitral tribunal both on procedure and on substance, shall be taken by majority vote of its members.
- The tribunal may take all appropriate measures in

order to establish the facts. It may, at the request of one of the Parties, recommend essential interim measures of protection.

- The Parties to the dispute shall provide all facilities necessary for the effective conduct of the proceedings
- The absence or default of a Party in the dispute shall not constitute an impediment to the proceedings.

The tribunal may hear and determine counter-claims arising directly out of the subject-matter of the dispute. Unless the arbitral tribunal determines otherwise because of the particular circumstances of the case, the expenses of the tribunal, including the remuneration of its members, shall be borne by the Parties to the dispute in equal shares. The tribunal shall keep a record of all its expenses, and shall furnish a final statement thereof to the Parties.

Any Party that has an interest of a legal nature in the subject-matter of the dispute which may be affected by the decision in the case, may intervene in the proceedings with the consent of the tribunal. The tribunal shall render its award within five months of the date on which it is established unless it finds it necessary to extend the time-limit for a period which should not exceed five months.T he award of the arbitral tribunal shall be accompanied by a statement of reasons. It shall be final and binding upon the Parties to the dispute. Any dispute which may arise between the Parties concerning the interpretation or execution of the award may be submitted by either Party to the arbitral tribunal which made the award or, if the latter cannot be seized thereof, to another tribunal constituted for this purpose in the same manner as the first.

Annex VII

List A: Wastes contained in this Annex are characterized as hazardous under Article 1, paragraph 1 (a), of this Convention, and their designation on this Annex does not preclude the use of Annex III to demonstrate that a waste is not hazardous.

A1 Metal and metal-bearing wastes:

A1010 Metal wastes and waste consisting of alloys of any of the following:

- Antimony
- Arsenic
- Beryllium
- Cadmium
- Lead
- Mercury
- Selenium
- Tellurium
- Thallium

but excluding such wastes specifically listed on list B.

A1020 Waste having as constituents or contaminants, excluding metal waste in massive form, any of the following:

- Antimony; antimony compounds
- Beryllium; beryllium compounds
- Cadmium; cadmium compounds
- Lead; lead compounds
- Selenium; selenium compounds
- Tellurium; tellurium compounds

A1030 Wastes having as constituents or contaminants any of the following:

- Arsenic; arsenic compounds
- Mercury; mercury compounds
- Thallium; thallium compounds

A1040 Wastes having as constituents any of the following:

- Metal carbonyls
- Hexavalent chromium compounds

A1050 Galvanic sludges

A1060 Waste liquors from the pickling of metals

A1070 Leaching residues from zinc processing, dust and sludges such as jarosite, hematite, etc.

A1080 Waste zinc residues not included on list B, containing lead and cadmium in concentrations sufficient to exhibit Annex III characteristics

A1090 Ashes from the incineration of insulated copper wire

A1100 Dusts and residues from gas cleaning systems of copper smelters

A1110 Spent electrolytic solutions from copper

	electrorefining and electrowinning operations
A1120	Waste sludges, excluding anode slimes, from electrolyte purification systems in copper electrorefining and electrowinning operations
A1130	Spent etching solutions containing dissolved copper
A1140	Waste cupric chloride and copper cyanide catalysts
A1150	Precious metal ash from incineration of printed circuit boards not included on list B
A1160	Waste lead-acid batteries, whole or crushed
A1170	Unsorted waste batteries excluding mixtures of only list B batteries. Waste batteries not specified on list B containing Annex I constituents to an extent to render them hazardous
A1180	Waste electrical and electronic assemblies or scrap containing components such as accumulators and other batteries included on list A, mercury-switches, glass from cathode-ray tubes and other activated glass and PCB-capacitors, or contaminated with Annex I constituents (e.g., cadmium, mercury, lead, polychlorinated biphenyl) to an extent that they possess any of the characteristics contained in Annex III (note the related entry on list B B1110)
A1190	Waste metal cables coated or insulated with plastics containing or contaminated with coal tar, PCB , lead, cadmium, other organohalogen compounds or other Annex I constituents to an extent that they exhibit Annex III characteristics.

A2 Wastes containing principally inorganic constituents, which may contain metals and organic materials:

A2010	Glass waste from cathode-ray tubes and other activated glasses
A2020	Waste inorganic fluorine compounds in the form of liquids or sludges but excluding such wastes specified on list B
A2030	Waste catalysts but excluding such wastes specified on list B
A2040	Waste gypsum arising from chemical industry

processes, when containing Annex I constituents to the extent that it exhibits an Annex III hazardous characteristic (note the related entry on list B B2080)

A2050 Waste asbestos (dusts and fibres)

A2060 Coal-fired power plant fly-ash containing Annex I substances in concentrations sufficient to exhibit Annex III characteristics (note the related entry on list B B2050)

A3 Wastes containing principally organic constituents, which may contain metals and inorganic materials:

A3010 Waste from the production or processing of petroleum coke and bitumen

A3020 Waste mineral oils unfit for their originally intended use

A3030 Wastes that contain, consist of or are contaminated with leaded anti-knock compound sludges

A3040 Waste thermal (heat transfer) fluids

A3050 Wastes from production, formulation and use of resins, latex, plasticizers, glues/adhesives excluding such wastes specified on list B (note the related entry on list B B4020)

A3060 Waste nitrocellulose

A3070 Waste phenols, phenol compounds including chlorophenol in the form of liquids or sludges

A3080 Waste ethers not including those specified on list B

A3090 Waste leather dust, ash, sludges and flours when containing hexavalent chromium compounds or biocides (note the related entry on list B B3100)

A3100 Waste paring and other waste of leather or of composition leather not suitable for the manufacture of leather articles containing hexavalent chromium compounds or biocides (note the related entry on list B B3090)

A3110 Fellmongery wastes containing hexavalent chromium compounds or biocides or infectious substances (note the related entry on list B B3110)

A3120 Fluff - light fraction from shredding

A3130 Waste organic phosphorous compounds

A3140 Waste non-halogenated organic solvents but

excluding such wastes specified on list B

A3150 Waste halogenated organic solvents

A3160 Waste halogenated or unhalogenated non-aqueous distillation residues arising from organic solvent recovery operations

A3170 Wastes arising from the production of aliphatic halogenated hydrocarbons (such as chloromethane, dichloro-ethane, vinyl chloride, vinylidene chloride, allyl chloride and epichlorhydrin)

A3180 Wastes, substances and articles containing, consisting of or contaminated with polychlorinated biphenyl (PCB), polychlorinated terphenyl (PCT), polychlorinated naphthalene (PCN) or polybrominated biphenyl (PBB), or any other polybrominated analogues of these compounds, at a concentration level of 50 mg/kg or more[8]

A3190 Waste tarry residues (excluding asphalt cements) arising from refining, distillation and any pyrolitic treatment of organic materials

A4010 Wastes from the production, preparation and use of pharmaceutical products but excluding such wastes specified on list B

A4020 Clinical and related wastes; that is wastes arising from medical, nursing, dental, veterinary, or similar practices, and wastes generated in hospitals or other facilities during the investigation or treatment of patients, or research projects

A4030 Wastes from the production, formulation and use of biocides and phytopharmaceuticals, including waste pesticides and herbicides which are off-specification, outdated[9], or unfit for their originally intended use

A4040 Wastes from the manufacture, formulation and use of wood-preserving chemicals[10]

A4050 Wastes that contain, consist of or are contaminated with any of the following:

- Inorganic cyanides, excepting precious-metal-bearing residues in solid form containing traces of inorganic cyanides

- Organic cyanides

A4060 Waste oils/water, hydrocarbons/water mixtures, emulsions

A4070 Wastes from the production, formulation and use of inks, dyes, pigments, paints, lacquers, varnish excluding any such waste specified on list B (note the related entry on list B B4010)

A4080 Wastes of an explosive nature (but excluding such wastes specified on list B)

A4090 Waste acidic or basic solutions, other than those specified in the corresponding entry on list B (note the related entry on list B B2120)

A4100 Wastes from industrial pollution control devices for cleaning of industrial off-gases but excluding such wastes specified on list B

Note: "Outdated" means unused within the period recommended by the manufacturer. [10]This entry does not include wood treated with wood preserving chemicals.

A4110 Wastes that contain, consist of or are contaminated with any of the following:

- Any congenor of polychlorinated dibenzo-furan
- Any congenor of polychlorinated dibenzo-dioxin

A4120 Wastes that contain, consist of or are contaminated with peroxides

A4130 Waste packages and containers containing Annex I substances in concentrations sufficient to exhibit Annex III hazard characteristics

A4140 Waste consisting of or containing off specification or outdated chemicals corresponding to Annex I categories and exhibiting Annex III hazard characteristics

A4150 Waste chemical substances arising from research and development or teaching activities which are not identified and/or are new and whose effects on human health and/or the environment are not known

A4160 Spent activated carbon not included on list B (note the related entry on list B B2060)

Wastes contained in the Annex will not be wastes covered

by Article 1, paragraph 1 (a), of this Convention unless they contain Annex I material to an extent causing them to exhibit an Annex III characteristic.

B1 Metal and metal-bearing wastes:

B1010 Metal and metal-alloy wastes in metallic, non-dispersible form:

- Precious metals (gold, silver, the platinum group, but not mercury)
- Iron and steel scrap
- Copper scrap
- Nickel scrap
- Aluminium scrap
- Zinc scrap
- Tin scrap
- Tungsten scrap
- Molybdenum scrap
- Tantalum scrap
- Magnesium scrap
- Cobalt scrap
- Bismuth scrap
- Titanium scrap
- Zirconium scrap
- Manganese scrap
- Germanium scrap
- Vanadium scrap
- Scrap of hafnium, indium, niobium, rhenium and gallium
- Thorium scrap
- Rare earths scrap
- Chromium scrap

B1020 Clean, uncontaminated metal scrap, including alloys, in bulk finished form (sheet, plate, beams, rods, etc), of:

- Antimony scrap
- Beryllium scrap
- Cadmium scrap
- Lead scrap (but excluding lead-acid batteries)
- Selenium scrap

- Tellurium scrap

B1030 Refractory metals containing residues

B1031 Molybdenum, tungsten, titanium, tantalum, niobium and rhenium metal and metal alloy wastes in metallic dispersible form (metal powder), excluding such wastes as specified in list A under entry A1050, Galvanic sludges

B1040 Scrap assemblies from electrical power generation not contaminated with lubricating oil, PCB or PCT to an extent to render them hazardous

B1050 Mixed non-ferrous metal, heavy fraction scrap, not containing Annex I materials in concentrations sufficient to exhibit Annex III characteristics

B1060 Waste selenium and tellurium in metallic elemental form including powder

B1070 Waste of copper and copper alloys in dispersible form, unless they contain Annex I constituents to an extent that they exhibit Annex III characteristics

B1080 Zinc ash and residues including zinc alloys residues in dispersible form unless containing Annex I constituents in concentration such as to exhibit Annex III characteristics or exhibiting hazard characteristic H4.3

B1090 Waste batteries conforming to a specification, excluding those made with lead, cadmium or mercury

B1100 Metal-bearing wastes arising from melting, smelting and refining of metals:

- Hard zinc spelter
- Zinc-containing drosses:
  - Galvanizing slab zinc top dross (>90% Zn)
  - Galvanizing slab zinc bottom dross (>92% Zn)
  - Zinc die casting dross (>85% Zn)
  - Hot dip galvanizers slab zinc dross (batch)(>92% Zn)
  - Zinc skimmings
- Aluminium skimmings (or skims) excluding salt

slag

- Slags from copper processing for further processing or refining not containing arsenic, lead or cadmium to an extent that they exhibit Annex IIIhazard characteristics
- Wastes of refractory linings, including crucibles, originating from copper smelting
- Slags from precious metals processing for further refining
- Tantalum-bearing tin slags with less than 0.5% tin

B1110 Electrical and electronic assemblies:

- Electronic assemblies consisting only of metals or alloys
- Waste electrical and electronic assemblies or scrap (including printed circuit boards) not containing components such as accumulators and other batteries included on list A, mercury-switches, glass from cathode-ray tubes and other activated glass and PCB-capacitors, or not contaminated with Annex I constituents (e.g., cadmium, mercury, lead, polychlorinated biphenyl) or from which these have been removed, to an extent that they do not possess any of the characteristics contained in Annex III (note the related entry on list A A1180)
- Electrical and electronic assemblies (including printed circuit boards, electronic components and wires) destined for direct reuse, and not for recycling or final disposal

B1115 Waste metal cables coated or insulated with plastics, not included in list A1190, excluding those destined for Annex IVA operations or any other disposal operations involving, at any stage, uncontrolled thermal processes, such as open-burning.

B1120 Spent catalysts excluding liquids used as catalysts, containing any of:

Transition metals,	Scandium	Titanium
	Vanadium	Chromium

excluding waste catalysts (spent catalysts, liquid used catalysts or other catalysts) on list A:	Manganese	Iron
	Cobalt	Nickel
	Copper	Zinc
	Yttrium	Zirconium
	Niobium	Molybdenum
	Hafnium	Tantalum
	Tungsten	Rhenium
Lanthanides (rare earth metals)	Lanthanum	Cerium
	Praseodymium	Neody
	Samarium	Europium
	Gadolinium	Terbium
	Dysprosium	Holmium
	Erbium	Thulium
	Ytterbium	Lutetium

B1130 Cleaned spent precious-metal-bearing catalysts

B1140 Precious-metal-bearing residues in solid form which contain traces of inorganic cyanides

B1150 Precious metals and alloy wastes (gold, silver, the platinum group, but not mercury) in a dispersible, non-liquid form with appropriate packaging and labelling

B1160 Precious-metal ash from the incineration of printed circuit boards (note the related entry on list A A1150)

B1170 Precious-metal ash from the incineration of photographic film

B1180 Waste photographic film containing silver halides and metallic silver

B1190 Waste photographic paper containing silver halides and metallic silver

B1200 Granulated slag arising from the manufacture of iron and steel

B1210 Slag arising from the manufacture of iron and steel including slags as a source of TiO2 and vanadium

B1220 Slag from zinc production, chemically stabilized, having a high iron content (above 20%) and processed according to industrial specifications (e.g., DIN 4301) mainly for construction

B1230 Mill scaling arising from the manufacture of iron and steel

B1240 Copper oxide mill-scale

B1250 Waste end-of-life motor vehicles, containing neither liquids nor other hazardous components

B2 Wastes containing principally inorganic constituents, which may contain metals and organic materials:

B2010 Wastes from mining operations in non-dispersible form:

- Natural graphite waste
- Slate waste, whether or not roughly trimmed or merely cut, by sawing or otherwise
- Mica waste
- Leucite, nepheline and nepheline syenite waste
- Feldspar waste
- Fluorspar waste
- Silica wastes in solid form excluding those used in foundry operations

B2020 Glass waste in non-dispersible form:

- Cullet and other waste and scrap of glass except for glass from cathode-ray tubes and other activated glasses

B2030 Ceramic wastes in non-dispersible form:

- Cermet wastes and scrap (metal ceramic composites)
- Ceramic based fibres not elsewhere specified or included

B2040 Other wastes containing principally inorganic constituents:

- Partially refined calcium sulphate produced from flue-gas desulphurization (FGD)
- Waste gypsum wallboard or plasterboard arising from the demolition of buildings
- Slag from copper production, chemically stabilized, having a high iron content (above 20%) and processed according to industrial specifications (e.g., DIN 4301 and DIN 8201) mainly for construction and abrasive applications

- Sulphur in solid form
- Limestone from the production of calcium cyanamide (having a pH less than 9)
- Sodium, potassium, calcium chlorides
- Carborundum (silicon carbide)
- Broken concrete
- Lithium-tantalum and lithium-niobium containing glass scraps

B2050 Coal-fired power plant fly-ash, not included on list A (note the related entry on list A A2060)

B2060 Spent activated carbon not containing any Annex I constituents to an extent they exhibit Annex III characteristics, for example, carbon resulting from the treatment of potable water and processes of the food industry and vitamin production (note the related entry on list A, A4160)

B2070 Calcium fluoride sludge

B2080 Waste gypsum arising from chemical industry processes not included on list A (note the related entry on list A A2040)

B2090 Waste anode butts from steel or aluminium production made of petroleum coke or bitumen and cleaned to normal industry specifications (excluding anode butts from chlor alkali electrolyses and from metallurgical industry)

B2100 Waste hydrates of aluminium and waste alumina and residues from alumina production excluding such materials used for gas cleaning, flocculation or filtration processes

B2110 Bauxite residue ("red mud") (pH moderated to less than 11.5)

B2120 Waste acidic or basic solutions with a pH greater than 2 and less than 11.5, which are not corrosive or otherwise hazardous (note the related entry on list A A4090)

B2130 Bituminous material (asphalt waste) from road construction and maintenance, not containing tar (note the related entry on list A, A3200)

B3 Wastes containing principally organic constituents, which may contain metals and inorganic materials:

B3010 Solid plastic waste:

The following plastic or mixed plastic materials, provided they are not mixed with other wastes and are prepared to a specification:

- Scrap plastic of non-halogenated polymers and co-polymers, including but not limited to the following:
  - Ethylene
  - Styrene
  - Polypropylene
  - Polyethylene terephthalate
  - Acrylonitrile
  - Butadiene
  - Polyacetals
  - Polyamides
  - Polybutylene terephthalate
  - Polycarbonates
  - Polyethers
  - Polyphenylene sulphides
  - Acrylic polymers
  - Alkanes C10-C13 (plasticiser)
  - Polyurethane (not containing CFCs)
  - Polysiloxanes
  - Polymethyl methacrylate
  - Polyvinyl alcohol
  - Polyvinyl butyral
  - Polyvinyl acetate
- Cured waste resins or condensation products including the following:
  - Polyvinyl acetate
  - Urea formaldehyde resins
  - Phenol formaldehyde resins
  - Melamine formaldehyde resins
  - Epoxy resins
  - Alkyd resins
  - Polyamides

- The following fluorinated polymer wastes
  - Perfluoroethylene/propylene (FEP)
  - Perfluoro alkoxyl alkane
  - Tetrafluoroethylene/per fluoro vinyl ether (PFA)
  - Tetrafluoroethylene/per fluoro methylvinyl ether (MFA)
  - Polyvinylfluoride (PVF)
  - Polyvinylidenefluoride (PVDF)

B3020 Paper, paperboard and paper product wastes

The following materials, provided they are not mixed with hazardous wastes:

Waste and scrap of paper or paperboard of:

- Unbleached paper or paperboard or of corrugated paper or paperboard
- Other paper or paperboard, made mainly of bleached chemical pulp, not coloured in the mass
- Paper or paperboard made mainly of mechanical pulp (for example, newspapers, journals and similar printed matter)
- Other, including but not limited to 1) laminated paperboard 2) unsorted scrap

B3030 Textile wastes

The following materials, provided they are not mixed with other wastes and are prepared to a specification:

- Silk waste (including cocoons unsuitable for reeling, yarn waste and garnetted stock)
  - Not carded or combed
  - Other
- Waste of wool or of fine or coarse animal hair, including yarn waste but excluding garnetted stock
  - noils of wool or of fine animal hair
  - other waste of wool or of fine animal hair
  - waste of coarse animal hair
- Cotton waste (including yarn waste & garnetted stock)

- yarn waste (including thread waste)
- garnetted stock
- other
- Flax tow and waste

- Tow and waste (including yarn waste and garnetted stock) of true hemp (Cannabis sativa L.)
- Tow and waste (including yarn waste and garnetted stock) of jute and other textile bast fibres (excluding flax, true hemp and ramie)
- Tow and waste (including yarn waste and garnetted stock) of sisal and other textile fibres of the genus Agave
- Tow, noils and waste (including yarn waste and garnetted stock) of coconut
- Tow, noils and waste (including yarn waste and garnetted stock) of abaca (Manila hemp or Musa textilis Nee)
- Tow, noils and waste (including yarn waste and garnetted stock) of ramie and other vegetable textile fibres, not elsewhere specified or included
- Waste (including noils, yarn waste and garnetted stock) of man-made fibres
  - Of synthetic fibres
  - Of artificial fibres
- Worn clothing and other worn textile articles
- Used rags, scrap twine, cordage, rope and cables and worn out articles of twine, cordage, rope or cables of textile materials
  - Sorted
  - Other

B3035 Waste textile floor coverings, carpets

B3040 Rubber wastes

The following materials, provided they are not mixed with other wastes:

- Waste and scrap of hard rubber (e.g., ebonite)
- Other rubber wastes (excluding such wastes specified elsewhere)

Chapter 5

Manufacture and Storage Rules

S.O. 966(E)

In exercise of the powers conferred by Section 6, 8 and 25 of the Environment (Protection) Act, 1986 (29 of 1966), the Central Government hereby makes the following rules, namely.

SHORT TITLE AND COMMENCEMENT

- These rules may be called the Manufacture, Storage and import of Hazardous Chemical Rules, 1989.
- They shall come into force on the date of their publication in the official Gazette.

DEFINITIONS

In these rules, unless he context otherwise requires:

- "Act" means the Environment (Protection) Act, 1986 (29 of 1986);
- "Authority" means an authority mentioned in Column 2 of Schedule 5;
- "export" with its grammatical variations and cognate expression, means taking out of India to a place outside India;
- "exporter" means any person under the jurisdiction of the exporting country and includes the exporting country who exports hazardous chemical;
- "Hazardous chemical" means-
  - Any chemical which satisfies any of the criteria

laid down in Part I of Schedule I and is listed in Column 2 of Part II of this Schedule;
  - Any chemical listed in Column 2 of Schedule 2;
  - Any chemical listed in Column 2 of Schedule 3;
- "Import" with its grammatical variations and cognate expression, means bringing into India from a place outside India;
- "Importer" means an occupier or any person who imports hazardous chemicals;
- "Industrial activity" means-
  - An operation of process carried out in an industrial installation referred to in Schedule 4 involving or likely to involve one or more or hazardous chemicals and includes on-site storage or on-site transport which is associated with that operation or process, as the case may be; or
  - Isolated storage; or
  - Pipeline;
- "Isolated storage" means storage of a hazardous chemical, other than storage associated with an installation on the same site specified in Schedule 4 where that storage involves atleast the quantities of that chemical set out in Schedule 2;
- "Major accident" means an occurrence including any particular major emission, fire or explosion involving one or more hazardous chemicals and resulting from uncontrolled developments in the course of an industrial activity or due to natural events leading to serious effects both immediate or delayed, inside or outside the installation likely to cause substantial loss of life and property including adverse effects on the environments;
- "Pipeline" means a pipe (together with any apparatus and works associated therewith) or system of pipes (together with any apparatus and work associated therewith) for the conveyance of a hazardous chemical other than a flammable gas as set out in Column 2 of Part II of Schedule 3 at a pressure of

less than 8 bars absolute: the pipeline also includes inter-state pipe

- "Schedule" means Schedule appended to these rules;
- "Site" means any location where hazardous chemicals are manufactured or processed, stored, handled, used, disposed of and includes the whole of an area under the control of an occupier and includes pier, jetty or similar structure whether floating or not;
- "Threshold quantity" means,-
  - In the case of a hazardous chemical specified in Column 2 of Schedule 2, the quantity of that chemical specified in the corresponding entry in Columns 3 & 4;
  - In the case of hazardous chemical specified in Column 2 of Part I of Schedule 3, the quantity of that chemical specified in the corresponding entry in Columns 3 & 4 of that part;
  - In the case of substances of a class specified in Column 2 of Part 11 of Schedule 3, the total quantity of all substances of that class specified in the corresponding entry in Column 3 & 4 of that part

DUTIES OF AUTHORITIES

Subject to the other provisions of these rules, the authority shall perform duties as specified in Column 3 of Schedule 5.

GENERAL RESPONSIBILITY

- This rule shall apply to,
  - An industrial activity in which a hazardous chemical, which satisfies any of the criteria laid down in Part I of Schedule I and is listed in Column 2 of Part II of this Schedule is or may be involved; and
  - Isolated storage in which there is involved a threshold quantity of a hazardous chemical listed in Schedule 2 in Column 2 which is equal to or more than the threshold quantity specified in the

Schedule for that chemical in Column 3 thereof.

- An occupier who has control of an industrial activity in term of sub-rule (I) shall provide evidence to show that he has,-
  - Identified the major accident hazards; and
  - Taken adequate steps to -
    - Prevent such major accidents and o limit their consequences to persons and the environment;
    - Provide to The persons working on the site with the information, training and equipment including antidotes necessary to ensure their safely.

NOTIFICATION

- Where a major accident occurs on a site or in a pipe line, the occupier shall forthwith notify the concerned authority as identified in Schedule S of that accident, and furnish thereafter to the concerned authority a report relating to the accidents in installments, if necessary, in Schedule 6.
- The concerned authority shall on receipt of the report in accordance with sub-rule I of this rule shall undertake a full analysis of the major accident and send the requisite information to the Ministry of Environment and Forests through appropriate channel.
- Where an occupier has notified a major accident to the concerned authority under respective legislation, he shall be deemed to have compiled with the requirements as per sub-rule I of this rule.

INDUSTRIAL ACTIVITY

- Rules 7 to 15 shall apply to,-
  - An industrial activity in which there is involved a quantity of hazardous chemical listed in Column 2 of Schedule 3 which is equal to or more than the quantity specified in the entry for

that chemical in Columns 3 & 4 (Rules 10-12 only for Column 4) and

- Isolated storage in which there is involved a quantity of a hazardous chemical listed in Column 2 of Schedule 2 which is equate to or more than the quantity specified in the entry for that chemical in Column 1

• For the purposes of rules 7 to 15, or

- "New industrial activity" means an industrial activity which-
  - Commences after the date of coming into operation of these rules; or
  - If commenced before that date is an industrial activity in which a modification has been made which is likely to cover major accident hazards and that activity shall be deemed to have commenced on the date on which the modification was made;

• An "existing industrial activity" means an industrial activity which is not a new industrial activity

NOTIFICATION OF SITES

(1) An occupier shall not undertake any industrial activity unless he has submitted A written report to the concerned authority containing the particulars specified in Schedule 7 at least 3 months before commencing that activity or before such shorter time as the concerned authority may agree and for the purpose of this paragraph an activity in which subsequently there is or is liable to be a threshold quantity or more of an additional hazardous chemical shall be deemed to be a different activity and shall be notified accordingly (2) No report under sub-rule (I) need to be submitted by the occupier if he submits a report under rule 10(1)

UPDATING OF THE SITE NOTIFICATION FOLLOWING CHANGES IN THE THRESHOLD QUANTITY

Where an activity has been reported in accordance with

rule 7(1) and the occupier makes a change in it (including an increase or decrease in the maximum threshold quantity of a hazardous chemical to which this rule applies which is or is liable to be at the site or in the pipeline or at the cessation of the activity, which affects the particulars specified in that report or any subsequent report made under this rule the occupier shall forthwith furnish a further report to the concerned authority.

TRANSITIONAL PROVISIONS

Where:

- At the date of coming into operation of these rules an occupier is in control of an existing industrial activity which is required to be reported under rule 7(1); or
- Within 6 months after that date an occupier commence any such new industrial activity; it shall be a sufficient compliance with that rule if he reports to the concerned authority as per the particulars in Schedule 7 within 3 months after the date of coming into operation of these rules or within such longer time as the concerned authority may agree in writing.

SAFETY REPORTS

(1) Subjects to the following paragraphs of this rule, an occupier shall not undertake any industrial activity to which this rule applies, unless he has prepared a safely report on that industrial activity containing The information specified in Schedule 8 and has sent a copy of that report to the concerned authority al least ninety days before commencing that activity. (2) In the case of a new industrial activity which an occupier commences, or by virtue of sub-rule (2) (a) (ii) of rule 6 is deemed to commence, within 6 months after coming into operation of these rules, it shall bc sufficient compliance with sub-rule (I) of this rule if the occupier sends to the concerned authority a copy of the report required in accordance with that sub-rule within ninety days after the date of coming into operation of these rules. (3) In The case of an existing industrial

activity, until five years from the date of coming into operation of these rules, it shall bc a sufficient compliance with sub-rule (I) of this rule in the occupier on or before ninety days from The date of the coming into operation of 1hcse rules sends to the concerned authority in information specified in Schedule 7 relating to that activity.

UPDATING OF REPORTS UNDER RULE 10

(1) Where an occupier has made a safety report in accordance with sub-rule (I) of rule 10 he shall not make any modification to The industrial activity to which that safely report relates which could materially affect the particulars in that report, unless the has made a further report to take account of those modifications and has sent a copy of that report to The concerned authority at least 90 days before making those modifications.

(2) Where an occupier has made a report in accordance with rule 10 and sub-rule (1) of this rule and that industrial activity is continuing the occupier shall within three years of the dale of the last such report, make a further report which shall have regard in particular to new technical knowledge which has affected the particulars in the previous report relating to safely and hazard assessment and shall within 30 days or in such longer lime as the concerned authority may agree in writing, send a copy of the report to the concerned authority

REQUIREMENTS FOR FURTHER INFORMATION TO BE SENT TO THE AUTHORITY

- Where, in accordance with rule 10, an occupier has sent a safely report relating to an industrial activity to the concerned authority, the concerned authority may, by a notice served on the occupier, requires him to provide such additional information as is specified in the notice and the occupied shall send that information to the concerned authority within such lime as is specified in The notice or within such extended time as the authority may subsequently specify

EMERGENCY PLAN BY THE OCCUPIER

- An occupier shall prepare and keep up-to-date an on-site emergency plan detailing how major accidents will be dealt with on the site on which the industrial activity is carried on and that plan shall include the name of The person who is responsible for safety on the site and the names of those who are authorised to take action in accordance with the plan in case of an emergency
- The occupier shall ensure that the emergency plan prepared in accordance with sub-rule (I) lakes into account any modification made in the industrial activity and that every person on the site who is affected by the plan-is informed of its relevant provisions.
- The occupier shall prepare the emergency plan required under sub-rule
  - In the case of a new industrial activity before that activity is commenced;
  - In the case of an existing industrial activity within 90 days of coming into operation of these rules.

PREPARATION OF OFF-SITE EMERGENCY

(1) It shall be the duty of the concerned authority as identified in Column 2 of Schedule 5 to prepare and keep up-to-date an adequate off-site emergency plan detailing how emergencies relating to a possible major accident on that site will be dealt with and in preparing that plan the concerned authority shall consult the occupier, and such other persons as it may deem necessary. (2) For the purpose of enabling The concerned authority to prepare the emergency plan required under sub-rule (1), the occupier shall provide the concerned authority with such information relating to the industrial activity under his control as the concerned authority may require, including the nature, extent and likely effects off-site of possible major accidents and the authority shall provide the occupier with any information from the off-site emergency

plan which relates to his duties under rule 13. (3) The concerned authority shall prepare its emergency plan required under sub-rule (1),- (a) in the case of a new industrial activity, before that activity is commenced; (b) in the case of an existing industrial activity, within six months of coming into operation Of these rules.

INFORMATION

(1) The occupier shall take appropriate steps to inform persons outside the site either directly or through District Emergency Authority who are likely to be in an area which may be affected by a major accident about (a) the nature of the major accident hazard; and (b) the safety measures and the "Do's' and 'Don'ts" which should be adopted in the event of a major accident (2) The occupier shall take the steps required under sub-rule (I) to inform persons about an industrial activity, before that activity is commenced, except, in the case of an existing industrial activity in which case the occupier shall comply with the requirements of sub-rule (I) within 90 days of coming into operation of these rules.

DISCLOSURES OF INFORMATION

- Where for the purpose of evaluating information notified under rule 5 or 7 to 15, the concerned authority discloses that information to some other person that other person shall not use that information for any purpose except for the purpose of the concerned authority disclosing it, and before disclosing the information the concerned authority shall inform that other person of his obligations under this paragraph.

COLLECTION AND DEVELOPMENT

- This rule shall apply to an industrial activity in which a hazardous chemical which satisfies any of the criteria laid down in part I of Schedule I and is listed in Column 2 of Part II of this Schedule is or may be involved.

- An occupier, who has control of an industrial activity in term of sub-rule 1 of this rule, shall arrange to obtain or develop information in the form of safety data sheet as specified in Schedule 9. The information shall be accessible upon request for reference.
- The occupier while obtaining or developing a safety data sheet as specified in Schedule 9 in respect of a hazardous chemical handled by him shall ensure that the information is recorded accurately and reflects the scientific evidence used in making the hazard determination. In case, any significant information regarding hazard Of a chemical is available, it shall be added to the material safety data shet as specified in Schedule 9 as soon as practicable.
- Every container of a hazardous chemical shall be clearly labelled or marked to identify,-
  - The contents of the container,
  - The name and address of manufacturer or importer Of the hazardous chemical;
  - The physical, chemical and toxicological data as per the criteria given at Part I of Schedule 1.
- In terms of sub-rule 4 Of this rule where it is impracticable to label a chemical in view of the size of the container or the nature of the package, provision should be made for other effective means like tagging or accompanying documents.

IMPORT OF HAZARDOUS CHEMICALS

- This rule shall apply to a chemical which satisfies any of the criteria laid down in Part I of Schedule I and is listed in Column 2 of Part II of this Schedule.
- Any person responsible for importing hazardous chemicals in India shall provide at the time of import or within thirty days from the date of import to the concerned authorities as identified in Column 2 of Schedule 5 the information pertaining to-
  - The name and address of the person receiving the consignment in India;

  - The port of entry in India;
  - Mode of transport from the exporting country to India
  - The quantity of chemical(s) being imported; and
  - Complete product safety information.
- If the concerned authority at the State is satisfied that the chemical being imported is likely to cause major accident, it may direct the importer to take such steps including stoppage of such imports as the concerned authority at the State may deem it appropriate.
- The concerned authority at the State shall simultaneously inform the concerned Port Authority to take appropriate steps regarding safe handling and storage of hazardous chemicals while off-loading the consignment with the port premises.
- Any person importing hazardous chemicals shall maintain the records of the hazardous chemicals imported as specified in Schedule 10 and the records so maintained shall be open for inspection by the concerned authority at the State or the Ministry of Environment and Forests or any officer appointed by them in this behalf.
- The importer of the hazardous chemical of a person working on his behalf shall ensure that transport of hazardous chemicals from port of entry to the ultimate destination is in accordance with the Central Motor Vehicles Rules, 1989 framed under the provisions of the Motor Vehicles Act, 1988.

IMPROVEMENT NOTICES

(1) If the concerned authority is of the opinion that a person has contravened the provisions of these rules, the concerned authority shall serve on him a notice (in this para referred to as "an improvement notice") requiring that person to remedy the contravention or, as the case may be, the matters occasioning it within such period as may be specified in the notice. (2) A notice served under sub-rule (1) shall clearly specify the measures to be taken by the occupier in remedying said contraventions.

MODIFYING POWERS

The Central Government may, at any-time, by notification in the Official Gazette, make suitable changes in the Schedules.

FEATURES AND DUTIES

SALIENT FEATURES OF THE RULES

Hazardous Chemicals are those chemicals which satisfies any of the criteria laid down in part-I of Schedule-I or listed in Column 2 of Part-II of Schedule-I and any chemical listed in Column-2 of Schedule-II and any chemical listed in Column 2 of Schedule-III.

DUTIES AND RESPONSIBILITY

This rule shall apply to a chemical which satisfies any of the criteria laid down in Part-I of Schedule 1 or listed in Column 2 of Part-II of this Schedule.

Any person responsible for importing hazardous chemicals in India shall provide before 30 days or as reasonably possible but not later than the date of import to the concerned authorities as identified in Column 2 of Schedule 5 the information pertaining to Te name and address of the person receiving the consignment in India;

The port of entry in India; Mde of transport from the exporting country to India; The quantity of chemical(s) being imported; and Complete product safety information If the concerned Authority of the State is satisfied that the chemical being imported is likely to cause major accidents, it may direct the importer to take such safety measures as the concerned Authority of the State may deem appropriate.

In case the concerned Authority at the State is of the opinion that the chemical should not be imported on safety or on environmental considerations, such Authority may direct stoppage of such import. The concerned Authority at the State shall simultaneously inform the concerned Port Authority to take appropriate steps regarding safe handling and storage of hazardous chemicals while off-loading the consignment with in the port premises. Any person importing hazardous chemicals shall maintain the records of the hazardous chemicals imported as specified in Schedule 10 and the records so maintained shall be open for inspection by the concerned authority at the State or the Ministry of Environment and Forests or any officer appointed by them in this behalf.

GENERAL RESPONSIBILITY

An industrial activity in which a hazardous chemical, which satisfies any of the criteria laid down in Part-I of Schedule 1 or listed in Column 2 of Part-II of this Schedule is, or may be, involved; and isolated storage of a hazardous chemical listed in Schedule 2 in a quantity equal to or more than the threshold quantity specified in Column 3, thereof. An occupier who has control of an industrial activity in terms of sub-rule (1) shall provide evidence to show that he has, identified the major accident hazards; and taken adequate steps to prevent such major accidents and to limit their consequences to persons and the environment; provide to the persons working on the site with the information, training and equipment including antidotes necessary to ensure their safety.

Responsibility of preparation of on-site emergency plan by the occupier in case of an accident etc. (Rule 13) An occupier shall prepare and keep up-to-date an on-site emergency plan containing details specified in Schedule-II and detailing how major accidents will be dealt with on the site on which the industrial activity is carried on an that plan shall include the name of the person who is responsible for safety on the site and the names of those who are authorized to take action in accordance with the plan in case of an emergency.

The occupier shall ensure that the emergency plan prepared in accordance with sub-rule (1) takes into account any modification made in the industrial activity and that every person on the site who is affected by the plan is informed of its relevant provisions. The occupier shall prepare the emergency plan required under sub-rule (1) 1. in the case of new industrial activity, before that activity is commenced; 2. in the case of an existing industrial activity within 90 days of commencing into operation of these rules.

The occupier shall ensure that a mock drill of the on-site emergency plan is conducted every six months; A detailed report of the mock drill conducted under sub-rule (4) shall be made immediately available to the concerned Authority. Responsibility of preparation of off-site emergency plan by the authorities in case of an accident etc. (Rule 14) It shall be the duty of the concerned authority as identified in Column 2 of Schedule 5 to prepare and keep up-to-date and adequate off-site emergency plan containing particulars specified in Schedule 12 and detailing how emergencies relating to a possible major accident on that site will be dealt with and in preparing that plan the concerned authority shall consult the occupier, and such other persons as it may deem necessary. For the purpose of enabling the concerned authority to prepare the emergency plan required under sub-rule(1), the occupier shall provide the concerned authority with such information relating to the industrial activity under his control as the concerned authority may require, including the nature, extent and likely effects off-site of possible major accidents and the authority shall provide the occupier with any information on the off-site emergency plan which relates to his duties under rule 13. The concerned authority shall prepare its emergency plan required under sub-rule(1) 1. In the case of a new industrial activity, before that activity is commenced; 2. In the case of an existing industrial activity, within six months of coming into operation to these rules. The concerned authority shall ensure that a rehearsal of the off-site emergency plan is conducted at least once in a calendar year.

CRITERIA AND LIST OF CHEMICALS

TOXIC CHEMICALS

Chemicals having the following values of acute toxicity and which, owing to their physical and chemical properties, are capable of producing major accidents hazards.

S.No.Degree of Toxicity Medium lethal dose by the oral route (oral toxicity) LD50 (mg/kg) body weight of test animals

Medium lethal dose by the dermal route (dermal toxicity) LD 50 (mg/kg) body weight of test animals Medium lethal concentration by inhalation route (four hours) LC 50 (mg/l) inhalation on test animals 1. Extremely toxic 1 - 50 1 - 200 0.1 - 0.5 2. Highly toxic 51 - 500 201 - 2000 0.5 - 2.0

(B) FLAMMABLE CHEMICALS

- Flammable gases; chemicals which in the gaseous state at normal pressure and mixed with air become flammable and the boiling point of which at normal pressure is 20°C or below;
- Highly flammable liquids: chemicals which have a flash point lower than 23°C and the boiling point of which at normal pressure is above 20° C;
- Flammable liquids: chemicals which have a flash point lower than 65°C- and which remain liquids under pressure, where particular processing conditions, such as high pressure and high temperature, may create major accident hazards.

EXPLOSIVES

Chemicals which may explode under the effect of flame, heat or photo-chemical conditions or which are more sensitive to shocks or friction than dinitrobenzene.

LIST OF HAZARDOUS

Sl. No.	Name of the Chemical
1	Acetone
2	Acetone Cynohydride
3	Acetyle Chloride
4	Acetylene (Ethyne)
5	Acrolein (2-Propenal)
6	Acrylonitrile
7	Aldicarb
8	Aldrin
9	Alkyl Phthalate
10	Allyl Alcohol

11	Allylamine
12	Alpha Naphthyl Thiourea (Antu)
13	Aminodiphenyl-4
14	Aminophenol-2
15	Amiton
16	Ammonia
17	Ammonium Nitrate
18	Ammonium Nitrates in fertilizers
19	Ammonium Sulfamate
20	Anabasine
21	Aniline
22	Anisidine-p
23	Antimony and Compounds
24	Antimony Hydride (Stibine)
25	Arsenic Hydride (Arsine)
26	Arsenic Pentoxide, Arsenic (v) Acid, and Salts
27	Arsenic Trioxide, Alsenious (iii) Acids and Salts
28	Asbestos
29	Azinophos-Ethyl
30	Azinphos-Methyl
31	Banum Azide
32	Benzene
33	Benzidine
34	Benzidine Salts
35	Benzoquinone
36	Benzoyl Chloride
37	Benzoyl Peroxide
38	Benzyl Chloride
39	Benzyl Cynide
40	Beryllium (Powders Compound)
41	Biphenyl
42	Bis (2-Clzloromethyl) Ketone
43	Bis (2, 4, 6-Trinitrophynile) Amine
44	Bis (2, Chloroethyle sulphide)
45	Bis (Chloromethyl) ether
46	Bis (tert-Butyl peroxy) Butane-2, 2
47	Bis (tert-Butyl peroxy) Cyclohexane-11
48	Bis-1, 2 Tribromophenoxy Ethane

49	Bis phenol
50	Boron and Compounds
51	Bromine
52	Bromine Pentafluoride
53	Bromoform
54	Butoadine
55	Butane
56	Butanethiol
57	Butanone-2
58	Butoxy Ethanol
59	Butyl Glycidal Ether
60	Butyl Peroxy acetate, tert
61	BUtyL Peroxyisobutyrate, tert
62	Butyl Peroxyisopropyl Carbonate, tert
63	Butyl Peroxymaleate, tert
64	Butyl Peroxypivalate, tcrt
65	Butyl Vinyl Ether
66	Buty-n-Mercaptan
67	Butylamine
68	C-9, Aromatic Hydrocarbon Fraction
69	Cadmium and Compounds
70	Cadmium Oxide (fumes)
71	Calcium Cynicde
72	Captan
73	Captofol
74	Carbaryl (Sevin)
75	Carbofuran
76	Carbon Disulphide
77	Carbon Monoxide
78	Carbon Tetrachloride
79	Carbophenothion
80	Cellulose Nitrate
81	Chlorats (used in explosives)
82	Chlordane
83	Chlorfenvinphos
84	Chlorinated Benzenes
85	Chlorine
86	Chlorine Di Oxide

87	Chlorine Oxide
88	Chlorine Trifluoride
89	Chloromequal Chloride
90	Chloroacetalchloride
91	Chloroacetaldehyde
92	Chloroanilin-2
93	Chloroaniline4
94	Chlorobenzene
95	Chlorodiphenyl
96	Chloropoxypropane
97	Chloroethanol
98	Chloroethyl
99	Chloroformate
100	Chorolfluorocarbons
101	Chloroform
102	Chloroformyl-4, Merpholine
103	Chloromethane
104	Chloromethyl Ether
105	Chloromethyl Methyl Ether
106	Chloronitrobenzene
107	Chloroprene
108	Chlorosulphonic Acid
109	Chlorotrinitro benzene
110	Chloroxuron
111	Chromium and Compounds
112	Cobalt and Compounds
113	Copper and Compounds
114	Coumafuryl
115	Coumaphos
116	Coumateralyl
117	Cresols
118	Cumidine
119	Cumene
120	Cynophos
121	Cynothoate
122	Cyanuric Fluoride
123	Cyclohexane
124	Cyclohexanol

125	Cyclohexane
126	Cycloheximide
127	Cyclopentadinene
128	Cyclopentane
129	Cyclotetramethylenetrinitramine
130	Cyclotriethylene Trinitramine
131	DDT
132	Dicarbomodiphenyl Oxide
133	Demeton
134	Di-Isobutyl Peroxide
135	Di n-Propyl Peroxydicarbonate
136	Di-sec-Butyl Peroxydicarbonate
137	Dalifos Mazodinitrophewl
138	Diszomethane
139	Dibenzyl Peroxydicarbonate
140	Diehloroaeetylene
141	Diehlorobenzene-0
142	Dichlorobenzene-2
143	Di-chloroethane
144	Dichlorethyl Ether
145	Dichlorophenol-2, 4
146	Dichlorophenol-2, 6
147	Dichlorophenoxy Acetic Acid, -2,4 (2,4-D)
148	Dichloropropane-1, 2
149	Diehlorosalicylic Acid, -3,5
150	Dichlorovos (DDVP)
151	Dicrotophos
152	Dieldrin
153	Diepoxybutane
154	Diethyl Peroxydicarbonate
155	Diethyl Glycol Dinitrate
156	Diethylene Triarnine
157	Diehyleneglycol Butyl Ether/Diethyleteglycol Butyl Acetate
158	Diethylenetriarnine (DETA)
159	Diglycidyl Ether
160	Dihydroperoxypropane, -2,2
161	Diisobutyryl Peroxide

162	Dimethoate
163	Dimethyl Phosphoramidocynidic Acid
164	Dimelhyl Phthalate
165	Dimethylcarbonyl
166	Dimethylnitrosamine
167	Dinitrophenol, Salts
168	Dinitroluene
169	Dinitro-o-Cresol
170	Dioxane
171	Dioxathion
172	Dioxalane
173	Diphacinone
174	Diphosphoramide Octamethyl
175	Dipropylene Glycolmethylether
176	Disulfoton
177	Endosulfan
178	Endrin
179	Epiehlorohydrine
180	EPN
181	Epoxypropane, 1, 2
182	Ehion
183	Ethyl Carbarnate f
184	Ethyl ether
185	Ethyl Hexanol, -2
186	Ethyl Mercaptan
187	Ethyl Methacrylate
188	Ethyl Nitrate
189	Ethylamine
190	Ethylene
191	Ethylene Chlorohydrine
192	Ethylene Diamine
193	Ethylene Dibromide
194	Ethylene Dichloride
195	Ethylene Glycol Dinitrate
196	Ethylene Oxide
197	Ethyleneimine
198	Ethylthiocynate
199	Fensulphothion

200	Fluenetil
201	Fluoro, -4,2-Hydroxybutyric Acid and Salts, Esters, Amides
202	Fluoroacetic Acid and Salts, Esters, Amides
203	Fluorobutyric Acid, -4, and Salts, Esters, Amides
204	Fluorocrotonic Acid, -4, and Salts, Esters, Amides
205	Formaldehyde
206	Glyconitrite (Hydroxyacetonitrite)
207	Guanyl, -1, 4 Nitrosaminoguanyl-1-Tetrazenc
208	Heptachlor
209	Haxachloro Cyclopentadiene
210	Hexachlorocyclohexane
211	Hexachlorocy cloamethane
212	Hexachlorodibenzo-p-Dioxin, -1, 2, 3, 7, 8, 9
213	Hexafluoropropene
214	Hexamethylphosphoramide
215	Hexamethyl, -3, 3, 6, 6, 9, 9, -1, 2, 4, 5-Tetroxacyclononane
216	Hexamethylenediamine
217	Hexane
218	Hexanitrosstibene, -2, 2, 4, 4, 6, 6,
219	Hexavalent Chromium
220	Hydrazine
221	Hyrazine Nitrate Hydrochloric Acid
222	Hydrogen
223	Hydrogen Bromide (Hydrobromic Acid)
224	Hydrogen Chloride (Liquified Gas)
225	Hydrogen Cynide
226	Hydrogen Fluoride
227	Hydrogen Selenide
228	Hydrogen Sulphide
229	Hydroquinone
230	Iodine
231	Isobenzan
232	Isodrin
233	Isophorone Diisocynate
234	Isopropyl Ether
235	Juglone (5-Hydroxynaphthalene-1, 4-Dione)

236	Lead (inorganic fumes & dusts)
237	Lead 2, 4, 6 -Trinitroresorcinoxide (Lead Styphnate)
238	Lead Azide
239	Leptophos
240	Lindane
241	Liquified Petroleum Gas (LPG)
242	Maleic Anhydride
243	Manganese & Compounds
244	Mercapto Benzothiawle
245	Mercury Alkyl
246	Mercury Fulminate
247	Mercury Methyl
248	Methacrylic Anhydride
249	Methacrylonitrite
250	Methacryloyl Chloride
251	Methamidophos
252	Methanesuphonyl Fluoride
253	Methanethiol
254	Methoxy Ethanol (2-Methyl Cellosive)
255	Methoxy ethyl mercuric Acetate
256	Methyl Acrylate
257	Melhyl Alcohol
258	Methyl Amylketone
259	Methyl Bromide (Bromomethane)
260	Methyl Chloride
261	Methyl Chloroform
262	Methyl Cyclohexene
263	Methyl Ethyl Ketone Peroxide
264	Methyl Hydrazine
265	Methyl Isobutyl Ketone
266	Methy Isobutyl Ketone Peroxide
267	Mthyl Isocycnate
268	Methyl Isothiocynate
269	Methyl Mercaptian
270	Methyl Methacrylate
271	Methyl Parathion

272	Methyl Phosphonic Dichloride
273	Methyl-N, 2, 4, 6,-Trinitroaniline
274	Methylene Chloride
275	Methylenebis, -4, 4, (2-Chloroaniline)
276	Methyltrichlcrosilane
277	Mevinphos
278	Molybdenum & Compounds
279	N-Methyl-N, 2, 4, 6-N-Tetranitroanilin
280	Naptha (Coal Tar)
281	Naphthylamine, 2
282	Nickel & Compounds
283	Nickel Tetracarbonyl
284	Noitroaniline-O
285	Nitroaniline-P
286	Nitrobenzene
287	Nitrochloroberizene-P
288	Nitrocyclohexane
289	Nitriothage
290	Nitrogen.Dioxide
291	Nitrogen Oxide
292	Nitrogen Trifluoride
293	Nitroglycerine
294	Nitrophenol-P
295	Nitropropane-1
296	Nitropropane-2
297	Nitrosodirnethylarnine
298	Nitrotolune
299	Octabrornophenyl Oxide
300	Oleurn
301	Oleylarnine
302	OO-Diethyl S-EthyIsulphonyImethyl phosbhorothioate
303	OO-Diethyl S-Ethylthiornethyl Phosphorothioate
304	OO-Diethyl S-Ethiomethyl'Phosphorathioate
305	OO-Diethyl S-1sopropyliniornethyl Phosphorolithioate

306	OO-diethyl S-Propylthiornethyl Phosphorodithioate
307	Oxyarnyl
308	Oxydisulioton
309	Oxygen (Liquid)
310	Oxygen Difluoride
311	Ozone
312	Paraoxon (Diethyl 4-Nitrophenyl Phosphate)
313	Paraquat
314	Parathion
315	Parathion Methyl
316	Paris green (Bis Aceto Hexametaatsinito Tetracopper)
317	Pentaborane
318	Pentabromodiphenyl Oxide
319	Pentabromophenol
320	Pentachloro Naphthalene
321	Pentachloroethane
322	Petachlorophenol
323	Pentacrythritol Tetranitrate
324	Pentane
325	Peracetic Acid
326	Perchloroethylene
327	Perchlorornethyl Mercaptan
328	Pentanone, 2,4-Methyl
329	Phenol
330	Phenyl Glycidal Ether
331	Phenylene p-Diarnine
332	Phenylmercury Acetate
333	Phorate
334	Phosacetim
335	Phosalone
336	Phosfolan
337	Phosgene (Carbonyl Chloride)
338	Phosmet
339	Phospamidon
340	Phosphine (Hydrogen Phosphide)

341	Phosphoric Acid and Esters
342	Phosphoric Acid, Bromethyl Bromo (2,2-dimethylpropyl) Bromoethyl Ester
343	Phosphoric Acid, Bromoethyl Bromo (2,2-Dimethylpropyl) Chlorethyethyl Ester
344	Phosphoric Acid, Chlorocthyl Bromo (2,2-Dimethoxylpropyl) Chloroethyl Ester
345	Phosporous & Compounds
346	Phostalan Pircic Acid (2,4,6-Trinitrophenol)
347	Polybrominaled Biphenyl
348	Potassium Arsenite
349	Potassium Chlorate
350	Promurit (1-(3, 4-Dichlorophenyl)-3-Triazenethiocarboxamide)
351	Propanesultone-1, 3
352	Propen,-1, 2-Chloro-1,3-Diol-Diacetate
353	Propylene Dichloride
354	Propylene Oxide
355	Propyleneimine
356	Pyrazoxon
357	Selenium Hexafluoride
358	Semicarbazide Hydrochloride
359	Sodium Arsenite
360	Sodium Azide
361	Sodium Chlorate
362	Sodium Cynide
363	Sodium Picramate
364	Sodium Selenite
365	Styrene, 1, 1, 2, 2-Tetrachloroethane
366	Sulfotep
367	Sulphur Dichloride
368	Sulphur Dioxide
369	Sulphur Trioxide
370	Sulphuric Acid
371	Sulphoxide, 3-Chloropropyloctyl
372	Tellurium
373	Tellurium Hexafluoride

374	Tepp
375	Terbufos
376	Tetrabromobisphenol-A
377	Tetrachloro, 2, 2, 5, 6, 2, 5-Cyclohexadiene-1, 4-Dione
378	Tetrachlorodibenzo-p Dioxin, 2, 3, 7, 8 (TCDD)
379	Tetraethyl Lead
380	Tetrafluoroethane
381	Tetramethylenedisulphotetramine
382	Tetramethyl Lead
383	Tetramnitromethane
384	Thalium & Compounds
385	Thionzin
386	Thionyl Chloride
387	Tirpate
388	Toluene
389	Toluidien-2, 4 Diisocynate
390	Toluidiene-O
391	Toluene 2, 6-Diisocynate
392	Trans-1, 4-Chlorobutene
393	Tri, -1 (Cyclohexyl) Stannyl-1H, 1, 2, 4-Trazole
394	Triamino, -1, 3, 5, 2, 4, 6-Trinitrobenzene
395	Tribromophenol, 2, 4, 6
396	Trichloro Acetyl Chloride
397	Trichloro Ethane
398	Trichloro Naphthalene
399	Ttichloro (chloromethyl) Silane
400	Trichlorodichlorophenylsilane
401	Triochloroethane, l, l, l
402	Trichloroethyl Silane
403	Trichloroethylene
404	Trichloromethanesulphenyl Chloride
405	Trichlorophenol, 2, 2, 6
406	Trichlorophenol, 2, 4, 5
407	Triethylamine
408	Triethylenemelamine
409	Trimethyl Chlorosilane

410	Trimethylopropane Phosphite
411	Trinitroaniline
412	Trinitroanisole, 2, 2, 4, 6
413	Trinolrobenzene
414	Trinitrobenzoic Acid
415	Trinitrocresol
416	Trinitrophenetole, 2, 4, 6
417	Trinitroesorcinol, 2, 4, 6 (Styphnic Acid)
418	Trinitrotoluene
419	Triorthocressyl Phosphate
420	Triphenylin Chloride
421	Turpenline Uranium & Compounds
422	Vanadium & Compounds
423	Vinyl Chloride
424	Vinyl Fluoride
425	Warfarin
426	Xylene
427	Xylidine
428	Zinc & Compounds
429	Zirconium & Compounds

Isolated storage at Installations other than those covered by Schedule 4

- The threshold quantities set out below relate to each installation or group of installations belonging to the same occupier where the distance between installation is not sufficient to avoid, in foreseeable circumstances, any aggravation of major accident hazards. These threshold quantities apply in any case to each group of installations belonging to the same occupier where the distance between the installations is less than 500 metres.
- For the purpose of determining the threshold quantity of hazardous chemical at an isolated storage, account shall also be taken of any hazardous chemical which is:
  - In that part of any pipeline under the control of the occupier having control of the site wh.ch is

within 500 metres of that site and connected to it;

- At any other site under the control of the same occupier any part of the boundary of which is within 500 metres of the said site; and
- In any vehicle, vessel, aircraft or hovercraft, under the control of the same occupier which is used for storage purpose either at the site or within 500 metres of it;

but no account shall be taken of any hazardous chemical which is in a vehicle, vessel, aircraft or a hovercraft used for transporting it.

Sl. No.	**Chemicals**	**Threshold Quantities (tonnes)**	
		For application of Rules 4, 5 and 7-9	**For Rules application of Rules 10 to 15**
1	**2**	**3**	**4**
1	Acrylonitrile	350	5,000
2	Ammonia	60	600
3	Ammonium nitrate (a)	350	2,500
4	Ammonium nitrate fertilizers (b)	1,250	10,000
5	Chlorine	10	25
6	Flammable gases as defined in Schedule 1, paragraph (b) (i)	50	300
7	Highly flammable liquids as defined in Schedule 1, paragraph (b) (ii)	10,000	100,000
8	Liquid oxygen	200	2,000
9	Sodium chlorate	25	250
10	Sulphur dioxide	20	500
11	Sulphur trioxide	15	100

- This applies to ammonium nitrate and mixtures of ammonium nitrates where the nitrogen content derived from the ammonium nitrate is grater than 28 per cent by weight and to aqueous solutions of ammonium nitrate where the concentration of ammonium nitrate is greater then 90 per cent by weight

- This applies to straight ammonium nitrate fertilizers and to compound fertilizers where the nitrogen content derived from the ammonium nitrate is greater than 28 per cent by weight (a compound-fertilizer contains ammonium nitrate together with phosphate and/or potash).

List of Hazardous Chemicals for Application of Rules 5 and 7 to 15

- The quantities set-out-below relate to each installation or group of installations belonging to the same occupier where the distance between the installations is not sufficient to avoid, in foreseeable circumstances, any aggravation of major-accident hazards. These quantities apply in any case to each group of installations belonging to the same occupier where the distance between the installations is less than 500 metres.
- For the purpose of determining the threshold quantity of a hazardous chemical in an industrial installation, account shall also be taken of any hazardous chemicals which is:-
  - In that part of any pipeline under the control of the occupier have control of the site, which is within 500 metres off that site and connected to it;
  - At any other site under the control of the same occupier any part of the boundary of which is within 500 metres of the said site; and
  - In any vehicle, vessel, aircraft or hovercraft under the control of the same occupier which is used for storage purpose either at the site or within 500 metres of it;

but no account shall be taken of any hazardous chemical which is in a vehicle, vessel, aircraft or hovercraft used for transporting it.

PART I

NAMED CHEMICALS

S.No.	Chemical	Threshold Quantity		CAS Number
		For Application of Rules, 5, 7-9 and 13-15	For Application of for Rules 10-12	
1	2	3	4	5
		Group 1-toxic Substances		
1	Aldicarb	100 kg		116-06-3
2	4-Aminodiphenyl	1 kg		96-67-1
3	Amiton	1 kg		78-53-5
4	Anabasine	100 kg		494-52-0
5	Arseinc pentoxide, Arsenic (V) acid & salts	500 kg		
6	Arsenic trioxide, Arseius (III) acid & salts	100 kg		
7	Arsine (Arsenic hydride)	10 kg		7784-42-1
8	Azinphos-ethyl	100 kg		2642-71-9
9	Azinphos-melhyl	100 kg		86-50-0
10	Benzidine	1 kg		92-87-5
11	Benzidine salts	1 kg		
12	Beryllium (powders, compounds}	10 kg		
13	Bis (2-chloroethyl) sulphide	1 kg		505-60-2
14	Bis (chloromethyl) ether	1 kg		542-88-1
15	Carbophuran	100 kg		1563-66-2
16	Carbophenothion	100 kg		786-19-6
17	Chlorefenvinphos	100 kg		470-90-6

18	4-(Chloroformyl) morpholine	1 kg	15159-40-7
19	Chloromethyl methyl ether	1 kg	107-30-2
20	Cobalt (metal, oxides, carbonates, sulphides, as powders)	1 t	
21	Crimidine	100 kg	535-89-7
22	Cynthoate	100 kg	3734-95-0
23	Cycloheximide	100 kg	66-81-9
24	Demeton	100 kg	8065-48-3
25	Dialifos	100 kg	10311-84-9
26	OO-Diethyl S-ethylsulphinyl-methyl phosphorothiate	100 kg	2588-05-8
27	OO-Diethyl S-ethylsulphonyl-methyl phosphorothioate	100 kg	2588-06-9
28	OO-Dielhyl S-ethyllhiomethyl Phosphorothioate	100 kg	2600-69-3
29	OO-Diethyl S-isopropylthiome thyl phosphoro dithioate	100 kg	78-52-4
30	OO-Diethyl S-propylthiomethyl phosphorodithio-ate	100 kg	3309-68-0
31	Dimefox	100 kg	115-26-4
32	Dimethylcarb -amoyl chloride	1 kg	79-44-7
33	Dimethylnitros amine	1 kg	62-75-9

34	Dimethyl phosphoramido-cynicidic acid	1 t	63917-41-9
35	Diphacinone	100 kg	82-66-6
36	Disulfoton	100 kg	298-04-4
37	EPN	100 kg	2104-64-5
38	Ethion	100 kg	563-12-2
39	Fensulfothion	100 kg	115-90-2
40	Fluenetil	100 kg	4301-50-2
41	Fluroacetic acid	1 kg	144-49-0
42	Fluoroacetic acid, salts	1 kg	
43	Fluoroacelic acid, esters	1 kg	
44	Fluoroacetic acid, amides	1 kg	
45	4-Fluorobutyric acid	1 kg	462-23-7
46	4-Fluorobutyric acid, salts	1 kg	
47	4-Fluorobutyric acid, esters	1 kg	
48	4-Fluorobutyric acid, amides	1 kg	
49	4-Florocrotonic acid	1 kg	37759-72-1
50	4-Fluorocrotonic acid, salts	1 kg	
51	4-Fluorocrotonic acid, esters	1 kg	
52	4-Fluorocrotonic acid, amides	1 kg	
53	4-Fluoro-2-hydroxybutyric acid, amides	1 kg	
54	4-Fluoro-2-hydroxybutyric acid, salts	1 kg	

	4-Fluoro-2-hydroxybutyric acid, esters	1 kg		
56	4-Fluoro-2-hydroxybutyric acid, amides	1 kg		
57	Glycolonitrile (Hydroxyaceto-nitrile)	100 kg		107-16-4
58	1, 2, 3, 7, 8, 9-Hexachlorodi benzo-p-dioxin	100 g		194-8-74-3
59	Hexamethyl phosphoramide	1 kg		680-31-9
60	Hydrogen sclenide	10 kg		7783-07-5
61	Isobenzan	100 kg		297-78-9
62	Isodrin	100 kg		465-73-6
63	Juglone (5-Hydroxynaphith alene 1, 4 dione)	100 kg		481-39-0
64	4, 4-Methylenebis (2-chloroniline)	10 kg		101-14-4
65	Methyl isocynate	150 kg	150 kg	624-83-9
66	Mevinphos	100 kg		7786-34-7
67	2-Naphlhylamine	1 kg		91 -59-8
68	2-Nickcl (metal, oxides, carbonates, sulphides, as powders)	1 t		
69	Nickel tetracarX powders)	10 kg		13463-39-3
70	Oxygendisulfoton	100 kg		2497-07-6
71	Oxygen difuoride	10 kg		7783-41-7
72	Paraxon (Diethyl 4-nitsphenyl phosphate)	100 kg		311 -45-5

73	Parathion	100 kg		56-38-2
74	Parathion-methyl	100 kg		298-00-0
75	Pentaborane	100 kg		19624-22-7
76	Phorate	100 kg		298-02-2
77	Phosacetim	100 kg		4104-14-7
78	Phosgene (carbonyl chloride)	750 kg	750 kg	75-44-5
79	Phosphamidon	100 kg		13171-41-6
80	Posphine (Hydrogen phosphide)	100 kg		7803-51 -2
81	Promurit (1-(3, 4-dichlorophenyl)-3 triazenethiocar boxamide)	100 kg		5836-73-7
82	1, 3-Propanesultone	1 kg		1120-7t-4
83	1 -Propen-2-chloro - 1, 3-diol diacetate	10 kg		10118-72-6
84	Pyrazoxon	100 kg		108-34-9
85	Selenium hexafluoride	10 kg		7783-79-1
86	Sodium selenite	100 kg		10102-18-8
87	Stibine (Antimony hydride)	100 kg		7803-52-3
88	Sulfotep	100 kg		3689-24-5
89	Sulphur dichloride	1 t		10545-99-0
90	Tellurium hexanuroride	100 kg		7783-80-4
91	TEPP	100 kg		107-49-3
92	2, 3, 7, 8-Tetrachlorodib-enzo-p-dioxin (TCDD)	1 kg		1746-01 -6
93	Tetramethylene disulphotetramine	1 kg		80-12-6

94	Thionazin	100 kg		297-97-2
95	Tirpate (2, 4-Dimethyl-l, 3-dilhiolane-2-carboxaldehyde O-methylcarbar noyloxime)	100 kg		26419-8
96	Trichloromethane sulphenyl chloride	100 kg		594-42-3
97	1-Tri (cyclohexyl) stannyl-l H-1, 2,. 4-triazole	100 kg		41083-11-8
98	Triethylenemel amine	10 kg		51-18-3
99	Warfarin	100 kg		81-81-2
	Group 2-Toxic Substances			
100	Acetonecyano hydrin (2-Cyanop ropan-2-01)	200 t		75-86-5
101	Acrolein (2-Propenal)	20 t		107-02-8
102	Acrylonitrile	20 t	200 t	107-13-1
103	Allyl alcohol (Propen-1-01)	200 t		107-18-6
104	Alylamine	200 t		107-11-9
105	Ammonia	50 t	500 t	7664-41-7
106	Bromine	40 t		7726-95-6
107	Carbon disulphide	20 t	200 t	75-15-0
108	Chlorine	10 t	25 t	7782-fO 5
109	Dipneyl ethane di-isocynate (MDI)	20 t		101-68-8
110	Ethylene dibromide (1, 2-Dibromoethane)	5 t		106-93-4
111	Ethyleneimine	50 t		151-56-4
112	Formaldehyde	5 t		50-00 0

	(concentration 90%)			
113	Hydrogen chloride (liquified gas)	25 t	250 t	7647-01-0
114	Hydrogen cynide	5 t	20 t	74-90-8
115	Hydrogen fluoride	5 t	50 t	7664-39-3
116	Hydrogen sulphide	5 t	50 t	7783-06-4
117	Methyl bromide (Bromomethane)	20 t		74-83-9
118	Nitrogen oxides	50 t		11104-93-1
119	Propylineimine	50 t		75-55-8
120	Sulphur dioxide	20 t	250 t	7446-09-5
121	Sulphur trioxide	15 t	75 t	7446-11-9
122	Tetraethyl Iead	5 t		78-00-2
123	Tetramethyl Iead	5 t		75-74-1
124	Toluene di-isocvnate (TDI)	10 t		584-84-9 75-01-4
	Group 3- Highly Reactive Substances			
125	Acetylene (ethyne)	5 t		74-86-2
126	a. Ammonium nitrate (1) b. Ammonium nitrate in form of fertiliser (2)	350 t 1250 t	2500 t	6484-52-2
127	2 2-Bis (tert-butylperoxy) butane) (eoncentration 70%)	5 t		2167-23-9
128	1 I Bis (tert-butylperoxy) cyclohexane (concentration 80%)	5 t		3006-86-8

129	tert-Butyl proxy acetate (concentration 70%)	5 t	107-71-1
130	Tert-Butyl peroxyisobutyrate (concentration-- 80%)	5 t	109-13-7
131	tert-Butyl peroxy isopropyl carbonate (concentration- 80%)	5 t	2372-21-6
132	tert-Butyl peroxymaleate (concentration- 80%)	5 t	1931-62-0
133	Tert-Butyl peroxypivalate (concentration 77%)	50 t	927-07-1
134	Dibenzyl peroxydic arbonate (concentration 90%)	5 t	2144-45-8
135	Di-sec-butyl peroxydicarbonate (concentration 80%)	5 t	19910-65-7
136	Diethyl peroxydic arbonate (concentration 30%)	50 t	14666-78-5
137	2, 2-dihydrope roxypropane (concentration 30%)	5 t	2614-76-08

138	Di-isobutyryl peroxide concentration 50%)	50 t		3437-84-1
139	Di-n-propyl peroxydi-carbonate (concentration 80%)	5 t		16066-38-9
140	Ethylene oxide	5 t	50 t	75-21-8
141	Ethyl nitrate	50 t		625-58-1
142	3, 3, 6, 6, 9, 9 Hexamcthyl-1, 2, 4, 5-tert oxacyclo nonane (concentration 75%)	50 t		22397-38-7
143	Hydrogen	2 t	50 t	1333-74-0
144	Liquid Oxygen	200 t		7782-41-7
145	Methyl ethyl ketone peroxide (concentration 60%)	50t		1338-23-4
146	Melhyl isobutyl ketone peroxide (concentration 60%)	50 t		37206-20-5
147	Peracelic acid (concentration 60%)	50 t		79-21-0
148	Propylene oxide	50 t		75-56-9
149	Sodium chlorate	25 t		7775-09-9
	Group 4-Explosive Substances			
150	Barium azide	50 t		18810-58-7
151	Bis (2,4, 6-trinilrophenyl) amine	50 t		131-073-7

152	Chlorotrinitro benzene	50 t		28260-61-9
153	Cellulose nitrate (containing 12.6% Nitrogen)	50 t		9004-70-0
154	Cyclotetramethyl eneteranitramine	50 t		2691-41-0
155	Cyclotrimetylene tiranitramine	50 t		121-82-1
156	Diazo dinitrophenol	10 t		7008-81-3
157	Diethylene glycol dinitrate	10 t		693-21-0
158	Dinitrophenol, salts	50 t		
159	Ethylene glycol dinitrate	10 t		628-96-6
160	1-Gyanyl-4-nitrosamino guanyl-1-tetrazene	10 t		109-27-3
161	2, 2', 4, 4,' 6, 6' -Hexanirostilbene	50 t		20062-22-0
162	Hydrazine nitrate	50 t		13464-97-6
163	Lead azide	50 t		13424-46-9
164	Lead styphnate (Lead 2, 4, 6-trinitroresorci noxide)	50 t		15245 44-0
165	Mercury fuliminate	10 t		20820-45-5 628-86-4
166	N-Methyl-N, 2, 4, 6-tetranitroaniline	50 t		479-45-8
167	Nitroglycerine	10 t	10 t	55-63-0
168	Pentacrythritol tetranitrate	50 t		78-11-5
169	Picric acid (2, 3, 6-	10 t		88-89-1

	Tr.nitrophenol)			
170	Sodium picramate	50 t		831-52-7
171	Styphnic acid) (2, 4, 6-Trinitroresorcinol	50 t		82-71-3
172	1, 3, 5-Triamino-2, 4, 6-trinitrob enzene	50 t		3058-38-6
173	Trinitroaniline-	50 t		2695242-1
174	2, 4, 6-Trinitroanisole	50 t		606-35-9
175	Trinitrobenzene	50 t		25377-32-6
176	Trinitrobenzoic acid	50 t		35860-50-5
				z129-66-8
177	Trinitrocresol	50 t		2890S-71-7
178	2,4, 6-Trinitrophenitolc	50 t		47324-3
179	2,4, 6 -Trinitrotulene	50 t	50 t	118-96-7

Classes of chemicals not specifically named in Part-I

1	2	3	4	5
	Group 5-Flammable Chemicals			
1	*Flammable gases:* Substances which in the gaseous state normal pressure and mixed with air become flammable and the boiling point of which at normal pressure is 20°C or below;	15 t	200 t	
2	*Highly flammable liquids:* Substances which have a flash point lower than 23°C and the boiling point Of which at normal pressure is above 20°C;	1000 t	50,000 t	
3	*Flammable liquids:* Substances which have a Rash	25 t	200 t	

point lower than 65ø C and which remain liquid under pressure, where particular processing conditions, such as high pressure and high temperature, may create major accident hazards.

- This applies to ammonium nitrate and mixtures of ammonium nitrate where the nitrogen content derived from the ammonium nitrate is greater than 28% by weight and aqueous solutions of ammonium nitrate where thc concentration of ammonium nitrate is greater than 90% by weight.
- This applies to straight ammonium nitrate fertilizers and to compound fertilizers where the nitrogen content derived from the ammonium nitrate is greater than 28% by weight (a compound fertilizer contains ammonium nitrate together with phosphate and/or potash).

SCHEDULE 4

- Installations for the production, processing or treatment of organic or inorganic chemicals using for this purpose, among others:
  - Alkylation
  - Amination by ammonolysis
  - Carbonylatin
  - Condensation
  - Dehydrogenation
  - Esterfication
  - Halogenation and manufacture of halogens
  - Hydrogenation
  - Hydrolysis
  - Oxidation
  - Polymerization
  - Sulphonation
  - Desulphurization, manufacture and transformation of sulphur-containing compounds

- Nitration and manufacture of nitrogen-containing compounds
- Manufacture of phosphorons-containing compounds
- Formulation of pesticides and of pharmaceutical products
- Distillation
- Extraction
- Solvation
- Mixing

• Installations for distillation, refining or other processing of petroleum or petroleum products.
• Installations for the total or partial disposal of solid or liquid substances by incineration or chemical decomposition.
• Installations for production, processing or treatment of energy gases, for example, LPG, LNG, SNG.
• Installations for the dry distillation of coal or lignite.
• Installations for the production of metals or non-metals by a wet process or by means of electrical energy.

SCHEDULE-5

S.No.Authority (ies) with legal backing Duties and corresponding Rule 1 Ministry of Environment and Forest under Environment (Protection) Act, 1986.(1) Notification of hazardous chemical-as per Rules 2(e)(i), 2(e) (ii) & 2(e) (iii) 2 Chief Controller Imports & Exports under Import & Export (Control) Act, 1947.Import of hazardous chemicals as per Rule 18. 3 Central Pollution Control Board or State Pollution Control Board under Environment (Protection) Act, 1986 as the case may be.(1) Enforcement of directions and procedures in respect of isolated storage of hazardous chemicals, regarding,

• Notification of major accidents as per Rules 5(1) and 5(2).
• Notification of sites as per Rules 7 to 9.
• Safety reports in respect of isolated storages as per Rule 10 to 12.

- Preparation of on-site emergency plans as per Rule 13.

(2) Import of hazardous Chemicals and enforcement of directions and procedures on import of hazardous chemicals as per Rule 18. 4 Chief Inspector or Factories appointed under the Factories Act, 1948. Enforcement of directions and procedures in respect of industrial installations and isolated storages covered under the Factories Act, 1948, dealing with hazardous chemicals and pipelines including inter-state pipelines regarding,-

- Notification of major accidents as per Rule 5(1) and 5(2).
- Notification of sites as per Rules 7-9.
- Safety reports as per Rules 10 to 12.
- Preparation of on-site emergency plans as per Rule 13.
- Preparation of off-site emergency - plans in consultation with District Collector or District Emergency Authority as per Sr. No. 9 of this schedule.

Chief Inspector of Dock Safety appointed under the Dock Workers (Safety, Health and Welfare) Act, 1986. Enforcement of directions and procedures in respect of industrial installations and isolated storages dealing with hazardous chemicals and pipelines inside a port regarding,-

- Notification of major accidents as per Rules 5(1) and 5(2).
- Notification of sites as per Rules 7 to 9.
- Safety reports as per Rules 10 to 12.
- Preparation of on-site emergency plans as per Rule 13.
- Preparation of off-site emergency plans in consultation with District Collector or District Emergency Authority as per Sr. No. 9 of this schedule.

Chief Inspector of Mines appointed under Mines Act, 1952.Enforcement of directions and procedures in the respect of industrial installations and isolated storages dealing with hazardous chemicals and pipelines inside a port regarding,-

- Notification of major accidents as per Rules 5(1) and 5(2).
- Notification of sites as per Rules 7 to 9.
- Safety reports as per Rules 10 to 12
- Preparation of on-site emergency plans as per Rule 13.
- Preparation of off-site emergency plans in consultation with District Collector or District Emergency Authority as per Sr. No. 9 of this schedule.

Atomic Energy Regulatory Board appointed under the Atomic Energy Act, 1972. Enforcement of directions and procedures as per the provisions of the Atomic Energy Act, 1972.

Chief Controller of Explosives appointed under the Indian Explosives Act and Rules, 1983. Enforcement of directions and procedures as per the provisions of the Indian explosives Act and Rules 1983.

District Collector or District Emergency Authority designated by the State Government. Preparation of off-site emergency plans as per Rule 14. Directorate Or Explosives Safety (DLS), Defence Research and Development of Organisation (DRDO). Department of defence Research & Development, Ministry of Defence. Enforcement of directions and procedures in respect of laboratories industrial establishment and isolated storages dealing with hazardous chemicals in the Ministry of Defence.

SCHEDULE 6

Information to be Furnished Regarding Notification of a Major Accident

SCHEDULE 7

Information to be Furnished for the Notification of Sites
PART I

Particulars to be included in a notification of a site:

- The name and address of the employer making the notification.

- The full postal address of the site where the notifiable industrial activity will be carried on.
- The area of the site covered by the notification and of any adjacent site which is required to be taken into account by virtue of b(ii) of Schedule 2 and 3.
- The date on which it is anticipated that the notifiable industrial activity will commence, or if it has already commenced a statement to that effect.
- The name and maximum quantity liable to be on the site of each dangerous substance for which notification is being made.
- Organisation structure namely organisation diagram for the proposed industrial activity and set up for ensuring safety and health.
- Information relating to the potential for major accidents, namely
  - Identification of major accident hazards;
  - The conditions or the events which could be significant in bringing one about;
  - A brief description of the measures taken.

Information relating to the site namely:

- A map of the site and its surrounding area to a scale large enough to show any features that may be significant in the assessment of the hazard or risk associated with the site,-
  - Area likely to be affected by the major accident.
  - population distribution in the vicinity.
- A scale plan of the site showing the location and quantities of all significant inventories of the hazardous chemicals;
- A description of the process or storage involving the hazardous chemicals and an indication of the conditions under which it is normally held;
- The maximum number of persons likely to be present on site.

The arrangement for training of workers and equipment necessary to ensure safety of such workers.

PART-II

Particulars to be included regarding pipeline:

- The names and the address of the persons making the notification.
- The full postal address of the place from which the pipeline activity is controlled addresses of the places where the pipeline starts and finishes and a map showing the pipeline route drawn to a scale of not less than 1: 400000
- The date on which it is anticipated that the notifiable activity will commence, or if it is already commenced a statement to that effect.
- The total length of the pipeline, its diameter and normal operating pressure and the name and maximum quantity liable to be in the pipeline of each hazardous chemical for which notification is being made.

SCHEDULE 8

Information to be Finished in a Safety Report

- The name and address of the person furnishing the information.
- Description of the industrial activity, namely-
  - Site,
  - Construction design,
  - Protection zones explosion protection, separation distances.
  - Accessibility of plant,
  - Maximum number of persons working on the site and particularly of those persons exposed to be hazard.
- Description of the processes, namely-
  - Technical purpose of the industrial activity,
  - Basic principles of the technological process,
  - Process and safety-related data for the individual process stages,
  - Process description,
  - Safety-related types of utilities.
- Description of the hazardous chemicals, namely-
  - Chemicals (quantities, substance data, safety-

related data, toxicological data and threshold values).
  - The form in which the chemical may occur on or into which they may be transformed in the event of abnormal conditions,
  - The degree of purity of the hazardous chemical
- Information on the preliminary hazard analysis, namely-
  - Types of accident
  - System elements or events that can lead to a major accident,
  - Hazards.
  - Safety-relevant components.
- Description of safety-relevant units, among others,
  - Special design criteria,
  - Controls and alarms,
  - Special relief systems,
  - Quick-acting valves,
  - Collecting tanks/dump tank,
  - Sprinkler system.
  - Fire-fighting etc.
- Information on the hazard assessment, namely--
  - Identification of hazards,
  - The cause of major accidents,
  - Assessment of hazards according to their occurrence frequency,
  - Assessment of accident consequences,
  - Safety systems,
  - Known accident history.
- Description of information on organisational systems used to carry on the industrial activity safety, namely-
  - Maintenance and inspection schedules,
  - Guidelines for the training of personnel,
  - Allocation and delegation of responsibility for plant safety,
  - Implementation of safety procedures.
- Information on assessment of the consequences of major accidents, namely-

  - Assessment of the possible release of hazardous chemicals or of energy
  - Assessment of the effects of the releases (size of the affected area, health effects, property damage)
- Information on the mitigation of major accidents, namely-
  - Fire brigade
  - Alarm systems,
  - Emergency plan containing system of organisation used to fight the emergency, the alarm and the communication rules, guidelines for fighting the emergency, information about hazardous chemicals, examples of possible accident sequences,
  - Coordination with the District Emergency authority and its off-site emergency plan,
  - Notification of the nature and scope of the hazard in the event of an accident,
  - Antidotes in the event of a release of a hazardous chemical.

SCHEDULE 9

Safety Data Sheet

SCHEDULE 10

Format for maintaining records of hazardous chemicals imported:

- Name and address of the Importer:
- Date and reference number of issuance of permission to import hazardous chemicals:
- Description of hazardous chemicals:
  - Physical form:
  - Chemical form:
  - Total volume and weight (in kilogrammes/ tonnes)
- Description of purpose of import:
- Description of storage of hazardous chemicals:
  - Date
  - Method of storage

Chapter 6

Scheme of Labeling

RESOLUTION

G.S.R. 85(E)

The Government have decided to institute a Scheme on Labelling of Environment Friendly Products. The scheme will operate on a national basis and provide accredition and labelling for household and other consumer products which meet certain environmental criteria along with quality requirements of the Indian Standards for that product. The Label shall be known as the "ECOMARK" and will be of the design to be notified.

Any product which is made, used or disposed of in a way that significantly reduces the harm it would otherwise cause the environment could be considered as Environment Friendly Product.

OBJECTIVES OF THE SCHEME

The specific objectives of the scheme are as follows:

- To provide an incentive for manufacturers and importers to reduce adverse environmental impact of products.
- To reward genuine initiatives by companies to reduce adverse environmental impact of their products.
- To assist consumers to become environmentally responsible in their daily lives by providing information to take account of environmental factors in their purchase decisions.

- To encourage citizens to purchase products which have less harmful environmental impacts.
- Ultimately to improve the quality of the environment and to encourage the sustainable management of resources.

ADMINISTRATIVE AND ORGANISATIONAL STRUCTURE

There will be three stages leading to the award of the "ECOMARK":

- A steering committee, set up in the Ministry of Environment and Forests, to determine the product categories for coverage under the scheme and also formulate strategies for promotion, implementation, future development and improvements in the working of the scheme.
- A technical committee, set up in the Central Pollution Control Board, to identify the specific product to be selected and the individual criteria to be adopted, including, wherever possible, inter-se priority between the criteria if there be more than one.
- The Bureau of Indian Standards to assess and certify the products and draw up a contract with the manufacturers, allowing the use of the label, on payment of a fee.

STEERING COMMITTEE

A steering Committee shall be set up in the Ministry of Environment and Forests by the Central Government to decide the products categories to be taken up under the scheme, and to formulate the strategies for promotion, future development and improvement of this scheme. The product categories will be notified from time to time.

The functions of the Steering Committee shall be as follows:

- Selection of the logo for the "ECOMARK".
- Activities related to creation of mass awareness for promotion and acceptance of the scheme.
- Determining the product category to be taken up under the scheme.

- Co-ordinating ways of ensuring that industry is actively involved in the scheme.
- Securing the involvement of other Ministries, Government Departments, Industry Associations and other Non-Governmental Organisations and Consumer organisations.
- Formulations of strategies for future development of the scheme.
- Identifying institutions in India or outside which are engaged in the standardization of any article or process or improvement of quality of any article or process and recommending assistance to build consumer awareness.
- Promoting programmes of Comparative Testing of products by Consumer Organisations and dissemination their results to the general public.
- Supporting any research for the formulation of ECOMARK products in the interest of Consumer groups.

The composition of the Committee shall be as follows :

- Secretary, Deptt. of Environment & Forests
  Chairman
- Secretary, Dcptt. of Civil Supplies (or his representative)
  Member
- Secretary, Ministry of Industry (or his representative)
  Member
- Secretary, Ministry of Chemicals & Petrochemicals (or his representative)
  Member
- Secretary, Ministry of Agriculture (or his representative) Member
- Secretary, Ministry of Information & Broadcasting (or his representative)
  Member
- Director General of Technical Development (or his representative)

Member

- Director General, Council of Scientific & Industrial Research (or his representative) Member
- Director General, Health Services (or his representative) Member
- Development Commissioner, Small Scale Industries (or his representative) Member
- Chairman, Central Pollution Control Board Member
- Not more than five non officials, to be nominated by the Central Government; to represent the interests of industry, consumer groups or other non governmental organisations; of which at least two will represent Consumer groups. Member
- Officer in charge, "ECOMARK" in the Ministry of Environment & Forests. Member-Secretary

In case of special requirement of expertise in specific fields, the committee may invite-experts as special invitees. The terms of the Committee shall be for three years or until reconstituted.

TECHNICAL COMMITTEE

A Technical Committee shall be constituted by the Central Government to identify the individual products and determine the criteria for awarding the ECOMARK. The Committee shall function in the Central Pollution Control Board, Delhi.

The following shall be the functions for the Technical Committee:

- Identification of specific products for classifying as environment friendly.
- Reviewing the existing state of knowledge and the environmental criteria being followed in other countries.
- Recommend the most appropriate criteria and parameters to designate various products as

environment friendly, including the most important criteria or individual products that have been specified for the purpose and their inter-se priority, whenever possible.

- Review the various technologies available for determining the criteria.
- Recommend various laboratories and analysts for product assessment in the Ministry of Environment and Forests.
- Evaluation of the environmental impact of the products and criteria from time to lime.
- To review from time to time the implementation of the schemes by the Bureau of Indian Standards (BIS), including the sample inspections done by it.
- Set up sub-committees for each product category if so required, including formulation of test programmes for comparative testing of products by consumer organisations.
- The technical committee may set up expert panels to advise it for specific products.

The composition of the Committee shall be:

- Chairman, Central Pollution Control Board. Chairman
- Director General, Bureau of Indian Standards, New Delhi Member
- Director, National Environmental Engineering Research Institute, Nagpur Member.
- Director, National Chemical Laboratory, Pune Member
- Director General, National Test House, Calcutta Member
- Director, Industrial Toxicology Institute, Lucknow Member
- Director, National Institute of Occupational Health, Ahmedabad Member
- Not more than five non-officials to represent the interest of industry & consumer groups, of which

atleast three will represent the Consumer groups be nominated by the Central Government. Research Member

- Officer in charge, (Eco-Mark scheme) Central Pollution Control Board. Member-Secretary

The Committee may co-opt experts on different products, as special invitees. The terms of the Committee shall be for three years or until reconstituted.

Administration

The Bureau of Indian Standards (BIS) shall implement the scheme.

Following shall be functions of the BIS:

- Assess the product for Ecomark, certify the product for award of the Ecomark;
- Review suspend or cancel a licence, for the use of the Ecomark;
- Mark inspections, and take such samples for analysis of any material or substances as may be necessary to see whether any article or product in relation to which the Ecomark has been used, conforms to the contract or whether the Ecomark is improperly used in relation to any article or process with or without a licence;

CERTIFICATION AND LICENCING

- Under the scheme the manufcturers shall apply for testing and certification of products which fall under the notified categories in terms of their compliance with published environmental criteria in the prescribed form. The terms and conditions governing operations of licences including fees shall be as per the Bureau of Indian Standards Act and the regulations framed there under.
- Testing and certification shall be carried out by the Bureau of Indian Standards. For product categories which have the Indian Standards mark, the Bureau of Indian Standards will ordinarily complete the task of certification within a period of three months.

Products certified as eligible for the ECOMARK shall be licenced to carry the ECOMARK for a prescribed time period.

- The product shall be reassessed after the prescribed period and the licence fee shall have to be paid again for the mark.

THE CRITERIA FOR ECOMARK

Environmental criteria for each product category will be notified by the Central Government and later on shall be translated into Indian Standards by the Bureau of Indian Standards. The criteria shall be for broad environmental levels and aspects, but will be specific at the product level.

Products will be examined in terms of the following main environmental impacts:

- That they have substantially less potential for pollution than other comparable products in production, usage and disposal.
- That they are recycled, recyclable, made from recycled products or biodegradable, where comparable products are not.
- That they make significant contribution to saving non-renewable resources, including non renewable energy sources and natural resources, compared with comparable products.
- That the product must contribute to a reduction of the adverse primary criteria which has thc highest environmental impact associated with the use of the product, and which will be specifically set for each of the product categories.

In determining the primary criteria for a product the following shall be taken:

- Production process including source of raw material;
- Case of Natural Resources;
- Likely impact on the environment;
- Energy conservation in the production of the product;
- Effect & extent of waste arising from the production process;

- Disposal of the product and its container;
- Utilization of "Waste" and recycled materials;
- Suitability for recycling or packaging
- Biodegradability;

The criteria shall be reviewed from time to time. The draft criteria shall be release for public comments for a period of sixty days.

PERIOD OF AWARD

The label shall be awarded for a minimum period of one year and shall roll forward annually. The Bureau of Indian Standards have the powers to withdraw the licence at any time if they find any misleading information. The award may also be withdrawn in case of any change in criteria due to the advancement of technology or any other valid reasons, in consultation with the technical committee. The time period of the award may be reviewed from time to time.

THE LOGO

The Logo for the 'ECOMARK" shall be as notified by the Central Government.

CONSUMER AWARENESS

The Ministry of Environment & Forests shall take appropriate measures to launch a country wide mass awareness campaign, including encouraging consumer groups.

Assistance will be given to consumer organisations for comparative testing of products and dissemination of information to the public.

ORDER

Ordered that the Resolution be published in the Gazette of India and a copy there of communicated to all concerned.

[No. 23/1/91-PL]

MUKUL SANWAL, Jt. Secy.

15th February,1991

Published in the Gazette No. 71 dt. 21-2-91].

G.S.R.768(E)

In exercise of the decision recorded in paragraph 5 of the Resolution of the Government of India in the Ministry of Environment & Forests, published vide GSR No.85(E), dated 21.2.1991 in the Gazette of India Extraordinary, Part II, Section 3, Sub-section(i), the Central Government hereby notifies the following criteria for labeling Cosmetics as Environment Friendly Products.

GENERAL REQUIREMENTS

- All the products manufactured shall meet the requirements of following Indian Standards of BIS pertaining to safety, quality and performance :-

Sl.No. 1.	Item 2.	IS CODE No. 3.
1.	Skin Powders	IS:3959:1979
2.	Skin powder for infants	IS:5339:1978
3.	Tooth Powder	IS:5383:1978
4.	Tooth Paste	IS:6356:1978
5.	Skin Creams	IS:6608:1976
6.	Hair Cils	IS:7123:1984
7.	Shampoo Soap based	IS:7669:1975
8.	Shampoo Synthetic Detergent based	IS:7884:1978
9.	Hair Creams	IS:7679:1975
10.	Oxidation Hair Dyes liquid	IS:8481:1977
11.	Cologne	IS:8482:1977
12.	Nail Polish (Nail Enamel)	IS:9245:1975
13.	After Shave lotion	IS:9255:1979
14.	Pomades & Brilliantines	IS:9339:1979
15.	Depliatorics Chemical	IS:9636:1988
16.	Shaving Creams	IS:9740:1981
17.	Cosmetic Pencils	IS:9832:1981
18.	Lipstick	IS:9875:1981

- All the ingredients that go into formulation of cosmetics shall comply with the provisions prescribed in IS 4707: Part I,II and III classification of cosmetics raw materials and adjuncts as well as the product specific requirements.

- The product package shall display a list of critical ingredients in descending order of quantity present. The list of such ingredients shall be identified by BIS.
- The product shall not be manufactured from any carcinogenic ingredients.
  Note: Central Drug Research Instt./Industrial Toxicological Research Instt. would furnish a list of carcinogenic ingredients to BIS and would also keep BIS informed about the changes therein.
- The product manufacturer must produce the consent as per the provisions of Water (Prevention and Control of Pollution) Act, 1974, Water (Prevention and Control of Pollution) Cess Act, 1977 and Air (Prevention and Control of Pollution) Act, 1981 alongwith the authorisation, if required under Environment(Protection)Act,1986 and rules made thereunder to BIS while applying for ECOMARK, Additionally, provisions of the Drugs and Cosmetics Act,1940 and rules thereunder shall also be complied with.
- The product package shall be suitably marked that ECOMARK label is applicable only to the contents, if the product package is not separately covered under the ECOMARK scheme.
- The material used for produce packaging shall meet the parameters evolved under the scheme of labeling Environment Friendly Packaging/packaging materials.

PRODUCT SPECIFIC REQUIREMENTS

All the cosmetics formulations shall comply with the requirements given below under (i) to (iii). Further in addition to compliance with the requirements under (i) to (iii) the respective cosmetics namely: Tooth Paste/Tooth Powder, Hair Dyes and Nail Polish shall comply with the requirements given below under (iv),(v) and (vi) respectively. (i) Product shall be dermatologically safe when tested by the method prescribed by IS 4011 :1982. (ii) Biodegradable surfactant agents wherever used in cosmetics formulation shall be as per their limit finished for synthetic detergents for ECOMARK by the Technical Committee. (iii) Heavy metals calculated as lead (Pb) and Arsenic (Ars) shall not exceed 10 and 1 ppm, respectively when tested by the respective methods, prescribed in Indian Standards. (iv) Tooth Paste/Tooth Powder :- For the purpose of formulation of these products, the ingredients listed in IS : 6356 (1979) and ISL : 5383 (1978) shall only be used.

Moreover, tooth paste shall not be fluoridated and presence of fluoride (F) as impurity shall not exceed the limit of 10 ppm. *Note*: This has been done with a view to ensure safety of these products from oral toxicity as the ingredients listed in the relevant Indian Standards are based on the consideration that are generally regarded as safe for such formulations. (v) Hair Dyes :- Lead based dyes shall not be used. (vi) Nail Polish :- Halogenated organic solvents shall not be used.

Note : Manufacturers will give necessary undertakings with supporting documents to BIS while applying for ECOMARK for requirements under (v) and (vi) above. 3. BIS may formulate/incorporate optional standards for environment friendly characteristics.

FILING OF OBJECTIONS

Any person interested in filling any objection against these criteria for labeling Cosmetics as environment friendly may do so in writing to the Deputy Secretary, Ministry of Environment & Forests, Paryavaran Bhawan, CGO Complex, Lodhi Road, New Delhi within sixty days from the date of publication of this notification in the official gazette.

Chapter 7

Role of Government

There is an ongoing debate about the appropriate role of government for solving environmental problems, with many environmentalists calling for increased government intervention and many people more predisposed to individual responsibility calling for less.

Without getting into a long discussion on political and economic philosophy (for now), here are a few observations on this important topic:

- Proponents of classic liberalism -- property rights, free markets, the rule of law, individual freedom -- assume that as information improves, private markets will lead to the increased preservation of environmental resources, and that externalities (e.g., pollution) will be internalized (e.g., taken into account by private actors) given a system of strong property rights. While much improvement in the environmental arena has occurred for this very reason, and much of this is due to property rights and better scientific knowledge, many famous economists vastly under-estimated the level of coordination required to tackle some of the world's most serious environmental problems. Issues such as global warming and the loss of biodiversity require much more government intervention then had previously been assumed. This is not to say that this government intervention won't rely heavily on the workings of the market system, but only that top-down regulation is absolutely necessary. There is simply no way to adequately address these issues without a strong commitment from the federal government, which will eventually include a high level of international cooperation. Policies such as absolute limits on CO_2, government funding of alternative-energy systems, and coordinated efforts to purchase and protect biodiversity hotspots around the world will need to be a major component of future government policy.

- Facing increased probabilities of natural disasters (many presumably due to global warming), the government should move us towards a more rational method of risk management in areas prone to natural disasters. It is highly inefficient, as well as an abrogation of government responsibility, to create incentives for people to live in areas that are both dangerous and prone to catastrophe by providing them with reconstruction aid every time disaster strikes. The government has two options; either require that all people living in hurricane zones, flood plains, or near fault lines purchase private insurance, or make it absolutely clear that people will not be compensated for their loss of property by the government if disaster strikes. Such a policy would no doubt lead to dramatic shifts in the population densities in many disaster-prone areas of the country, and perhaps some one-time assistance for relocation would be required. The net effect would be to dramatically reduce future losses of life and property and save the government hundreds of billions in future costs. It would also force private actors (notably insurance companies) to fully take into account the effects of environmental externalities that until now have largely been ignored.
- Regarding personal health and risk, the government must play a much more active role than typically advocated by some of the strongest proponents of free markets. Milton Friedman famously noted that

there is no use for the Food and Drug Administration since companies whose products lead to illness will be forced out of the market (i.e., products that make people sick will not be bought). What he failed to realise is that if someone gets sick, it is extremely difficult to trace the source of the illness, and without government regulation many companies that poison consumers could in fact operate profitably for long periods of time. But Friedman did have a point in that as people look more and more toward government to regulate the economy, they sometimes do decrease the effort they invest in making wise choices for themselves (e.g., does anyone really need the government to tell them that "fast food" is bad for you?). This being said, it is clear that in this highly complex and inter-connected system, where we all are exposed to thousands of chemicals a year, many of which interact in ways that aren't yet fully understood, where it is hard to trace the origin of products, and where the effects of these products often don't manifest for years, the government must play an active role in regulation. The information problems are too complex for individuals to cope with (and, unfortunately, governments, at this point). The Food and Drug Administration, the Environmental Protection Agency, and the U.S. Department of Agriculture should all be well-funded, be decoupled from conflicts of interest with industry, and their mandate to protect the public welfare through rational risk assessment should be strengthened.

PERCEIVED ROLE OF GOVERNMENT

To better understand what action the government might take on the environment, respondents were asked whether they agreed or disagreed with a number of regulatory and policy options that could be introduced to protect the environment.

Most Victorians (89%) agreed the government should consider environmental concerns when making decisions.

ROLE OF GOVERNMENT INTERVENTION

In environmental cases, a policy framework is sometimes more effective when there is less government intervention. As the level of government intervention diminishes, this allows more flexibility for corporations to achieve efficiency. Furthermore the traditional command and control approach has proven to be costly, bureaucratic and often inefficient.

It is important to address the fact that there are numerous benefits that can be achieved for both policy makers and industries, if a policy framework is based on market forces. However it is important that there is a need for some government intervention, but should be as minimal as possible. I have chosen to examine the article from the New York Times entitled RU.S. Seeking Options of Pollution RulesS.Although pollution is detrimental to our environment, you have to take into account that it is almost impossible to entirely prevent pollution.

This is scientifically impossible and it would have severely negative economic impact on the industries. So the core issue becomes the fact no matter what, there will always be pollution, as long as these industries exist. So we should focus on how we can minimize this and yet at the same time have an efficient market system? Furthermore, we should also focus on how we can accomplish this so that sustainable growth and development can take place. So there is definitely a need for some form of government intervention to enforce and monitor this.

Reason being that there is always an element of equality that has to be enforced, when dealing with cases such as this. For instance, larger corporations may have an advantage over smaller corporation, since they have stronger influence on politicians and lobbyists. So the governmentUs role should be to ensure that all industries (regardless size and/or power) have equal opportunities to benefit from this type of approach.Role of Government Intervention in Environmental

Issues In environmental cases, a policy framework is sometimes more effective when there is less government intervention. As the level of government intervention diminishes, this allows more flexibility for corporations to achieve efficiency. Furthermore the traditional command and control approach has proven to be costly, bureaucratic and often inefficient. It is important to address the fact that there are numerous benefits that can be achieved for both policy makers and industries, if a policy framework is based on market forces. However it is important that there is a need for some government intervention, but should be as minimal as possible.

I have chosen to examine the article from the New York Times entitled RU.S. Seeking Options of Pollution RulesS.Although pollution is detrimental to our environment, you have to take into account that it is almost impossible to entirely prevent pollution. This is scientifically impossible and it would have severely negative economic impact on the industries. So the core issue becomes the fact no matter what, there will always be pollution, as long as these industries exist. So we should focus on how we can minimize this and yet at the same time have an efficient market system?

Furthermore, we should also focus on how we can accomplish this so that sustainable growth and development can take place. So there is definitely a need for some form of government intervention to enforce and monitor this.Reason being that there is always an element ofequality that has to be enforced, when dealing with cases such as this.For instance, larger corporations may have an advantage over smaller corporation, since they have stronger influence on politicians and lobbyists. So the governmentUs role should be to ensure that all industries (regardless size and/or power) have equal opportunities to benefit from this type of approach.

Chapter 8

Legal Aspects

ENVIRONMENT

DEFINITION

Legal aspects are an indispensable part of a successful business environment in any country. They reflect the policy framework and the mind set of the Governmental structure of that country. They ensure that every company is functioning as per the statutory framework of the country. Every enterprise must take into account this legal set up while framing the basic aims and objectives of its company.

This is because, it is necessary for efficient and healthy functioning of the organisation and helps it to know about the rights, responsibilities as well as the challenges that it may have to face. In India, the most important law which regulates all aspects relating to a company is the Companies Act,1956. It contains provisions relating to formation of a company, powers and responsibilities of the directors and managers, raising of capital, holding company meetings, maintenance and audit of company accounts, powers of inspection and investigation of company affairs, reconstruction and amalgamation of a company and even winding up of a company.

The Indian Contract Act,1872, is another legislation which regulates all the transactions of a company. It lays down the general principles relating to the formation and enforceability of contracts; rules governing the provisions of an agreement and offer; the various types of contracts including those of indemnity and guarantee, bailment and pledge and agency.

It also contains provisions pertaining to breach of a contract. The other major legislations are:- the Industries (Development and Regulation) Act 1951; Trade Unions Act; the Competition Act, 2002; the Arbitration and Conciliation Act, 1996; the Foreign Exchange Management Act (FEMA),1999; laws relating to intellectual property rights; as well as laws relating to labour welfare.

Over the years, there has been an increasing consciousness and realisation that environmental quality and economic development are complementary and not mutually exclusive. This is because, with technological advancements, environ--mental challenges are also on rise. As a result, there is a need to bring about necessary changes in the industrial and agricultural production patterns, utility services, consumer behaviour and life styles of the people keeping in view our social and developmental priorities for conservation and sustainable use of natural resources. Hence, environmental regulations and standards have been set up by environmental bodies world around. Indian industry and business too are under increasing pressure of meeting these environmental standards and regulations.

Recognising the importance of environment, its protection has been given a Constitutional status. The 'Directive Principles of State Policy' state that, it is the duty of the State 'to protect and improve the environment and to safeguard the forests and wildlife of the country'. It is also the 'Fundamental duty' of every citizen 'to protect and improve the natural environment including forests, lakes, rivers and wildlife'.

In India, the Ministry of Environment and Forests (MoEF) is the apex administrative body for:

- RSegulating and ensuring environmental protection;
- Formulating the environmental policy framework in the country;
- Undertaking conservation & survey of flora, fauna, forests and wildlife; and
- Planning, promotion, co-ordination and overseeing the implementation of environmental and forestry programmes. The Ministry is also the Nodal agency

in the country for the United Nations Environment Programme (UNEP). The organizational structure of the Ministry covers number of Divisions, Directorate, Board, Subordinate Offices, Autonomous Institutions, and Public Sector Undertakings to assist it in achieving all these objectives.

Besides, the responsibility for prevention and control of industrial pollution is primarily executed by the Central Pollution Control Board (CPCB) at the Central Level, which is a statutory authority, attached to the MoEF. The State Departments of Environment and State Pollution Control Boards are the designated agencies to perform this function at the State Level.

Central government has enacted several laws for environmental protection. The Environment (Protection) Act, 1986, is the umbrella legislation which authorizes the Central Government to protect and improve environmental quality, control and reduce pollution from all sources, and prohibit or restrict the setting and /or operation of any industrial facility on environmental grounds. According to the Act, the term "environment" includes water, air and land and the inter-relationship which exists among and between water, air and land, and human beings, other living creatures, plants, micro-organism and property.

The main provisions of the Act are:

- The Central Government shall have the power to take all such measures as it deems necessary or expedient for the purpose of protecting and improving the quality of the environment and preventing, controlling and abating environmental pollution.
- No person carrying on any industry, operation or process shall discharge or emit any environmental pollutants or permit to do so in excess of such standards as may be prescribed.
- Where the discharge of any environmental pollutant in excess of the prescribed standards occurs or is apprehended to occur due to any accident or other unforeseen act or event, the person responsible for

such discharge and the person in charge of the place at which such discharge occurs or is apprehended to occur, shall be bound to prevent or mitigate the environmental pollution caused as a result of such discharge and shall also forthwith intimate the fact of such occurrence or apprehension of such occurrence; and be bound, if called upon, to render all assistance to such authorities or agencies as may be prescribed.

- No person shall handle or cause to be handled any hazardous substance except in accordance with such procedure and after complying with such safeguards as may be prescribed.
- The Central Government or any officer empowered by it in this behalf, shall have power to take, for the purpose of analysis, samples of air, water, soil or other substance from any factory, premises or other place in such manner as may be prescribed.
- The Central Government may, by notification in the Official Gazette, establish one or more environmental laboratories; and recognise one or more laboratories or institutes as environmental laboratories to carry out the functions entrusted to an environmental laboratory under this Act.
- Whoever fails to comply with or contravenes any of the provisions of this Act, or the rules made or orders or directions issued thereunder, shall, in respect of each such failure or contravention, be punishable with imprisonment or with fine or with both.

The other important environmental legislations may be categorised as follows:

WATER POLLUTION

ACTS

1. No.36 of 1977, [7/12/1977] - The Water (Prevention and Control of Pollution) Cess Act, 1977, amended 1992 No. 19 of 2003, [17/3/2003] - The Water (Prevention and Control of

Pollution) Cess (Amendment) Act, 2003 An Act further to amend the Water(Prevention and Control of Pollution) Cess Act, 1977. *BE it enacted by parliament in the Fifty-fourth Year of the Republic of India as follows*:

Short Title and Commencement

- This Act may be called the Water(Prevention and Control of Pollution) Cess (Amendment) Act, 2003.
- It shall come into force on such date as the Central Government may, by notification in the Official Gazette, appoint.

Amendment of Section 2

In the Water (Prevention and Control of Pollution) Cess Act, 1977.(hereinafter referred to as the principal Act), in section 2, for clause(C), the following clause shall be substituted, namely:

'(C) "industry" includes any operation or process, or treatment and disposal system, which consumes water or gives rise to sewage effluent or trade effluent, but does not include any hydel power unit;'.

Substitution of Certain Expression

In the principal Act, for the words "specified industry", wherever they occur, the word "industry" shall be substituted.

PRELIMINARY

Short Title, Application and Commencement

(1) Short title, application and commencement. This Act may be called the Water (Prevention and Control of s Pollution) Act, 1974. (2) It applies in the first instance to the whole of the States of Assam, Bihar, Gujarat, Haryana, Himachal Pradesh, Jammu and Kashmir, Karnataka, Kerala, Madhya Pradesh, Rajasthan, Tripura and West Bengal and the Union territories; and it shall apply to such other State which adopts this Act by resolution passed in that behalf under clause (1) of article 252 of the Constitution. (3) It shall come into force,

at once in the States of Bihar, Gujarat, Haryana, Himachal Pradesh, Jammu and Kashmir, Karnataka, Kerala, Madhya Pradesh, Rajasthan, Tripura and West Bengal and in the Union territories, and in any other State which adopts this Act under clause (1) of article 252 of the Constitution on the date of such adoption and any reference in this Act to the commencement of this Act shall, in relation to any State or Union territory, mean the date on which this Act comes into force in such State or Union territory.

Definitions

In this Act, unless the context otherwise requires:

(a) "Board" means the Central Board or State Board; 1[(b) " Central Board" means the Central Pollution Control Board Constituted under section3;] (c) "members" means a member of a Board and includes the chairman thereof; 2[(d) "occupier", in relation to any factory or premises, means the person who has control over the affairs of the factory or the premises, and includes, in relation to any substance, the person in possession of the substance.] 3 [(dd) "outlet" includes any conduit pipe or channel, open or closed carrying sewage or trade effluent or any other holding arrangement which causes, or is likely to cause, pollution;] (e) "pollution" means such contamination of water or such alteration of the physical, chemical or biological properties of water or such discharge of any sewage or trade effluent or of any other liquid, gaseous or solid substance into water (whether directly or indirectly) as may, or is likely to, create a nuisance or render such water harmful or injurious to public health or safety, or to domestic, commercial, industrial, agricultural or other legitimate uses, or to the life and health of animals or plants or of aquatic organisers; (f) "prescribed" means prescribed by rules made under this Act by the Central Government or, as the case may be, the State Government, (g) "sewage effluent" means effluent from any sewerage system or sewage disposal works and includes sullage from open drains; 4[(gg) "sewer" means any conduit pipe or channel, openor closed, carrying sewage or trade effluent;] 5[(h) "State Board" means a State Pollution

Control Board constituted under section 4"]; (i) "State Government" in relation to a Union territory means the Administrator thereof appointed under article 239 of the Constitution; (j)"stream" includes- (i) river; (ii) Water course (whether flowing or for the time] being dry); (iii) inland water (whether natural or artificial);] (iv) subterranean waters; (v) sea or tidal waters to such extent or, as the case may be, to such point as the State Government may, by notification in the Official Gazette, specify in this behalf ; (k) "trade effluent" includes any liquid, gaseous or solid substance which is discharged from any premises used for carrying on any 6["Industry, operation or process, or treatment and disposal system" other than domestic sewage.

THE CENTRAL & STATE BOARDS FOR PREVENTION & CONTROL OF WATER POLLUTION

CONSTITUTION OF CENTRAL BOARD

(1) The Central Government shall, with effect from such date (being a date not later than six months of the commencement of this Act is the States of Assam, Bihar, Gujarat, Haryana, Himachal Pradesh, Jammu and Kashmir, Karnataka, Kerala, Madhya Pradesh, Rajasthan, Tripura and West Bengal and in the Union territories) as it may, by notification in the Official Gazette, appoint, constitute a Central Board to be called the 1[Central Pollution Control Board] to exercise the powers conferred on and perform the functions assigned to that Board under this Act. (2) The Central Board shall consist of the following members, namely:- (a) a full-time chairman, being a person having special knowledge or practical experience in respect of 2[matters relating to environmental protection] or a person having knowledge and experience in administering institutions dealing with the matters aforesaid, to be nominated by the Central Government; (b) 3[such number of officials, not exceeding five] to be nominated by the Central Government to represent that Government; (c) such number of persons, not exceeding five to be nominated by the Central Government, from amongst

the members of the State Boards, of whom no exceeding two shall be from those referred to in clause (c) of sub-section (2) of section 4; (d) 4[such number of non-officials, not exceeding three] to be nominated by the Central Government, to represent the interests of agriculture, fishery or industry or trade or any other interest which, in the opinion of the Central Government, ought to be represented; (e) two persons to represent the companies or corporations owned, controlled or managed by the Central Government, to be nominated by that Government; 5[(f) a full-time member-secretary, possessing qualifications, knowledge and experience of scientific, engineering or management aspects of pollution control, to be appointed by the Central Government] (3) The Central Board shall be a body corporate with the name aforesaid having perpetual succession and a common seal with power, subject to the provisions of this Act, to acquire, hold and dispose of property and to contract, and may, by the aforesaid name, sue or be sued.

CONSTITUTION OF STATE BOARDS

(1) The State Government shall, with effect from such date 6 as it may, by notification in the Official Gazette, appoint, constitute a 7[State Pollution Control Board], under such name as may be specified in the notification, to exercise the powers conferred on the perform the functions assigned to that Board under this Act. (2) A State Board shall consist of the following members, namely:- (a) a 8 chairman, being a person having special knowledge or practical experience in respect of 9[matters relating to environmental protection] or a person having knowledge and experience in administering institutions dealing with the matters aforesaid, to be nominated by the State Government. 10[Provided that the chairman may be either whole-time or part-time as the State Government may think fit;] (b) 11[such number of officials, not exceeding five,] to be nominated by the State Government to represent that Government; (c) 12[such number of persons, not exceeding five] to be nominated by the State Government from amongst the members of the local authorities functioning

within the State; (d) 13[such number of non-officials, not exceeding three] to be nominated by the State Government to represent the interest of agriculture, fishery or industry or trade or any other interest which, in the opinion of the State Government, ought to be represented; (e) two persons to represent the companies or corporations owned, controlled or managed by the State Government, to be nominated by that Government; 14[(f) a full-time member-secretary, possessing qualifications, knowledge and experience of scientific, engineering or management aspects of pollution control, to be appointed by the State Government (3) Every State Board shall be a body corporate with the name specified by the State Government in the notification under sub-section (1), having perpetual succession and a common seal with power, subject to the provisions of this Act, to acquire, hold and dispose of property and to contract, and may, by the said name, sue or be sued. (4) Notwithstanding anything contained in this section, no State Board shall be constituted for a Union territory and in relation to a Union territory, the Central Board shall exercise the powers and perform the functions of a State Board for that Union territory: Provided that in relation to a Union territory the Central Board may delegate all of any of its powers and functions under this sub-section to such person or body of persons as the Central Government may specify.

TERMS AND CONDITIONS OF MEMBERS

(1) Save as otherwise provided by or under this Act, a member of a Board, other than, a member-secretary, shall hold office for a term of three years from the date of this nomination: Provided that a member shall, notwithstanding the expiration of his term, continue to hold office until his successor enters upon his office. 15[(2) The term of office of a member of a Board nominated under clause (b) or clause (e) of sub-section (2) of Section 3 or clause (b) or clause (e) of sub-section (2) of section 4 shall come to an end as soon as he ceases to hold the office under the Central Government or the State Government or, as the case may be, the company or corporation owned, controlled or managed by the Central Government or the State

Government, by virtue of which he was nominated] (3) The Central Government or, as the case may be, the State Government may, if it thinks fit, remove any member of a Board before the expiry of his term of office, after giving him a reasonable opportunity of showing cause against the same. (4) A member of a Board, other than the member-secretary, may at any time resign his office by writing under his hand addressed-- (a) in the case of chairman, tot he Central Government or, as the case may be, the State Government; and (b) in any other case, to the chairman of the Board; and the seat of the chairman or such member shall thereupon become vacant. (5) A member of a Board, other than the member-secretary, shall be deemed to have vacated his seat if he is absent without reason, sufficient in the opinion of the Board, from three consecutive meetings of the Board, 16[or where he is nominated under clause (c) or clause (e) of sub-section (2) of section (3) or under clause (c) or clause (e) of sub-section (2) of section 4, if he ceases to be a member of the State Board or of the local authority or, as the case may be, of the company or corporation owned, controlled or managed by the Central Government or the State Government and such vacation of seat shall, in either case, take effect from such date as the Central Government or, as the case may be, the State Government may, by notification in the Official Gazette, specify] (6) A casual vacancy in a Board shall be filled by a fresh nomination and the person nominated to fill the vacancy shall hold office only for the remainder of the term for which the member in a whose place he was nominated. (7) A member of a Board 17[shall be eligible for renomination]. (8) The other terms and conditions of service of a member of a Board, other than the chairman and member-secretary, shall be such as may be prescribed. (9) The other terms and conditions of service of the chairman shall be such as may be prescribed.

DISQUALIFICATIONS

(1) No person shall be a member of a Board, who-- (a) is, or at any time has been adjudged insolvent or has suspended payment of his debts or has compounded with his creditors,

or (b) is of unsound mind and stands so declared by a competent court, or (c) is, or has been, convicted of an offence which, in the opinion of the Central Government or, as the case may be, of the State Government, involves moral turpitude, or (d) is, or at any time has been, convicted of an offence under this Act, or (e) has directly or indirectly by himself or by any partner, any share or interest in any firm or company carrying on the business of manufacture, sale or hire of machinery, plant, equipment, apparatus or fittings for the treatment of sewage or trade effluents, or (f) is a director or a secretary, manager or other salaried officer or employee of any company or firm having any contract with the Board, or with the Government constituting the Board, or with a local authority in the State, or with a company or corporation owned, controlled or managed by the Government, for the carrying out of sewerage schemes or for the installation of plants for the treatment of sewage or trade effluents, or (g) has so abused, in the opinion of the Central Government or as the case may be, of the State Government, his position as a member, as to render his continuance on the Board detrimental to the interest of the general public. (2) No order of removal shall be made by the Central Government or the State Government, as the case may be, under this section unless the member concerned has been given a reasonable opportunity of showing cause against the same. (3) Notwithstanding anything contained in sub-section (1) and (7) of section 5, a member who has been removed under this section shall not be eligible for renomination as a member.

VACATION OF SEAT BY MEMBERS

If a member of a Board becomes subject to any of the disqualifications specified in section 6, his seat shall become vacant.

MEETINGS OF BOARDS

A Board shall meet at least once in every three months and shall observe such rules of procedure in regard to the transaction of business at its meetings as may be prescribed:

Provided that if, in the opinion of the chairman, any business of an urgent nature is to be transacted, he may convene a meeting of the Board at such time as he thinks fit for the aforesaid purpose.

CONSTITUTION OF COMMITTEES

- A Board may constitute as many committees consisting wholly of members or wholly of other persons or partly of members and partly of other persons, and for such purpose or purposes as it may think fit.
- A committee constituted under this section shall meet at such time and at such place, and shall observe such rules of procedure in regard to the transaction of business at its meetings, as may be prescribed.
- The members of a committee (other than the members of Board) shall be paid such fees and allowances, for attending its meetings and for attending to any other work of the Board as may be prescribed.

EMPORARY ASSOCIATION OF PERSONS WITH BOARD FOR PARTICULAR PURPOSES

(1) A Board may associate with itself in such manner, and for such purposes, as may be prescribed any person whose assistance or advice it may desire to obtain in performing any of its functions under this Act. (2) A person associated with the Board under sub-section (1) for any purpose shall have a right to take part in the discussions of the Board relevant to that purpose, but shall not have a right to vote at a meeting of the Board, and shall not be a member for any other purpose. 18[(3) A person associated with the Board under sub-section (1) for any purpose shall be paid such fees and allowances, for attending its meetings and for attending to any other work of the Board, as may be prescribed]

VACANCY IN BOARD

No act or proceeding of a Board or any committee thereof shall be called in question on the ground merely of the existence of any vacancy in, or any defect in the constitution of, the Board or such committee, as the case may be. 19[11A.Delegation of powers to Chairman The chairman of a Board shall exercise such powers and perform such duties as may be prescribed or as may, from time to time, be delegated to him by the Board]

MEMBER-SECRETARY AND OFFICERS

- Terms and conditions of service of the member-secretary shall be such as may be prescribed.
- The member-secretary shall exercise such powers and perform such duties as may be prescribed or as may, from time to time, he delegated to him by the Board or its chairman.
- Subject to such rules as may be madé by the Central Government or, as the case may be, the State Government in this behalf, a Board may appoint such officers and employees as it considers necessary for the efficient performance of its functions

  21[(3A) The method of recruitment and the terms and conditions of service (including the scales or pay) of the officers (other than the member-secretary) and other employees of the Central Board or a State Board shall be such as may be determined by regulations made by the Central Board or, as the case may be, by the State Board:

  Provided that no regulation made under this sub-section shall take effect unless:

  (a) In the case of a regulation made by the Central Board, it is approved by the Central Government; and

  (b) In the case of a regulation made by a State Board, it is approved by the State Government

22[(3B) The Board may, by general or special order, and subject to such conditions and limitations, if any, as may be specified in the order, delegate to any officer of the Board such of its powers and functions under this Act as it may deem necessary

- Subject to such conditions as may be prescribed, a Board may from time to time appoint any qualified person to be a consulting engineer to the Board and pay him such salaries and allowances and subject him to such other terms and conditions of service as it thinks fit.

JOINT BOARDS

Constitution of Joint Board

(1) Notwithstanding anything contained in this Act, an agreement may be entered into (a) by two or more Governments of contiguous States, or (b) by the Central Government (in respect of one or more Union territories) and one or more Government of State Government contiguous to such Union territory or Union territories, to be in force for such period and to be subject to renewal for such further period if any, as may be specified in the agreement to provide for the constitution of a Joint Board (i) in a case referred to in clause (a), for all the participating States, and (ii) in a case referred to in clause (b), for the participating Union territory or Union territories and the State or States. (2) An agreement under this section may -- (a) provide, in a case referred to in clause (a) of sub-section (1), for the apportionment between the participating States and in a case referred to in clause (b) of that sub-section, for the apportionments between the Central Government and the participating State Government or State Governments, of the expenditure in connection with the Joint Board; (b) determine, in a case referred to in clause (a) of sub-section (1), which of the participating State Governments and in a case referred to in clause (b) of that sub-section, whether the Central Government or the participating State Government (if there are more than one participating State, also which of the participating State Governments) shall exercise and perform the several powers and functions of the State Government under this Act and the references in this Act to the State Government shall be construed accordingly; (c) provide for consultation, in a case referred to in clause (a) of

sub-section (1), between the participating State Governments and in a case referred to in clause (b) of that sub-section, between the Central Government and the participating State Government or State Governments either generally or with reference to particular matters arising under this Act;- (d) make such incidental and ancillary provisions, not inconsistent with this Act, as may be deemed necessary or expedient for giving effect to the agreement. (3) An agreement under this section shall be published, in a case referred to in clause (a) of sub-section (1), in the Official Gazette of the participating States and in a case referred to in clause (b) of that sub-section, in the Official Gazette of participating Union territory or Union territories and participating State or States.

Composition of Joint Boards

(1) A Joint Board constituted in pursuance of an agreement entered into under clause (a) of sub-section (1) of section 13 shall consist of the following members, namely: (a) a full-time chairman, being a person having special knowledge or practical experience in respect of 1[matters relating to environmental protection] or a person having knowledge and experience in administering institutions dealing with the matters aforesaid, to be nominated by the Central Government; (b) two officials from each of the participating States to be nominated by the concerned participating State Government to represent that Government; (c) one person to be nominated by each of the participating State Governments from amongst the members of the local authorities functioning within the State concerned; (d) one non-official to be nominated by each of the participating State Governments to represent the interests or agriculture, fishery or industry or trade in the State concerned or any other interest which, in the opinion of the participating State Government, is to be represented; (e) two persons to be nominated by the Central Government to represent the companies or corporations owned, controlled or managed by the participating State Government; 2[(f) a full-time member-secretary, possessing qualifications, knowledge and experience of scientific, engineering or management

aspects of pollution control, to be appointed by the Central Government] (2) A Joint Board constituted in pursuance of an agreement entered into under clause (b) of sub-section (1) of section 13 shall consist of the following members, namely:- (a) a full-time chairman, being a person having special knowledge or practical experience in respect of 3[matters relating to environmental protection] or a person having knowledge and experience in administering institutions dealing with the matters aforesaid, to be nominated by the Central Government; (b) two officials to be nominated by the Central Government from the participating Union territory or each of the participating union territories, as the case may be, and two officials to be nominated, from the participating State or each of the participating States, as the case may be by the concerned participating State Government; (c) one person to be nominated by the Central Government from amongst the members of the local authorities functioning within the participating Union territory or each of the participating Union territories, as the case may be and one person to be nominated, from amongst the members of the local authorities functioning within the participating State or each of the participating States, as the case may be, by the concerned participating State Government; (d) one non-official to be nominated by the Central Government and one person to be nominated by the participating State Government or State Governments to represent the interests of agriculture, fishery or industry or trade in the Union territory or in each of the Union territories or the State or in each of the States, as the case may be, or any other interest which in the opinion in the Central Government or, as the case may be, of the State Government is to be represented. (e) two persons to be nominated by the Central Government to represent the companies or corporations owned, controlled or managed by the Central Government and situate in the participating Union territory or territories and two persons to be nominated by Central Government to represent the companies or corporations owned, controlled or managed by the participating State Government; 4[(f) a full-time member-secretary, possessing qualifications, knowledge and experience of scientific, engineering or management aspects of pollution control, to be appointed by the Central Government.] (3) When a Joint Board is constituted in pursuance of an agreement under clause (b) of sub-section (1) of section 13, the provisions of sub-section (4) of section 4 shall cease to apply in relation to the Union territory for which the Joint Board is constituted. (4) Subject to the provisions of sub-section (3), the provisions of sub-section (3) of section 4 and sections 5 to 12 (inclusive) shall apply in relation tot he Joint Board and its member-secretary as they apply in relation to a State Board and its member-secretary. (5) Any reference in this Act to the State Board shall, unless the context otherwise requires, be construed as including a Joint Board.

Special Provision

Notwithstanding anything contained in this Act where any Joint Board is constituted under section 13 --

- The Government of the State for which the Joint Board is constituted shall be competent to give any direction under this Act only in cases where such direction relates to a matter within the exclusive territorial jurisdiction of the State;
- The Central Government alone shall be competent to give any direction under this Act where such direction relates to a matter within the territorial jurisdiction of two or more States or pertaining to a Union territory.

POWERS AND FUNCTIONS OF BOARDS

Functions of Central Board

(1) Subject to the provisions of this Act, the main function of the Central Board shall be to promote cleanliness of streams and wells in different areas of the States. (2) In particular and without prejudice to the generality of the foregoing function, the Central Board may perform all or any of the following functions, namely:-- (a) advise the Central Government on any matter concerning the prevention and control of water

pollution; (b) co-ordinate the activities of the State Boards and resolve disputes among them; (c) provide technical assistance and guidance to the State Boards, carry out and sponsor investigations and research relating to problems of water pollution and prevention, control or abatement of water pollution; (d) plan and organise the training of persons engaged or to be engaged in programs for the prevention, control or abatement of water pollution on such terms and conditions as the Central Board may specify; (e) organise through mass media a comprehensive programme regarding the prevention and control of water pollution; 1[(ee) perform such of the functions of any State Board as may be specified in an order made under sub-section (2) of section 18]; (f) collect, compile and publish technical and statistical data relating to water pollution and the measures devised for its effective prevention and control and prepare manuals, codes or guides relating to treatment and disposal of sewage and trade effluents and disseminate information connected therewith; (g) lay down, modify or annul, in consultation with the State Government concerned, the standards for a stream or well: Provided that different standards may be laid down for the same stream or well or for different streams or wells, having regard to the quality of water, flow characteristics of the stream or well and the nature of the use of the water in such stream or well or streams or wells; (h) plan and cause to be executed a nation-wide programme for the prevention, control or abatement of water pollution; (i) perform such other functions as may be prescribed. (3) The Board may establish or recognise a laboratory or laboratories to enable the Board to perform its functions under this section fficiently, including the analysis of samples of water from any stream or well or of samples of any sewage or trade effluents.

Functions of State Board

- Subject to the provisions of this Act, the functions of a State Board shall be
  - To plan a comprehensive programme for the prevention, control or abatement of pollution of

streams and wells in the State and to secure the execution thereof;

- To advise the State Government on any matter concerning the prevention, control or abatement of water pollution;
- To collect and disseminate information relating to water pollution and the prevention, control or abatement thereof;
- To encourage, conduct and participate in investigations and research relating to problems of water pollution and prevention, control or abatement of water pollution;
- To collaborate with the Central Board in organising the training of persons engaged or to be engaged in programmes relating to prevention, control or abatement of water pollution and to organise mass education programmes relating thereto;
- To inspect sewage or trade effluents, works and plants for the treatment or sewage and trade effluents and to review plans, specifications or other data relating to plants set up for the treatment of water, works for the purification thereof and the system for the disposal of sewage or trade effluents or in connection with the grant of any consent as required by this Act;
- Lay down, modify or annul effluent standards for the sewage and trade effluents and for the quality of receiving waters (not being water in an inter-State stream) resulting from the discharge of effluents and to classify waters of the State;
- To evolve economical and reliable methods of treatment of sewage and trade effluents, having regard to the peculiar conditions of soils, climate and water resources of different regions and more specially the prevailing flow characteristics of water in streams and wells which render it

impossible to attain even the minimum degree of dilution;

- To evolve methods of utilisation of sewage and suitable trade effluents in agriculture;
- To evolve efficient methods of disposal of sewage and trade effluents on land, as are necessary on account of the predominant conditions of scant stream flows that do not provide for major part of the year the minimum degree of dilution;
- To lay down standards of treatment of sewage and trade effluents to be discharged into any particular stream taking into account the minimum fair weather dilution available in that stream and the tolerance limits of pollution permissible in the water of the stream, after the discharge of such effluents;
- To make, vary or revoke any order --
  - For the prevention, control or abatement of discharge of waste into streams or wells;
  - Requiring any person concerned to construct new systems for the disposal of sewage and trade effluents or to modify, alter or extend any such existing system or to adopt such remedial measures as are necessary to prevent control or abate water pollution;
- To lay down effluent standards to be complied with by persons while causing discharge of sewage or sullage or both and to lay down, modify or annul effluent standards for the sewage and trade effluents;
- To advice the State Government with respect to the location of any industry the carrying on of which is likely to pollute a stream or well;
- To perform such other functions as may be prescribed or as may, from time to time be entrusted to it by the Central Board or the State Government.

• The Board may establish or recognise a laboratory

or laboratories to enable the Board to perform its functions under this section efficiently, including the analysis of samples of water from any stream or well or of samples of any sewage or trade effluents.

POWERS TO GIVE DIRECTIONS

2[1)] In the performance of its functions under this Act -- (a) the Central Board shall be bound by such directions in writing the Central Government may give to it; and (b) every State Board shall be bound by such directions in writing as the Central Government or the State Government may give to it: Provided that where a direction given by the State Government is inconsistent with the direction given by the Central Board, the matter shall be referred to the Central Government for its decision. 3[(2) Where the Central Government is of the opinion that and State Board has defaulted in complying with any directions given by the Central Government under sub-section (1) and as a result of such default a grave emergency has arisen and it is necessary or expedient so to do in the public interest, it may, by order, direct the Central Board to perform any of the functions of the State Board in relation to such area for such period and for such purposes, as may be specified in the order. (3) Where the Central Board performs any of the functions of the State Board in pursuance of a direction under sub-section (2), the expenses, if any, incurred by the Central Board with respect to performance of such functions may, if the State Board is empowered to recover such expenses, be recovered by the Central Board with interest (at such reasonable rate as the Central Government may, by order, fix) from the date when a demand for such expenses is made until it is paid from the person or persons concerned as arrears of land revenue or of public demand. (4) For the removal of doubts, it is hereby declared that any directions to perform the functions of any State Board given under sub-section (2) in respect of any area would not preclude the State Board from performing such functions in any other area in the State or any of its other functions in that area.

PREVENTION AND CONTROL OF WATER POLLUTION

Power of State Government to Restrict the Application of the Act to Certain Areas:

(1) Notwithstanding contained in this Act, if the State Government, after consultation with, or on the recommendation of, the State Board, is of opinion that the provisions of this Act need not apply to the entire State, it may, by notification in the Official Gazette, restrict the application of this Act to such area or areas as may be declared therein as water pollution, prevention and control area or areas and thereupon the provisions of this Act shall apply only to such area or areas. (2) Each water pollution, prevention and control area may be declared either by reference to a map or by reference to the line of any watershed or the boundary of any district or partly by one method and partly by another. (3) The State Government may, by notification in the Official Gazette- (a) alter any water pollution prevention and control area whether by way of extension or reduction; or (b) define a new water pollution, prevention and control area in which may be merged one or more water pollution, prevention and control areas, or any part or parts thereof.

POWER TO OBTAIN INFORMATION

(1) For the purpose of enabling a State Board to perform the function conferred on it by or under this Act, the State Board or any officer empowered by it in that behalf, may make surveys of any area and gauge and keep records of the flow or volume and other characteristics of an stream or well in such area, and may take steps for the measurement and recording of the rainfall in such area or any part thereof and for the installation and maintenance for those purposes of gauges or other apparatus and works connected therewith, and carry out stream surveys and may take such other steps as may be necessary in order to obtain any information required for the purposes aforesaid. (2) A State Board may give directions requiring any person who in its opinion is abstracting water from any such stream or well in the area in quantities which

are substantial in relation to the flow or volume of that stream or well or is discharging sewage or trade effluent into any such stream or well, to give such information as to the abstraction or the discharge at such times and in such form as may be specified in the directions. (3) Without prejudice to the provisions of sub-section (2), a State Board may, with a view to preventing or controlling pollution of water, give directions requiring any person in charge of any establishment where any 1[industry, operation or process, or treatment and disposal system is carried on, to furnish to it information regarding the construction, installation or operation of such establishment or of any disposal system or of any extension or addition thereto in such establishment and such other particulars as may be prescribed.

Samples of Effluents and Procedure

(1) A State Board or any officer empowered by it in this behalf shall have power to take for the purpose of analysis samples of water from any stream or well or samples of any sewage of trade effluent which is passing from any plant or vessel or from or over any place into any such stream or well. (2) The result of any analysis of a sample of any sewage or trade effluent taken under sub-section (1) shall not be admissible in evidence in an legal proceeding unless the provisions of sub-sections (3), (4) and (5) are complied with. (3) Subject to the provisions of sub-sections (4) and (5), when a sample (composite or otherwise as may be warranted by the process used) of any sewage or trade effluent is taken for analysis under sub-section (1), the person taking the sample shall -- (a) serve on the person in charge of, or having control over, the plant or vessel or in occupation of the place (which person is hereinafter referred to as the occupier) or any agent of such occupier, a notice, then and there in such form as may be prescribed of his intention to have it so analysed; (b) in the presence of the occupier or his agent, divided the sample into two parts; (c) cause each part to be placed in a container which shall be marked and sealed and shall also be signed both by the person taking the sample and the occupier or his agent;

(d) send one container forthwith,-- (i) in a case where such sample is taken from any area situated in a Union territory, to the laboratory established or recognised by the Central Board under section; and (ii) in any other case, to the laboratory established or recognised by the State Board under section 17; (e) on the request of the occupier or his agent, send the second container -- (i) in a case where such sample is taken from any area situated in a Union territory, to the laboratory established or specified under sub-section (1) of section 51; and (ii) in an other case, to the laboratory established or specified under sub-section (1) of section 52. 2[(4) When a sample of any sewage of trade effluent is taken for analysis under sub-section (1) and the person taking the sample serves on the occupier or his agent, a notice under clause (a) of sub-section (3) and the occupier or his agent wilfully absents himself, then -- (a) the sample so taken shall be placed in a container which shall be marked and sealed and shall also be signed by the person taking the sample and the same shall be sent forthwith by such person for analysis to the laboratory referred to in sub-clause (i) or sub-clause (ii), as the case may be, of clause (e) of sub-section (3) and such person shall inform the Government analyst appointed under sub-section (1) or sub-section (2), as the case may be, of section 53, in writing about the wilful absence of the occupier or his agent; and (b) the cost incurred in getting such sample analysed shall be payable by the occupier or his agent and in case of default of such payment, the same shall be recoverable from the occupier or his agent, as the case may be, as an arrear of land revenue or of public demand: Provided that no such recovery shall be made unless the occupier or, as the case may be, his agent has been given a reasonable opportunity of being heard in the matter. (5) When a sample of any sewage or trade effluent is taken for analysis under sub-section (1) and the person taking the sample serves on the occupier or his agent a notice under clause (a) of sub-section (3) and the occupier or his agent who is present at the time of taking the sample does not make a request for dividing the sample into two parts as provided in clause (b) of sub-section (3), then, the sample so taken shall be placed in a container which shall be marked and sealed and shall also be signed by the person taking the sample and the same shall be sent forthwith by such person for analysis to the laboratory referred to in sub-clause (i) or sub-clause (ii), as the case may be, of clause (d) of sub-section (3).

REPORTS OF RESULTS

(1) Where a sample of any sewage or trade effluent has been sent for analysis to the laboratory established or recognised by the Central Board or, as the case may be, the State Board, the concerned Board analyst appointed under sub-section (3) of section 53 shall analyse the sample and submit a report in the prescribed form of the result of such analysis in triplicate to the Central Board or the State Board, as the case may be. (2) On receipt of the report under sub-section (1), one copy of the report shall be sent by the Central Board or the State Board, as the case may be, to the occupier or his agent referred to in section 21, another copy shall be preserved for production before the court in case any legal proceedings are taken against him and the other copy shall be kept by the concerned Board. (3) Where a sample has been sent for analysis under clause (e) of sub-section (3) or sub-section (4) of section 21 to any laboratory mentioned therein, the Government analyst referred to in that sub-section shall analyse the sample and submit a report in the prescribed form of the result of the analysis in triplicate to the Central Board or, as the case may be, the State Board which shall comply with the provisions of sub-section (2). (4) If there is any inconsistency or discrepancy between, or variation in the results of, the analysis carried out by the laboratory established or recognised by the Central Board or the State Board, as the case may be, and that of the laboratory established or specified under section 51 or section 52, as the case may be, the report of the latter shall prevail. (5) Any cost incurred in getting any sample analysed at the request of the occupier or his agent shall be payable by such occupier or his agent and in case of default the same shall be recoverable from him as arrears of land revenue or of public demand.

Power of Entry and Inspection

- Subject to the provisions of this section, any person empowered by a State Board in this behalf shall have a right at any time to enter, with such assistance as he considers necessary, any place--
  - For the purpose of performing any of the functions of the Board entrusted to him;
  - For the purpose of determining whether and if so in what manner, any such functions are to be performed or whether any provisions of this Act or the rules made thereunder of an notice, order, direction or authorisation served, made, given, or granted under this Act is being or has been complied with;
  - For the purpose of examining any plant, record, register, document or any other material object or for conducting a search of any place in which he has reason to believe that an offence under this Act or the rules made thereunder has been or is being or is about to be committed and for seizing any such plant, record, register, document or other material object, if he has reason to believe that it may furnish evidence of the commission of an offence punishable under this Act or the rules made thereunder: Provided that the right to enter under this sub-section for the inspection of a well shall be exercised only at reasonable hours in a case where such well is situated in any premises used for residential purposes and the water thereof is used exclusively for domestic purposes.
- The provisions of 3[the Code of Criminal Procedure, 1973, or, in relation to the State of Jammu and Kashmir, the provisions of any corresponding law in force in that State, shall, so far as may be, apply to an search or seizure under this section as they apply to any search or seizure made under the authority of a warrant issued under 4[section 94] of

the said Code, or, as the case may be, under the corresponding provisions of the said law.

Prohibition on Use of Stream or Well

(1) Subject to the provisions of this section -- (a) no person shall knowingly cause or permit any poisonous, noxious or polluting matter determined in accordance with such standards as may be laid down by the State Board to enter (whether directly or indirectly) into any 5[stream or well or sewer or on land]; or (b) no person shall knowingly cause or permit to enter into any stream any other matter which may tend, either directly or in combination with similar matters, to impede the proper flow of the water of the stream in a manner leading or likely to lead to a substantial aggravation of pollution due to other causes or of its consequences. (2) A person shall not be guilty of an offence under sub-section (1), by reason only of having done any of the following acts, namely;-- (a) constructing, improving a maintaining in or across or on the bank or bed of any stream any building, bridge, weir, dam, sluice, dock, pier, drain or sewer or other permanent works which he has a right to construct, improve or maintain; (b) depositing any materials on the bank or in the bed of any stream for the purpose of reclaiming land or for supporting, repairing or protecting the bank or bed of such stream provided such materials are not capable of polluting such stream; (c) putting into an stream any sand or gravel or other natural deposit which has flowed from or been deposited by the current of such stream; (d) causing or permitting, with the consent of the State Board, the deposit accumulated in a well, pond or reservoir to enter into any stream. (3) The State Government may, after consultation with, or on the recommendation of, the State Board, exempt, by notification in the Official Gazette, any person from the operation of sub-section (1) subject to such conditions, if any, as may be specified in the notification and any conditions so specified may by a like notification and be altered, varied or amended.

Restrictions on New Outlets and New Discharges

6[(1) Subject to the provisions of this section, no person

shall, without the previous consent of the State Board,-- (a) establish or take any steps to establish any industry, operation or process, or any treatment and disposal system or an extension or addition thereto, which is likely to discharge sewage or trade effluent into a stream or well or sewer or on land (such discharge being hereafter in this section referred to as discharge of sewage); or (b) bring into use any new or altered outlets for the discharge of sewage; or (c) begin to make any new discharge of sewage; Provided that a person in the process of taking any steps to establish any industry, operation or process immediately before the commencement of the Water (Prevention and Control of Pollution) Amendment Act, 1988, for which no consent was necessary prior to such commencement or, if he has made an application for such consent, within the said period of three months, till the disposal of such application. (2) An application for consent of the State Board under sub-section (1) shall be made in such form, contain such particulars and shall be accompanied by such fees as may be prescribed. (3) The State Board may make such inquiry as it may deem fit in respect of the application for consent referred to in sub-section (1) and in making any such inquiry shall follow such procedure as may be prescribed.

7[(4) The State Board may-- (a) grant its consent referred to in sub-section (1), subject to such conditions as it may impose, being-- (i) in cases referred to in clauses (a) and (b) of sub-section (1) of section 25, conditions as to the point of discharge of sewage or as to the use of that outlet or any other outlet for discharge of sewage; (ii) in the case of a new discharge, conditions as to the nature and composition, temperature, volume or rate of discharge of the effluent from the land or premises from which the discharge or new discharge is to be made; and(iii) that the consent will be valid only for such period as may be specified in the order, and any such conditions imposed shall be binding on any person establishing or taking any steps to establish any industry, operation or process, or treatment and disposal system or extension or addition thereto, or using the new or altered outlet, or discharging the effluent from the land or premises aforesaid; or (b) refuse such consent for reasons to be recorded in writing. (5) Where, without the consent of the State Board, any industry operation or process, or any treatment and disposal system or any extension or addition thereto, is established, or any steps for such establishment have been taken or a new or altered outlet is brought into use for the discharge of sewage or a new discharge of sewage is made, the State Board may serve on the person who has established or taken steps to establish any industry, operation or process, or any treatment and disposal system or any extension or addition thereto, or using the outlet, or making the discharge, as the case may be, a notice imposing any such conditions as it might have imposed on an application for its consent in respect of such establishment, such outlet or discharge. (6) Every State Board shall maintain a register containing particulars or conditions imposed under this section and so much of the register as relates to any outlet, or to any effluent, from any land or premises shall be open to inspection at all reasonable hours by any person interested in, or affected by such outlet, land or premises, as the case may be, or by any person authorised by him in this behalf and the conditions so contained in such register shall be conclusive proof that the consent was granted subject such conditions] (7) The consent referred to in sub-section (1) shall, unless given or refused earlier, be deemed to have been given unconditionally on the expiry of a period of four months of the making of an application in this behalf complete in all respects to the State Board. (8) For the purposes of this section and sections 27 and 30 -(a) the expression "new or altered outlet" means any outlet which is wholly or partly constructed on or after the commencement of this Act or which (whether so constructed or not) is substantially altered after such commencement; (b) the expression "new discharge" means a discharge which is not, as respects the nature and composition, temperature, volume, and rate of discharge of the effluent substantially a continuation of a discharge made within the preceding twelve months (whether by the same or different outlet), so however that a discharge which is in other respects a continuation of previous discharge made as aforesaid shall not be deemed to be a new discharge by reason of any reduction of the temperature or volume or rate of discharge of the effluent as compared with the previous discharge.

Provision of Sewage or Trade Effluent

Where immediately before the commencement of this Act any person was discharging any sewage or trade effluent into a 8[stream or well or sewer or on land], the provisions of section 25 shall, so far as may be, apply in relation to such person as they apply in relation to the person referred to in that section subject to the modification that the application for consent to be made under sub-section (2) of that section 9[shall be made on or before such date as may be specified by the State Government by notification in this behalf in the Official Gazette.

Refusal or Withdrawal

10[(1) A State Board shall not grant its consent under sub-section (4) of section 25 for the establishment of any industry, operation or process, or treatment and disposal system or extension or addition thereto, or to the bringing into use of a new or altered outlet unless the industry, operation or process, or treatment and disposal system or extension or addition thereto, or the outlet is so established as to comply with an conditions imposed by the Board to enable it to exercise its right to take samples of the effluent. 11[(2) A State Board may from time to time review -- 12[(a) any condition imposed under section 25 or section 26 and may serve on the person to whom a consent under section 25 or section 26 is granted a notice making any reasonable variation of or revoking any such condition. (b) the refusal of any consent referred to in sub-section (1) of section 25 or section 26 or the grant of such consent without any condition, and may make such orders as it deemed fit] (3) Any conditions imposed under section 25 or section 26 shall be subject to any variation made under sub-section (2) and shall continue in force until revoked under that sub-section.

Appeals

(1) Any person aggrieved by an order made by the State

Board under Section 25, section 26 or section 27 may within thirty days from the date on which the order is communicated to him, prefer an appeal to such authority (hereinafter referred to as the appellate authority) as the State Government may think fit to constitute:

Provided that the appellate authority may entertain the appeal after the expiry of the said period of thirty days if such authority is satisfied that the appellant was prevented by sufficient cause from filing the appeal in time. 13[(2) An appellate authority shall consist of a single person or three persons as the State Government may think fit, to be appointed by that Government. (3) The form and manner in which an appeal may be preferred under sub-section (1), the fees payable for such appeal and the procedure to be followed by the appellate authority shall be such as may be prescribed. (4) On receipt of an appeal preferred under sub-section (1), the appellate authority shall, after giving the appellant and the State Board an opportunity of being heard, dispose of the appeal as expeditiously as possible. (5) If the appellate authority determines that any condition imposed, or the variation of any condition, as the case may be, was unreasonable, then,-- (a) where the appeal is in respect of the unreasonableness of any condition imposed, such authority may direct either that the condition shall be treated as annulled or that there shall be substituted for it such condition as appears to it to be reasonable; (b) where the appeal is in respect of the unreasonableness of any variation of a condition, such authority may direct either that the condition shall be treated as continuing in force unvaried or that it shall be varied in such manner as appears to it to be reasonable.

Revision

- The State Government may at any time either of its own motion or on an application made to it in this behalf, call for the records of any case where an order has been made by the State Board under section 25, section 26 or section 27 for the purpose of satisfying itself as to the legality or propriety of any such order and may pass such order in relation thereto as it may think fit: Provided that the State Government shall not pass any order under this sub-section without affording the State Board and the person who may be affected by such order a reasonable opportunity of being heard in the matter.

- The State Government shall not revise any order made under section 25, section 26 or section 27 where an appeal against that order lies to the appellate authority, but has not been preferred or where an appeal has been preferred such appeal is pending before the appellate authority.

Power of State Board

(1) Where under this Act, any conditions have been imposed on any person while granting consent under section 25 or section 26 and such conditions require such person to execute any work in connection therewith and such work has not been executed within such time as may be specified in this behalf, the State Board may serve on the person concerned a notice requiring him within such time (not being less than thirty days) as may be specified in the notice to execute the work specified therein] (2) If the person concerned fails to execute the work as required in the notice referred to in sub-section (1), then, after the expiration of the time specified in the said notice, the State Board may itself execute or cause to be executed such work. (3) All expenses incurred by the State Board for the execution of the aforesaid work, together with interest, at such rate as the State Government may, by order, fix, from the date when a demand for the expenses is made until it is paid, may be recovered by that Board from the person concerned, as arrears of land revenue, or of public demand.

Furnishing of Information to State Board and Other Agencies in Certain Cases

15[(1) If at any place where any industry, operation or process, or any treatment and disposal system or any extension or addition thereto is being carried on, due to accident or other unforeseen act or event, any poisonous, noxious or polluting matter is being discharged, or is likely to be discharged into a stream or well or sewer or on land and, as a result of such discharge, the water in any stream or well is being polluted, or is likely to be polluted, then the person incharge of such place shall forthwith intimate the occurrence of such accident, act or event to the State Board and such other authorities or agencies as may be prescribed] (2) Where any local authority operates any sewerage system or sewage works the provisions of sub-section (1) shall apply to such local authority as they apply in relation to the person in charge of the place where an industry or trade is being carried on.

Emergency Measures

(1) Where it appears to the State Board that any poisonous, noxious or polluting matter is present in 16[any stream or well or on land by reason of the discharge of such matter in such stream or well or on such land or has entered into that stream or well due to any accident or other unforeseen act or event, and if the Board is of opinion that it is necessary or expedient to take immediate action, it may for reasons to be recorded in writing, carry out such operations as it may consider necessary for all or any of the following purposes, that is to say --

- Removing that matter from the 17[stream or well or on land and disposing it of in such manner as the Board considers appropriate;
- Remedying or mitigating any pollution caused by its presence in the stream or well;
- Issuing orders immediately restraining or prohibiting the persons concerned from discharging any poisonous, noxious or polluting matter 18[into the steam or well or on land] or from making insanitary use of the stream or well.

(2) The power conferred by sub-section (I) does not include the power to construct any works other than works of a temporary character which are removed on or before the completion of the operations. Power of board to make application to courts for restraining apprehended pollution of

water in streams of wells. 19[(1) Where it is apprehended by a Board that the water in any stream or well is likely to be polluted by reason of the disposal or likely disposal of any matter in such stream or well or in any sewer, or on any land, or otherwise, the Board may make an application to a court, not inferior to that of a Metropolitan Magistrate or a Judicial Magistrate of the first class, for restraining the person who is likely to cause such pollution from so causing.] (2) On receipt of an application under sub-section (I) the court make such order as it deems fit. (3) Where under sub-section (2) the court makes an order restraining any person from polluting the water in any stream or well, it may in that order- (i) direct the person who is likely to cause or has caused the pollution of the water in the stream or well, to desist from taking such action as is likely to cause pollution or, as the case may be, to remove such stream or well. (ii) authorise the Board, if the direction under clause (i) (being a direction for the removal of any matter from such stream or well) is not complied with by the person to whom such direction is issued, to undertake the removal and disposal of the matter in such manner as may be specified by the court. (4) All expenses incurred by the Board in removing any matter in pursuance of the authorisation under clause (ii) of sub-section (3) or in the disposal of any such matter may be defrayed out of any money obtained by the Board from such disposal and any balance outstanding shall be recoverable from the person concerned as arrears of land revenue or of public demand.

Power to Give Directions

Notwithstanding anything contained in any other law, but subject to the provisions of this Act, and to any directions that the Central Government may give in this behalf, a Board may, in the exercise of its powers and performance of its functions under this Act, issue any directions in writing to any person, officer or authority, and such person, officer or authority shall be bound to comply with such directions. Explanation.-For the avoidance of doubts, it is hereby declared that the power to issue directions under this section includes the power to direct-

(a) the closure, prohibition or regulation of any industry, operation or process; or (b) the stoppage or regulation of supply of electricity, water or any other service.]

FUNDS, ACCOUNTS AND AUDIT

Contributions by Central Government

The Central Government may, after due appropriation made by Parliament by law in this behalf, make in each financial year such contribution to the Central Board as it may think necessary to enable the Board to perform its functions under this Act.

Contributions by State Government

The State Government may, after due appropriation made by the Legislature of the State by law in this behalf, make in each financial year such contributions to the State Board as it may think necessary to enable that Board to perform its functions under this Act.

Fund of Central Board

- The Central Board shall have its own fund, and all sums which may, from time to time, be paid to it by the Central Government and all other receipts (by way of gifts, grants, donations, benefactions 1[fees] or (otherwise) of that Board shall be carried to the fund of the Board and all payments by the Board shall be made therefrom.
- The Central Board may expend such sums as it thinks fit for performing its functions under this Act, 1[and, where any law for the time being in force relating to the prevention, control of abatement or air pollution provides for the performance of any function under such law by the Central Board, also for performing its functions under such [law] and such sums shall be treated as expenditure payable out of the funds of that Board.

Fund of State Board

- The State Board shall have its own fund, and the

sums which may, from time to time, be paid to it by the State Government and all other receipts (by way of gifts, grants, donations, benefactions 2[fees] or (otherwise) of that Board shall be carried to the fund of the Board and all payments by the Board shall be made therefrom.

- The State Board may expend such sums as it thinks fit for performing its functions under this Act, 2[and, where any law for the time being in force relating to the prevention, control or abatement of air pollution provides for the performance of any function under such law by the State Board, also for performing its functions under such law] and such sums shall be treated as expenditure payable out of the fund of that Board.

Borrowing Powers of Board

A Board may, with the consent of, or in accordance with, the terms of any general or special authority given to it by the Central Government or, as the case may be, the State Government, borrow money from any source by way of loans or issue of bonds, debentures or such other instruments, as it may deem fit, for the performance of all or any of its functions under this Act].

Budget

The Central Board or, as the case may be, the State Board shall, during each financial year, prepare, in such form and at such time as may be prescribed, a budget in respect of the financial year next ensuing showing the estimated receipt and expenditure, and copies thereof shall be forwarded to the Central Government, or as the case may be, the State Government.

Annual Report

(1) The Central Board shall, during each financial year, prepare, in such form as may be prescribed, an annual report giving full account of its activities under this Act during the

previous financial year and copies thereof shall be forwarded to the Central Government within four months from the last date of the previous financial year and that Government shall cause every such report to be laid before both Houses of Parliament within nine months from the last date of the previous financial year. (2) Every State Board shall, during each financial year, prepare, in such form as may be prescribed, an annual report giving full account of its activities under this Act during the previous financial ear and copies thereof shall be forwarded to the State Government within four months from the last date of the previous financial year and that Government shall cause every such report to be laid before the State legislature within a period of nine months from the last date of the previous financial year]

Account and Audit

(1) Every Board shall maintain proper accounts and other relevant records and prepare an annual statement of accounts in such form as may be prescribed by the Central Government or, as the case may be, the State Government. (2) 1 of 1956. The accounts of the Board shall be audited by an auditor duly qualified to act as an auditor of companies under section 226 of the Companies Act, 1956. (3) The said auditor shall be appointed by the Central Government or, as the case may be, the State Government on the advice of the Comptroller and Auditor-General of India. (4) Every auditor appointed to audit the accounts of the Board under this Act shall have the right to demand the production of books, accounts, connected vouchers and other documents and papers and to inspect any of the offices of the Board. (5) Every such auditor shall send a copy of his report together with an audited copy of the accounts to the Central Government or, as the case may be, the State Government. (6) The Central Government shall, as soon as may be after the receipt of the audit report under sub-section (5), cause the same to be laid before both Houses of Parliament. (7) The State Government shall, as soon as may be after the receipt of the audit report under sub-section (5), cause the same to be laid before the State Legislature.

PENALTIES AND PROCEDURE

Failure to comply with directions under sub-section (2) or sub-section (3) of section of 20, or orders issued under clause (c) of sub-section (1) of 32 or directions issued under sub-section (2) of section 33 or section 33A. (1) Whoever fails to comply with any direction given under sub-section (2) or sub-section (3) of section 20 within such time as may be specified in the direction shall, or conviction, be punishable with imprisonment for a term which may extend to three months or with fine which may extend to ten thousand rupees or with both and in case the failure continues, with an additional fine which may extend to five thousand rupees for every day during which such failure continues after the conviction for the first such failure. (2) Whoever fails to comply with any order issued under clause (c) of sub-section (1) of section 32 or any direction issued by a court under sub-section (2) of section 33 or any direction issued under section 33A shall, in respect of each such failure and on conviction, be punishable with imprisonment for a term which shall not be less than one year and six months but which may extend to six years and with fine, and case the failure continues, with an additional fine which may extend to five thousand rupees for every day during which such failure continues after the conviction for the first such failure. (3) If the failure referred to in sub-section (2) continues beyond a period of one year after the date of conviction, the offender shall, on conviction, be punishable with imprisonment for a term which shall not be less than two years but which may extend to seven years and with fine]

Penalty for Certain Acts

(1) Whoever -- (a) destroys, pulls down, removes, injures or defaces any pillar, post or stake fixed in the ground or any notice or other matter put up, inscribed or placed, by or under the authority of the Board, or (b) obstructs any person acting under the orders or directions of the Board from exercising his powers and performing his functions under this Act, or (c) damages any works or property belonging to the Board, or (d) fails to furnish to any officer or other employees of the

Board any information required by him for the purpose of this Act, or (e) fails to intimate the occurrence of an accident or other unforeseen act or even under section 31 to the Board and other authorities or agencies as required by that section, or (f) in giving any information which he is required to give under this Act, knowingly or wilfully makes a statement which is false in any material particular, or (g) for the purpose of obtaining any consent under section 25 or section 26, knowingly or willfully makes a statement which is false in any material particular shall be punishable with imprisonment for a term which may extend to three months or with fine which may extend to 2[ten thousand rupees or with both.] (2) Where for the grant of a consent in pursuance of the provisions of section 25 or section 26 the use of a meter or gauge or other measure or monitoring device is required and such device is used for the purposes of those provision, any person who knowingly or willfully alters or interferes with that device so as to prevent it from monitoring or measuring correctly shall be punishable with imprisonment for a term which may extend to three months or with fine which may extend to 2[ten thousand rupees] or with both.

Penalty for Contravention

Whoever contravenes the provisions of section 24 shall be punishable with imprisonment for a term which shall not be less than 3[one year and six months] but which may extend to six years and with fine.

Penalty for Section 25 or Section 26

Whoever contravenes the provision of section 25 or section 26 shall be punishable with imprisonment for a term which shall not be less than 4[two years] but which may extend to six years and with fine.

Enhanced Penalty After Previous Conviction

If any person who has been convicted of any offence under section 24 or 25 or section 26 is again found guilty of an offence involving a contravention of the same provision, he shall, on the second and on every subsequent conviction, be punishable with imprisonment for a term which shall not be less than 4[one and half years] but which may extend to seven years and with fine: Provided that for the purpose of this section no cognizance shall be taken of any conviction made more than two years before the commission of the offence which is being punished.

Penalty for Contravention of Certain Provisions of the Act

5[Whoever contravenes any of the provisions of this Act or fails to comply with any order or direction given under this Act, for which no penalty has been elsewhere provided in this Act, shall be punishable with imprisonment which may extend to three months or with fine which may extend to ten thousand rupees or with both and in the case of a continuing contravention or failure, with an additional fine which may extend to five thousand rupees for every day during which such contravention or failure continues after conviction for the first such contravention or failure

Publication of Names of Offenders

If any person convicted of an offence under this Act commits a like offence afterwards it shall be lawful for the court before which the second or subsequent conviction takes place to cause the offender's name and place of residence, the offence and the penalty imposed to be published at the offender's expense in such newspapers or in such other manner as the court may direct and the expenses of such publication shall be deemed to be part of the cost attending the conviction and shall be recoverable in the same manner as a fine.

Offences by Companies

1) Where an offence under this Act has been committed by a company, every person who at the time the offence was committed was in charge of, and was responsible to the company for the conduct of, the business of the company, as well as the company, shall be deemed to the guilty of the

offence and shall be liable to be proceeded against and punished accordingly: Provided that nothing contained in this sub-section shall render any such person liable to any punishment provided in this Act if he proves that the offence was committed without his knowledge for that he exercised all due diligence to prevent the commission of such offence. (2) Notwithstanding anything contained in sub-section (1), where an offence under this Act has been committed by a company and it is proved that the offence has been committed with the consent or connivance of, or is attributable to any neglect on the part of, any director, manager, secretary or other officer of the company, such director, manager, secretary or other officer shall also be deemed to be guilty of that offence and shall be liable to be proceeded against and punished accordingly.

Explanation: For the purpose of this section,

- Company" means any body corporate, and includes a firm or other association of individuals; and
- "Director" in relation to a firm means a partner in the firm.

Offences by Government Departments

Where an offence under this Act has been committed by any Department of Government, the Head of the Department shall be deemed to be guilty of the offence and shall be liable to be proceeded against and punished accordingly: Provided that nothing contained in this section shall render such Head of the Department liable to any punishment if he proves that the offence was committed without his knowledge or that he exercised all due diligence to prevent the commission of such offence.

Cognizance of Offences

(1) No court shall take cognizance of any offence under this Act except on a complaint made by-- (a) a Board or any officer authorised in this behalf by it; (b) any person who has given notice of not less than sixty days, in the manner prescribed, of the alleged offence and of his intention to make a complaint, to the Board or officer authorised as aforesaid,

and no court inferior to that of a Metropolitan Magistrate or a Judicial Magistrate of the first class shall try any offence punishable under this Act] 7[(2) Where a complaint has been made under clause (b) of sub-section (1), the Board shall, on demand by such person, make available the relevant reports in its possession to that person: Provided that the Board may refuse to make any such report available to such person if the same is, in its opinion, against the public interest 8[(3) 2 of 1974. Notwithstanding anything contained in section 29 of the Code of Criminal Procedure, 1973"], it shall be lawful for any 9[Judicial Magistrate of the first class or for any Metropolitan Magistrate"] to pass a sentence of imprisonment for a term exceeding two years or of fine exceeding two thousand rupees on any person convicted of an offence punishable under this Act.

Members, Officers and Servants of Board to be Public Servants

All members, officers and servants of a Board when acting or purporting to act in pursuance of any of the provisions of this Act (45 of 1860) and the rules made thereunder shall be deemed to be public servants within the meaning of section 21 of the Indian Penal Code.

MISCELLANEOUS

Central Water Laboratory

- The Central Government may, by notification in the Official Gazette --
  - Establish a Central Water Laboratory; or
  - Specify any laboratory or institute as a Central Water Laboratory, to carry out the functions entrusted to the Central Water Laboratory under this Act.
- The Central Government may, after consultation with the Central Board, make rules prescribing--
  - The functions of the Central Water Laboratory;
  - The procedure for the submission to the said laboratory of samples of water or of sewage or

trade effluent for analysis or tests, the form of the laboratory's report thereunder and the fees payable in respect of such report;
- Such other matters as may be necessary or expedient to enable that laboratory to carry out its functions.

State Water Laboratory

- The State Government may, by notification in the Official Gazette --
  - Establish a State Water Laboratory; or
  - Specify any State laboratory or institute as a State Water Laboratory, to carry out the functions entrusted to the State Water Laboratory under this Act.
- The State Government may, after consultation with the State Board, make rules prescribing --
  - The functions of the State Water Laboratory;
  - The procedure for the submission to the said laboratory of samples of water or of sewage or trade effluent for analysis or rests, the form of the laboratory's report thereon and the fees payable in respect of such report;
  - Such other matters as may be necessary or expedient to enable that laboratory to carry out its functions.

Analysts

(1) The Central Government may, by notification in the Official Gazette appoint such persons as it thinks fit and having the prescribed qualifications to be Government analysts for the purpose of analysis of samples of water or of sewage or trade effluent sent for analysis to any laboratory established or specified under sub-section (1) of section 51. (2) The State Government may, by notification in the Official Gazette, appoint such persons as it thinks fit and having the prescribed qualifications to be Government analysts for the purpose of analysis of water or of sewage or trade effluent sent for analysis

to any laboratory established or specified under sub-section (1) of section 52. (3) Without prejudice to the provisions of sub-section (3) of section 12, the Central Board or, as the case may be, the State Board may, by notification in the Official Gazette, and with the approval of the Central Government or the State Government, as the case may be, appoint such persons as it thinks fit and having the prescribed qualifications to be Board analysts for the purpose of analysis of samples of water or of sewage or trade effluent sent for analysis to any laboratory established or recognised under section 16, as the case may be, under section 17.

Reports of Analysts

Any document purporting to be report signed by a Government analyst or, as the case may be, a Board analyst may be used as evidence of the facts stated therein in any proceeding under this Act.

Local Authorities to Assist

All local authorities shall render such help and assistance and furnish such information to the Board as it may require for the discharge of its functions, and shall make available to the Board for inspection and examination such records, maps, plans and other documents as may be necessary for the discharge of its functions.

Compulsory Acquisition of Land for The State Board

Any land required by a State Board for the efficient performance of its function under this Act shall be deemed to be needed for a public purpose and such land shall be acquired for the State Board under the provisions of the Land Acquisition Act, 1894 (1 of 1984), or under any other corresponding law for the time being in force.

Returns and Reports

The Central Board shall furnish to the Central Government, and a State Board shall furnish to the State

Government and to the Central Board such reports, returns, statistics, accounts and other information with respect to its fund or activities as that government, or, as the case may be, the Central Board may, from time to time, require.

Bar of Jurisdiction

No civil court shall have jurisdiction to entertain any suit or proceeding in respect of any matter which an appellate authority constituted under this Act is empowered by or under this Act to determine, and no injunction shall be granted by any court or other authority in respect of any action taken or to be taken in pursuance of any power conferred by or under this Act.

Protection of Action Taken in Good Faith

No suit or other legal proceedings shall lie against the Government or any officer of Government or any member or officer of a Board in respect of anything which is in good faith done or intended to be done in pursuance of this Act or the rules made thereunder.

Overriding Effect

The provisions of this Act shall have effect notwithstanding anything inconsistent therewith contained in any enactment other than this Act.

Power of central government to supersede the central board and joint boards:

(1)If at any time the Central Government is of opinion -- (a) That the Central Board or any Joint Board has persistently made default in the performance of the functions imposed on it by or under this Act; or (b) That circumstances exist which render it necessary in the public interest so to do, the Central Government may, by notification in the Official Gazette, supersede the Central Board or such Joint Board, as the case may be, for such period not exceeding one year, as may be specified in the notification: Provided that before issuing a notification under this sub-section for the reasons mentioned in clause , the Central Government shall give a reasonable opportunity to the Central Board or such Joint Board, as the case may be, to show cause why it should not be superseded and shall consider the explanations and objections if any, of the Central Board or such Joint Board, as the case may be.

(2)Upon the publication of notification under sub-section (1) superseding the Central Board or any Joint Board, (a)All the members shall, as from the date of supersession vacate their offices as such; (b)All the powers, functions and duties which may, by or under this Act, be exercised, performed or discharged by the Central Board or such Joint Board, shall, until the Central Board or the Joint Board, as the case may be, is reconstituted under sub-section (3) be exercised, performed or discharged by such person or persons as the Central Government may direct; (c) All property owned or controlled by the Central Board or such Joint Board shall, until the Central Board or the Joint Board, as the case may be, is reconstituted under sub-section (3) vest in the Central Government. (3)On the expiration of the period of supersession specified in the notification issued under sub-section (1), the Central Government may -- (a) extend the period of supersession for such further term, not exceeding six months, as it may consider necessary; or (b) reconstitute the Central Board or the Joint Board, as the case may be, by fresh nomination or appointment, as the case may be, and in such case any person who vacated his office under clause (a) of sub-section (2) shall not be deemed disqualified for nomination or appointment: Provided that the Central Government may at any time before the expiration of the period of supersession, whether originally specified under sub-section (1) or as extended under this sub-section, take action under clause (b) of this sub-section.

Power of State Government to Supersede State Board

(1) If at any time the State Government is of opinion -- (a) that the State Board has persistently made default in the performance of the functions imposed on it by or under this Act; or (b) that circumstances exist which render it necessary in the public interest so to do, the State Government may, by

notification in the Official Gazette, supersede the State Board for such period, not exceeding one year, as may be specified in the notification: Provided that before issuing a notification under this sub-section for the reasons mentioned in clause (a), the State Government shall give a reasonable opportunity to the State Board to show cause why it should not be superseded and shall consider the explanations and objections, if any, of the State Board. (2) Upon the publication of a notification under sub-section (1) superseding the State Board, the provisions of sub-sections (2) and (3) of section 61 shall apply in relation to the supersession of the State Board as they apply in relation to the supersession of the Central Board or a Joint Board by the Central Government.

LEGAL LAWS IN INDIA

There was a time when environment was treated as a bottomless phenomenon. The quantity of consumers was simply trifling before the sheer magnitude of natural resources to be consumed. Management of natural resources such as forests or minerals was done by locals who made use of them. There was no profit motive behind exploiting environmental resources. There were no market forces driving the engines of mass production. Environment was local. It was managed by locals based on local indigenous knowledge. Time as well as modern science has proved that traditional local management of environment and natural resources is the best. Whether it be Indians of Brazil or Africans or Asians, they are the best caretakers of their resources because their knowledge of their environment is time tested. Market forces, profit motive, mass production and modern technology have damaged our natural environment to an alarming extent. Since our attention has been drawn to this damage, we must use modern techniques, modern communication and capital to preserve and improve our natural environment.

India is equipped with a solid brigade of legal provisions and policy documents designed to protect and improve the natural environment. Article 48(a) directs the State to take strong measures not only for its protection but also work actively for its improvement. Article 51(a) incurs a corresponding duty on the citizen to do the same. We have an Air (Prevention and Control of Pollution) Act and a similar Water Act. We have an Environmental Protection Act of 1986 amended from time to time to control hazardous pollutants. Each one of our nine five year plans contains a chapter on safeguarding the environment.

We have Forest Acts stretching from 1861 to 1988. We have State and Central boards for the prevention of pollution. Our Judiciary has been exceptionally active in allowing public interest litigations that have resulted in the State being directed to take measures for its improvement or to refrain from taking measures that would degenerate our ecology. However, the core issues effecting or rather controlling India's natural environment have remained the same.

Who should control India's forest wealth? Should the traditional local tribal manage forest resources with his age-old knowledge reducing the government to a mere assistant? On the other hand, should forests be managed by the Central government? Before the British came to India, forests were the property of locals who survived on them as well as took loving care of them. As British gained control of India, they simply threw the tribal out of this management.

Their concern was entirely different. They gave contracts for felling forests and such felling was immense all across Indian sub-continent. They wanted to increase revenue by selling timber and converting forestland into agricultural land. Timber was required for the expansion of railways, construction of bridges and buildings. Right from the forest Act of 1861 till 1927, the British disassociated the local traditional dweller from its management.

All these Acts contain a provision of arrest without warrant for anyone who encroached upon forestland without permission from the British officer. Whether it be a cattle grazier or a woman collecting dry wood for fuel. The same practice has continued after independence. Forest wealth has been centralized and the local dweller is as angry with the administration as ever. Since he gets no incentive by protecting his forest, he does not bother about it anymore. Until this issue of local versus government control is resolved, forest resources will continue to be exploited and mismanaged in India.

Weakness of laws and administrative rules is the second main problem. Laws are not weak by chance. They are left weak deliberately. For example, the boards entrusted with preventing water and air pollution have proved ineffective. Not by chance but because they have not been empowered sufficiently. They can detect pollution but not prosecute the culprit. Prosecution must proceed in an ordinary court and it lingers on for years allowing the hazardous unit to continue operation. So many procedural anomalies have been left in the body of these acts that the sufferers of environment degeneration have no alternative but to appeal in the Supreme Court through Public interest litigation to get a remedy.

Finally, there is the economic and development imperative. Often we must reject an environment friendly technology that is expensive as well as monopolised and patented by a multi national company whose objective is to get returns on its research rather than protect the ecology. This means that we must adopt a technology, which is less expensive but harms the environment because production has to continue in today's capitalist market driven economy. We have to feed our population. We have to raise their living standard. We have to boost our exports. We must repay our international loans lest the big brother will make a Mexico or a Banana republic out of us.

REGULATORY LAW

Over the years, together with a spreading of environmental consciousness, there has been a change in the traditionally-held perception that there is a trade-off between environmental quality and economic growth as people have come to believe that the two are necessarily complementary. The current focus on environment is not new—environmental considerations have been an integral part of the Indian culture. The need for conservation and sustainable use of natural resources has been expressed in Indian scriptures, more than three thousand years old and is reflected in the constitutional, legislative and policy framework as also in the international commitments of the country. Even before India's independence in 1947, several environmental legislation existed but the real impetus for bringing about a well-developed framework came only after the UN Conference on the Human Environment (Stockholm, 1972).

Under the influence of this declaration, the National Council for Environmental Policy and Planning within the Department of Science and Technology was set up in 1972. This Council later evolved into a full-fledged Ministry of Environment and Forests (MoEF) in 1985 which today is the apex administrative body in the country for regulating and ensuring environmental protection.

After the Stockholm Conference, in 1976, constitutional sanction was given to environmental concerns through the 42nd Amendment, which incorporated them into the Directive Principles of State Policy and Fundamental Rights and Duties. Since the 1970s an extensive network of environmental legislation has grown in the country. The MoEF and the pollution control boards (CPCB i.e. Central Pollution Control Board and SPCBs i.e. State Pollution Control Boards) together form the regulatory and administrative core of the sector. A policy framework has also been developed to complement the legislative provisions. The Policy Statement for Abatement of Pollution and the National Conservation Strategy and Policy Statement on Environment and Development were brought out by the MoEF in 1992, to develop and promote initiatives for the protection and improvement of the environment.

The EAP (Environmental Action Programme) was formulated in 1993 with the objective of improving environmental services and integrating environmental considerations in to development programmes. Other measures have also been taken by the government to protect and preserve the environment. Several sector-specific policies have evolved, which are discussed at length in the concerned chapters. This chapter attempts to highlight only legislative initiatives towards the protection of the environment.

LEGISLATION FOR ENVIRONMENTAL PROTECTION IN INDIA

Water

Water quality standards especially those for drinking water are set by the Indian Council of Medical Research. These bear close resemblance to WHO standards. The discharge of industrial effluents is regulated by the Indian Standard Codes and recently, water quality standards for coastal water marine outfalls have also been specified.

In addition to the general standards, certain specific standards have been developed for effluent discharges from industries such as, iron and steel, aluminium, pulp and paper, oil refineries, petrochemicals and thermal power plants. Legislation to control water pollution are listed below.

Water (Prevention and Control of Pollution) Act, 1974

This Act represented India's first attempts to comprehensively deal with environmental issues. The Act prohibits the discharge of pollutants into water bodies beyond a given standard, and lays down penalties for non-compliance. The Act was amended in 1988 to conform closely to the provisions of the EPA, 1986.

It set up the CPCB (Central Pollution Control Board) which lays down standards for the prevention and control of water pollution. At the State level, the SPCBs (State Pollution Control Board) function under the direction of the CPCB and the state government.

Water (Prevention and Control of Pollution) Cess Act, 1977

This Act provides for a levy and collection of a cess on water consumed by industries and local authorities. It aims at augmenting the resources of the central and state boards for prevention and control of water pollution. Following this Act, *The Water (Prevention and Control of Pollution) Cess Rules* were formulated in 1978 for defining standards and indications for the kind of and location of meters that every consumer of water is required to install.

AIR

Air (Prevention and Control of Pollution) Act, 1981

To counter the problems associated with air pollution, ambient air quality standards were established, under the 1981 Act. The Act provides means for the control and abatement of air pollution. The Act seeks to combat air pollution by prohibiting the use of polluting fuels and substances, as well as by regulating appliances that give rise to air pollution. Under the Act establishing or operating of any industrial plant in the pollution control area requires consent from state boards. The boards are also expected to test the air in air pollution control areas, inspect pollution control equipment, and manufacturing processes.

National Ambient Air Quality Standards (NAAQS) for major pollutants were notified by the CPCB in April 1994. These are deemed to be levels of air quality necessary with an adequate margin of safety, to protect public health, vegetation and property (CPCB 1995 cited in Gupta, 1999). The NAAQS prescribe specific standards for industrial, residential, rural and other sensitive areas. Industry-specific emission standards have also been developed for iron and steel plants, cement plants, fertilizer plants, oil refineries and the aluminium industry. The ambient quality standards prescribed in India are similar to those prevailing in many developed and developing countries.

To empower the central and state pollution boards to meet grave emergencies, the *Air (Prevention and Control of Pollution) Amendment Act*, 1987, was enacted. The boards were authorized to take immediate measures to tackle such emergencies and recover the expenses incurred from the offenders. The power to cancel consent for non-fulfilment of the conditions prescribed has also been emphasized in the Air Act Amendment.

The Air (Prevention and Control of Pollution) Rules formulated in 1982

Defined the procedures for conducting meetings of the boards, the powers of the presiding officers, decision-making, the quorum; manner in which the records of the meeting were to be set etc. They also prescribed the manner and the purpose of seeking assistance from specialists and the fee to be paid to them.

Complementing the above Acts is the *Atomic Energy Act* of 1982, which was introduced to deal with radioactive waste. In 1988, the *Motor Vehicles Act*, was enacted to regulate vehicular traffic, besides ensuring proper packaging, labelling and transportation of the hazardous wastes. Various aspects of vehicular pollution have also been notified under the EPA of 1986. Mass emission standards were notified in 1990, which were made more stringent in 1996.

In 2000 these standards were revised yet again and for the first time separate obligations for vehicle owners, manufacturers and enforcing agencies were stipulated. In addition, fairly stringent Euro I and II emission norms were notified by the Supreme Court on April 29, 1999 for the city of Delhi. The notification made it mandatory for car manufacturers to conform to the Euro I and Euro II norms by May 1999 and April 2000, respectively, for new non-commercial vehicle sold in Delhi.

FORESTS AND WILDLIFE

The Wildlife (Protection) Act, 1972, Amendment 1991

The WPA (Wildlife Protection Act), 1972, provides for protection to listed species of flora and fauna and establishes a network of ecologically-important protected areas. The WPA empowers the central and state governments to declare any area a wildlife sanctuary, national park or closed area. There is a blanket ban on carrying out any industrial activity inside these protected areas. It provides for authorities to administer and implement the Act; regulate the hunting of wild animals;

protect specified plants, sanctuaries, national parks and closed areas; restrict trade or commerce in wild animals or animal articles; and miscellaneous matters. The Act prohibits hunting of animals except with permission of authorized officer when an animal has become dangerous to human life or property or so disabled or diseased as to be beyond recovery (WWF-India, 1999). The near-total prohibition on hunting was made more effective by the Amendment Act of 1991.

The Forest (Conservation) Act, 1980

This Act was adopted to protect and conserve forests. The Act restricts the powers of the state in respect of de-reservation of forests and use of forestland for non-forest purposes (the term 'non-forest purpose' includes clearing any forestland for cultivation of cash crops, plantation crops, horticulture or any purpose other than re-afforestation).

GENERAL

Environment (Protection) Act, 1986 (EPA)

This Act is an umbrella legislation designed to provide a framework for the co-ordination of central and state authorities established under the Water (Prevention and Control) Act, 1974 and Air (Prevention and Control) Act, 1981. Under this Act, the central government is empowered to take measures necessary to protect and improve the quality of the environment by setting standards for emissions and discharges; regulating the location of industries; management of hazardous wastes, and protection of public health and welfare. From time to time the central government issues notifications under the EPA for the protection of ecologically-sensitive areas or issues guidelines for matters under the EPA.

Some notifications issued under this Act are:

- *Doon Valley Notification* (1989), which prohibits the setting up of an industry in which the daily consumption of coal/fuel is more than 24 MT (million tonnes) per day in the Doon Valley.
- *Coastal Regulation Zone Notification* (1991), which

regulates activities along coastal stretches. As per this notification, dumping ash or any other waste in the CRZ is prohibited. The thermal power plants (only foreshore facilities for transport of raw materials, facilities for intake of cooling water and outfall for discharge of treated waste water/cooling water) require clearance from the MoEF.

- *Dhanu Taluka Notification* (1991), under which the district of Dhanu Taluka has been declared an ecologically fragile region and setting up power plants in its vicinity is prohibited.
- *Revdanda Creek Notification (1989),* which prohibits setting up industries in the belt around the Revdanda Creek as per the rules laid down in the notification.
- *The Environmental Impact Assessment of Development Projects Notification,* (1994 and as amended in 1997). As per this notification: All projects listed under Schedule I require environmental clearance from the MoEF.
- Projects under the delicenced category of the New Industrial Policy also require clearance from the MoEF.
- All developmental projects whether or not under the Schedule I, if located in fragile regions must obtain MoEF clearance.
- Industrial projects with investments above Rs 500 million must obtain MoEF clearance and are further required to obtain a LOI (Letter Of Intent) from the Ministry of Industry, and an NOC (No Objection Certificate) from the SPCB and the State Forest Department if the location involves forestland. Once the NOC is obtained, the LOI is converted into an industrial licence by the state authority.

Index

A

B

C

D

E

F

I

J

L

M

O

P